HRAC2

D0685507

Shot in
OKLAHOMA

STORIES & STORYTELLERS

Teresa Miller, Series Editor

Shot in OKLAHOMA

A CENTURY OF SOONER STATE CINEMA

JOHN WOOLEY

UNIVERSITY OF OKLAHOMA PRESS : NORMAN

Also by John Wooley

Dark Within: A Novel (Tulsa, 2000)
Awash in the Blood (Tulsa, 2002)
(with Michael H. Price) *The Big Book of Biker Flicks: 40 of the Best
Motorcycle Movies of All Time* (Tulsa, 2005)
Voices from the Hill: The Story of Oklahoma Military Academy (Tulsa, 2005)
From the Blue Devils to Red Dirt: The Colors of Oklahoma Music (Tulsa, 2006)
Ghost Band: A Novel (Tulsa, 2006)

This book is published with the generous assistance of the
Wallace C. Thompson Endowment Fund, University of Oklahoma Foundation.

Library of Congress Cataloging-in-Publication Data

Wooley, John.
Shot in Oklahoma : a century of sooner state cinema / John Wooley.
    p. cm—(Stories & storytellers series ; 7)
Includes bibliographical references and index.
Includes filmography.
ISBN 978-0-8061-4174-9 (pbk. : alk. paper)
1. Motion pictures—Oklahoma—History.
2. Motion picture industry—Oklahoma—History.
I. Title.
PN1993.5.U7725W65 2011
792.09766—dc22

                    2010045271

Shot in Oklahoma: A Century of Sooner State Cinema is Volume 7
in the Stories & Storytellers series.

The paper in this book meets the guidelines for permanence and durability of the Committee on Production Guidelines for Book Longevity of the Council on Library Resources, Inc. ∞
Copyright © 2011 by John Wooley. Published by the University of Oklahoma Press, Norman, Publishing Division of the University. Manufactured in the U.S.A.

All rights reserved. No part of this publication may be reproduced, stored in a retrieval system, or transmitted, in any form or by any means, electronic, mechanical, photocopying, recording, or otherwise—except as permitted under Section 107 or 108 of the United States Copyright Act—without the prior written permission of the University of Oklahoma Press.
1 2 3 4 5 6 7 8 9 10

For my fellow travelers Jonathan and Steven
and for Janis, the light on our path

Contents

Illustrations

Preface and Acknowledgments

For more than two decades as an entertainment writer for the Tulsa World, I made much of my living talking to Oklahoma people who were actively engaged in making music and movies and then putting their words down on paper for others to read—a gig I remain very grateful for. Out of that experience came my Oklahoma Centennial book, From the Blue Devils to Red Dirt: The Colors of Oklahoma Music (2006), and now Shot in Oklahoma: A Century of Sooner State Cinema, a record of the first seven decades of feature filmmaking in Oklahoma (including a few side trips into theatrical shorts and TV shows). My newspaper years taught me the importance of getting fresh material from primary sources wherever possible, a lesson I've applied here. (Any unattributed interviews were done by me for this book; otherwise, my sources are clearly identified within the text.) My aversion to throwing away any notes, transcriptions, or files relating to old stories I've done certainly borders on the obsessive (just ask my wife), but some of that archival stuff has come in pretty handy many years later, and I was delighted to have it when it came time to write this book.

It all started with Teresa Miller, my longtime friend and fellow author, who thought that my idea for a book on Sooner State movies might find a home with her Stories & Storytellers series at the University of Oklahoma Press. I thank Teresa for her encouragement and for so many other things. She, for instance, connected me with now-retired publisher John Drayton, a fair and wise man whose early counsel meant a great deal to me and to *Shot in Oklahoma*. Winding its way toward publication, this project got lots of help—from acquisitions editor Jay Dew, who stepped in when John Drayton left; manuscript editor Emily Jerman, who shepherded the book, and me, with grace and good humor; copyeditor Rosemary Wetherold, who was as kind as she was thorough (which is saying something); and production manager Emmy Ezzell. My gratitude also goes to Amy Hernandez, Anna María Rodríguez, Diane Cotts, Minna Fielding, and Lisa Tullius, all at OU Press. I should also mention another friend, the late Kirk Bjornsgaard, an acquisitions editor with OU Press who kept a line of communication open with me for years regarding possible book projects.

Without the permission of the ownership and management of the *Tulsa World*, much of the research for *Shot in Oklahoma* would have been far more difficult, so my thanks go to the Lorton family, executive editor Joe Worley, managing editor Susan Ellerbach, Sunday editor Debbie Jackson, and photo department head Tom Gilbert, among many others. News clerks Keith Binning and Hilary Pittman provided invaluable help, and Rachelle Vaughan went absolutely above and beyond, taking a personal interest in this book and guiding me into research avenues I would otherwise have missed. Thanks, Rachelle.

My friends at the *Tulsa World* not only allowed me to use material I gathered while on the newspaper's payroll but also helped me uncover other pertinent stories published over the years by Oklahoma's daily papers. I remain extremely grateful to the *World*'s editors and news clerks, as well as to the legions of writers and reporters—from the *World* and elsewhere—who covered Sooner cinema events as they were happening. Their words shine like nuggets, and I'm happy to be the guy who dug them out.

Special gratitude goes to Randy Johnston, old pal and film fan, whose supplemental material helped form the bedrock of this book; Bill Moore, the now-retired moving-picture archivist at the Oklahoma Historical Society, who took the time to show me some rare archival material and otherwise provided me with important background material, and whose repeated citations in this book are a testament to his importance as an Oklahoma film historian; Mike Ransom and his fine website, www.tulsatvmemories.com, who jumped in with amazing research on Tulsa-related filmmaking; Jim Vance, who contributed in an impressive number of different ways; and Michael Wallis, whose guidance, kindness, and friendship—not to mention his own writing—were an inspiration.

Others who contributed significantly to *Shot in Oklahoma* in one way or another include Dollie Banner at Jerry Ohlinger's Movie Material Store, Jack and Carole Bender, Dr. Bob Blackburn and Larry O'Dell at the Oklahoma Historical Society, Bob and Don Blair of VCI Entertainment, Karen Bryan at Tulsa Central Library, Thomas Conner, Billy Coppedge, Rob Craig, Simon Christopher Dew, Jim Downing, James Edwards, Dr. Caroline Frick, David F. Friedman, Tom Golden at *Oklahoma Magazine*, Gregory Gray, Scott Gregory, Cassie Hagerdon, Joey Hambrick, Kathy Harger at Tulsa Central Library, S. E. Hinton, Dale Ingram, Dennis King, Randy Krehbiel, Katie Kyle, Jim Lazalier, Christopher and Linda Lewis, Dr. Guy Logsdon, Richard Matthy, John McMahan, Paul McSpadden, Dr. John L. Myers, Joshua Peck at the Tulsa Historical Society, Dale Pelton, Bill Pitcock IV, Michael H. Price, Gary D. Rhodes, Ayn Robbins, Rick Scott, Harvey Shell, Jill Simpson at the Oklahoma Film and Music Office, Michael Smith, Mickie Smith at OETA, Tim Spindle at Tulsa Central Library, Vern Stefanic, Paul Stevenson, Suzanne Wallis, Buck Walton, Lee Woodward, Jonathan Wooley, Marcia Becton Wright, David Yeagley, and anyone I inadvertently left off this list—you know you who are, and you have my apologies in advance.

To all of you: thanks are inadequate. But they're the best I've got, and they come from the heart.

Shot in OKLAHOMA

Introduction

Before we can begin any discussion of the birth of Oklahoma's film industry, we have to go back, if only for a moment, to the beginning of American movies themselves. That takes us to West Orange, New Jersey, and the man whose name is synonymous with invention, Thomas Alva Edison. By 1891, when Edison—with a substantial assist from his British assistant William Kennedy Laurie Dickson—gave the world the movie camera, he'd already been responsible for such society-altering creations as the phonograph (1877) and the first commercially viable electric light bulb (1879). Employing a variation of the Greek word kinesis, meaning "motion," he first dubbed his creation the kinetograph. The peep-show cabinets, designed to show the films taken with the kinetograph to a single viewer at a time, were called kinetoscopes.

In 1894 the first Kinetoscope Parlor opened in New York, with the coin-operated cabinets offering patrons a variety of brief one-scene Edison movies. Kinetoscopes soon began popping up all over, mostly in amusement parlors, which were frequented—as film historian Anthony Slide pointed out in his book *Early American Cinema* (1970)—by people who generally belonged to the lower socioeconomic classes. (In fact, Slide contended, "The middle and upper classes were not to 'discover' the movies until D. W. Griffith produced *The Birth of a Nation* in 1915, but that does not mean that the cinema was in any way unpopular with a vast number of people before that date" [pp. 7–8]).

A year or so later, Edison came up with a projector—or "vitascope"— that could show the films on a wall or screen, enabling more than one person to see a particular moving picture at one time. That invention, debuting publicly in a New York music hall in April 1896 with scenes of rolling waves, a dancer, and a boxing match, did nothing less than kick-start the beginning of the motion picture industry in this country.

(The pioneering Lumière brothers, based in France, had actually beaten Edison by a few months, first projecting their own movies to Paris café audiences on December 28, 1895.)

With the invention of the projector, films could be, and were, shown to crowds in concert halls, as parts of traveling vaudeville shows and carnivals, and even outdoors. Eventually, of course, venues would pop up that were devoted exclusively to exhibiting movies. Perhaps the most famous of these was the Nicolet Theatre in Pittsburgh, which opened in 1905, its management charging patrons a nickel to come in and glimpse the wonders dancing across its screen. Soon, similar venues known as nickelodeons—reflecting both the cost of admission and the name of the place where it all started—began exploding across America's landscape.

Back in the early 1890s, in Edison's pioneering New Jersey film studio Black Maria (a term used at the time for hearses and police paddy wagons), the inventor, his assistant Dickson, and others had begun knocking out short movies for the kinetoscope trade. One of these, described by Gordon Hendricks in a 1959 issue of the magazine *Image*, foreshadowed not only the coming appetite for western movies but also the involvement of Oklahoma's 101 Ranch and its staff and employees. Wrote Hendricks about the 1894 Edison short *Bucking Bronco*: "Taken during a visit of members of the Buffalo Bill Wild West Show in West Orange. Lee Martin, of Colorado, is riding 'Sunfish,' while Frank Hammitt stands on the fence and fires a pistol. In the background, press agent Madden waves his stick. The riders were paid $35—including transportation for the horses—for their work" (p. 8).

In the beginning, it was enough simply to give the peep-show crowd something that moved, and there was plenty of kinetic energy on display in *Bucking Bronco*'s brief running time. As films began their move from arcades to screens, however, they grew longer, their images beginning to coalesce around stories. It didn't happen a second too soon, either. Edison himself figured movies to be only a passing fancy, an amusement hall diversion that would eventually wear out its welcome, and early indications seemed to prove him right. Then along came Edwin S. Porter, who produced and directed for Edison's outfit one of the most groundbreaking pictures in the history of cinema, 1903's *The Great Train Robbery*.

Brought in for around $150, the eleven-minute film was revolutionary for a number of reasons. It told a complete story, highlighting a train robbery by outlaws on horseback and continuing through their pursuit and ultimate capture by the forces of justice. It was also one of the first movies to use editing as a narrative aid; instead of shooting everything in sequence, the normal way of making a movie at the time, Porter filmed the robbery and getaway scenes separate from the ones showing the organization of the posse, then edited them together so that the shots of the outlaws' attempts to get away alternated with the scenes of the posse forming and then riding in pursuit. The use of editing to heighten suspense and storytelling quickly became standard in movies, but at the time of *The Great Train Robbery* it was nothing less than a stroke of genius.

The thing, however, that makes *The Great Train Robbery* most relevant to the beginnings of the movie industry in Oklahoma was its Wild West–flavored, cowboys-and-outlaws setting. A few years after the turn of the last century, a general feeling had begun to creep into the American culture that suggested the days of the real Old West were over, that progress and technology had rendered the frontier, and the rugged individualists who tamed it and lived and loved and fought in it, obsolete. As Michael Wallis put it in his definitive work on Oklahoma's 101 Ranch, *The Real Wild West* (1999):

> By 1909, some people realized that the passing of what came to be called the Old West was at hand. Perhaps some of them saw the writing on the wall when Frederic Remington, creator of more than twenty-seven hundred works of art that symbolized the American West of myth, died that year at age forty-eight in Connecticut. Still others recognized that the end was in sight because of the advancement of modern technology. As more rail and telephone lines crisscrossed the land, Henry Ford mass-produced Model T automobiles, and pioneer aviators made further advances, the rural West quickly became far less isolated. (p. 339)

As often happens when people begin to feel that something has slipped away from their lives, any sense of loss was accompanied by a complementary ache of nostalgia—which is after all, as the novelist John O'Hara once observed, a kind of homesickness, a yearning for something you realize you'll never really have again. This nostalgia, shared by both those who had experienced the West and those who only knew it from books, newspapers, and touring wild-west shows, made *The Great Train Robbery* a runaway success and showed the nascent filmmaking world that there was a real appetite in the country for western stories utilizing the familiar narrative elements of robbery, saloons, gunplay, chases on horseback, fisticuffs, and the ultimate triumph of white-hatted emissaries of justice. Audiences wanted to see people and situations on-screen that reminded them of western frontier life, so that they could vicariously live, at least for a few moments, in a place that had essentially passed from the American scene.

And that's as good an opportunity as any to segue into the story of the 101 Ranch, and the profound effect it had on early Oklahoma filmmaking.

ONE

Dawn at the 101 Ranch

The first film shot in Oklahoma was on the famous 101 Ranch near Ponca City in May of 1904. Thomas Edison sent a film crew to capture the magic of that ranch and share it with the world.

> —Bill Moore, moving-images archivist, Oklahoma Historical Society, quoted in Scott Pitcock's "Oklahoma on the Silver Screen," *Oklahoma Magazine* (March 2007)

It's my belief that the Miller Brothers as a unit, the whole 101 Ranch operation, could unquestionably be considered a pioneer of the film industry in Oklahoma. And over and above that, it was right up there near the top in the western-movie genre nationally.

> —Michael Wallis, author of *The Real Wild West*

Taking up 110,000 acres that sprawled over parts of four counties in north-central Oklahoma, the 101 Ranch in the early 1900s was a self-contained livestock and farming operation that might as well have been its own city. Remarkably diversified, it was home to not only thousands of employees and the Miller family, who owned it, but also to a school, a general store, a meat-packing plant, a dude ranch, and a rodeo showground, among other things. For some years, it had both its own newspaper and its own money, the latter good for making purchases in the ranch's store and at participating establishments in nearby towns, including the 101's hometown of Bliss (now Marland) and the neighboring Ponca City. (The brass coins issued by the ranch were popularly referred to as "broncs," and the paper money as "bucks." It's been suggested that the slang term for dollar bills may have sprung from the latter.)

In 1903, the year *The Great Train Robbery* hit American screens, the patriarch of the ranch family, Col. George W. Miller, died, leaving the operation to sons Joe, Zack, and George. The next year, according to the Oklahoma Historical Society's Bill Moore, a camera-toting entourage from Edison's New Jersey studio traveled to the 101 to shoot some western-themed shorts.

"They shot several films there during that time period," Moore said recently. "One was called *A Brush between Cowboys and Indians*. Obviously, in the period we're talking about, around the turn of the century, film is in its early stages. So, as far as production values go, they're very crude, to say the least. The camera's set up for a wide shot, and it just pretty much stays there. You don't have cutaways, you don't have close-ups, you don't have establishing shots, because it's too early in the process.

"To us, it's something that's a minute long, and it looks like they just had some guys run across the river and go past the camera," he added with a chuckle. "It's the single scene in the film. But to them, it was a complete movie."

A Brush between Cowboys and Indians is also noteworthy because it featured a former vaudevillian named Gilbert M. Anderson, who'd had a small part in *The Great Train Robbery* the year before. He would go on to much greater fame a few years later, after leaving Edison, co-founding a Chicago-based film company called Essanay and becoming Broncho Billy Anderson, the first real cowboy-movie hero. Chances are good that Anderson was also involved in the other shorts filmed at the ranch by Edison in '04, all with similar self-explanatory titles. They included *Bucking Bronco*, *Driving Cattle to Pasture*, *Rounding Up and Branding Cattle*, *Western Stage Coach Hold Up*, and *Cowboys and Indians Fording a River in a Wagon*, the titles reflecting activities that surely seemed wildly exotic to city-dwelling audiences.

Moore said he could only make an educated guess about why the Edison crew came all the way to Oklahoma to shoot these pictures. "Westerns were popular, any kind of western action," he explained. "That's why the wild-west shows were so popular. People in the cities wanted to see that kind of stuff."

As noted earlier, Edison had used some members of the Buffalo Bill Wild West Show to make at least one of his company's early kinescope films, but the traveling show was apparently visiting the East Orange area at the time, so Edison's people were able to film real cowboys without ever having to leave their home turf. The specific reason that Edison would send a crew all the way from New Jersey to Oklahoma remains something of a mystery, especially since the 101 Ranch would not start sending out its own wild-west show until 1906. However, a clue may lie in a trip that Joe, the eldest of the three Miller brothers, took in May of 1904, the same month Edison visited the ranch.

It was then, as Wallis observed in *The Real Wild West*, that Miller traveled to St. Louis, Missouri, for a meeting of the country's newspaper editors, in order to promote the idea that their next annual meeting ought to be held in Oklahoma Territory and include a trip to the 101, where visitors would be able to see real-life cowboys and Indians in a spectacular show—and dine on buffalo meat as well. His pitch to the group, the National Editorial Association, was a success, and the next year the conventioneers traveled to Oklahoma for their get-together. Of course, the itinerary did include a visit to the 101 Ranch, where the visitors were treated to a heavily promoted day of parades, Indian dances, trick riding, and other specialty acts; a buffalo hunt featuring the famed Apache chief Geronimo; and, to cap things off, a simulated Indian attack on a wagon train. Drawn by extensive regional and national publicity for the event, thousands of curiosity seekers from all over joined the editors and publishers at the event. "By best estimates," Wallis wrote, "at least sixty-five thousand men, women, and children showed up at the 101 Ranch, making it the largest gathering of its kind in the history of the Twin [Oklahoma and Indian] Territories" (p. 249).

The runaway success of that outdoor spectacle created a major buzz across the country. The fact that newspaper executives were honored guests at the blowout, of course, didn't hurt the ranch as far as publicity was concerned. It should be noted that the huge cast of cowboys entertaining the vast crowd included two eventual film stars, Tom Mix and Bill Pickett—both just beginning their association with the 101.

This extravaganza unfolded in June of 1905, more than a year after the Edison unit had visited the ranch. But it's possible that news of Joe Miller's sales pitch to the National Editorial Association the previous year, which included a no-doubt glowing description of the authentic western-style entertainment the 101 Ranch could offer, enticed Edison into sending his camera crew halfway across the country to capture on film some real cowboys and Indians, with their horses and buffaloes, ranch houses, and teepees.

Perhaps, also, Edison was solicited by George Miller, the youngest of the three brothers and the one who, according to Bill Moore, was the first to see the potential in the 101 as a filmmaking site. "He was always trying to convince Joe that motion pictures would be a real benefit to the ranch," Moore said. "And he was working hard at it, sending out letters to film companies."

It's not much of a stretch to speculate that one of those letters found William Selig, owner of the Selig Polyscope Company in Chicago. Selig had been producing films since 1896; one of his more audacious efforts, 1909's *Hunting Big Game in Africa*, was an alleged documentary showing former president Teddy Roosevelt shooting a lion on a big-game safari in Africa. Roosevelt shot the lion, all right, but none of that was in the movie. Selig had faked his version of the lion-bagging—let's be generous and call it an *homage*—in Chicago, utilizing hometown talent (including a guy who looked a little like Teddy R.), some tropical plants, and an aged lion he'd bought, as Wallis wrote, "at a bargain price" (p. 342).

Hunting Big Game in Africa turned out to be a popular success, bogus though it may have been, and its box office take encouraged Selig not only to acquire an entire zoo for the purposes of filmmaking but also to send camera crews out to various spots around the globe, where they shot footage that could be incorporated into future movies. Less exotic than Africa, but much closer to home, was the 101 Ranch, where a crew showed up in the spring of 1909 to shoot some background scenes of authentic ranch life for use in upcoming Selig opuses.

Thus began a practice that would continue for decades—that of a movie company coming from elsewhere to Oklahoma to film background, or second-unit, footage. (The two terms, while sometimes used interchangeably, aren't quite the same. Film shot by a second-unit crew usually includes more than just scenery and settings—stunts, for instance, are traditionally done by a second unit. Still, as indicated by the term, second-unit material isn't as important to the film as what's being shot on the main sets with the major actors.) Evidence does exist that suggests at least one of these Selig westerns, *The Stampede* (1909), was primarily shot at the ranch.

Apparently, Selig met up with Tom Mix during this time. Mix, a Pennsylvania native and former Oklahoma City bartender, had been just one of many cowboys in the 101's big 1905 wild-west show, eventually signing on with the Miller brothers full-time and working primarily in the dude ranch part of their sprawling business. In *The Life and Legend of Tom Mix* (1972), Paul E. Mix remarked that the future movie star lacked most of the traditional cowpoke skills during his early days on the spread:

> His first job for the ranch was to act as a host for "dude" cowboys and cowgirls on vacation from the East. Colonel Zack Miller didn't think much of Tom as a cowboy. Tom looked the part however and proved himself to be an excellent host for the ranch. One oldtimer said, "Tom's duties at the ranch consisted mostly of just hanging around and looking pretty. He was not much of a cowboy as such when he first came to work for the 101. People used to say that Tom could get lost in an 800-acre pasture." (p. 47)

It's not clear whether Mix was working for the 101 full-time when he first became acquainted with William Selig. We do know, however, that he and the filmmaker got together somewhere around the middle of 1909, which was proving to be a busy year for the soon-to-be cowboy-movie star. Mix had gotten married—for the third time—in January, to a cowgirl from Dewey, Oklahoma, named Olive Stokes. There were dozens of the circus-like wild-west shows touring the country then, including the three-year-old Miller Brothers 101 Ranch Real Wild West Show, and Mr. and Mrs. Mix hooked up with one out of Texas for a few months before quitting and forming their own. They worked for still another wild-west outfit in '09, and sometime after that, Mix returned to the 101.

In *The Real Wild West*, Wallis wrote that Selig immediately saw the potential Mix had for the movies and "put the handsome cowboy to work as an extra and a scout for film locations for a low-key movie entitled *Ranch Life in the Great Southwest*" (p. 343). Wallis's description of Mix's duties on the film was amplified in the 1979 book *Photostory of the Screen's Greatest Cowboy Star—Tom Mix*, written, compiled, and published by longtime western-movie aficionado Mario DeMarco: "The film company hired Tom to handle the live stock and at the same time act as a safety man in keeping animals from hurting the members of the cast and crew. (This was quite common in those early flicks because Tom once related how he was locked in a small building and several wolves were put in with him. The cameras kept grinding while the scared Mix battled these hungry animals with his bare hands!)" (p. 12). That parenthetical anecdote probably illustrates a penchant Mix had for, as today's business jargon would put it, "inflating his resume." Wallis was a bit more blunt about it in *The Real Wild West*, writing that "Mix had invented various aspects of his life and spiced up his professional resume with exaggerations and, in some instances, outright lies" (p. 343).

There is, for example, the one about Mix's law enforcement career. In the credits for the August 1910–released *Ranch Life in the Great Southwest*, his first picture, he's billed as a former deputy United States marshal. No record exists, however, to support that title. He did serve for a time as a deputy sheriff and night marshal in his third wife's hometown of Dewey, seventy-five miles east of the 101 Ranch, after he and Olive returned to Oklahoma from their wild-west show adventures.

DeMarco wrote that, after being hired to work on *Ranch Life in the Great Southwest*, Tom "realized that 'picture making' was the answer to his dreams" and asked the director for a role in the movie (p. 12). This appears to have been the case. And if the movies indeed gave Mix a raison d'être, director Francis Boggs nudged him along by casting the cowpoke in a bronc-busting sequence for the one-reel opus. (A reel of film ran approximately ten minutes.)

Was *Ranch Life in the Great Southwest* shot on the grounds of the 101? Probably not, although it was definitely filmed in the Sooner State. Western-movie historian Buck Rainey, for one, believed that it was done at a location other than the Miller spread. In his *Saddle Aces of the Cinema* (1980), Rainey wrote: "Tom and Olive had a small spread in the Cherokee Territory, and it was this fact that led to his entrance into the movies. The Selig Company was looking for a ranch on which to shoot a picture and for someone who knew the surrounding country. Tom Mix volunteered his ranch and himself" (p. 60).

Regardless of exactly where it was lensed, however, *Ranch Life in the Great Southwest* was the beginning of a spectacular career for Tom Mix. In no time at all, he was starring for Selig and director Boggs in such western-themed films as *The Trimming of Paradise Gulch*, *The Long Trail*, and *Pride of the Range*, the latter featuring another 101 ranch hand who would go on to fame as a movie cowboy, Hoot Gibson. By 1913, Mix was a major player for the Selig Company, later achieving even greater fame at Twentieth Century-Fox—where, as Rainey put it, he "remained the most popular screen cowboy until the advent of sound" (p. 61).

In the late 1920s, as the talkie era dawned, Fox pulled the plug on its western movies, and Mix, after making a series of silents with another studio, hit the sawdust trail, finding new life as a circus attraction. After that, he tried adapting to the new talking-picture format, and he might have made it if he hadn't been seriously injured in a fall with his horse while shooting *Rustler's Roundup* (1933), his final feature film. Upon re-covering, Mix returned to the world of circuses and personal-appearance tours until his death in a one-car accident in 1940. In 1968 the Tom Mix Museum opened in Dewey, the town where Mix met Olive Stokes and served for a short time as a law enforcement officer. The museum contin-ues today under the auspices of the Oklahoma Historical Society and the local Tom Mix Museum Board of Directors.

Another filmmaker associated with the 101 Ranch may not be nearly as well known as Edison or Selig, but his contribution to Sooner cin-ema is powerful and undeniable. Bennie Kent, the story goes, became a filmmaker after a camera operator from a visiting studio abandoned his equipment during a shoot at the 101. "Kent was on the ranch when some of these films were being shot," explained Bill Moore, "and the story he told to a newspaper reporter was that one of the photographers had stomped off the set—upset about something, I guess—and one of the Millers said, 'Well, Kent knows how to frame a shot. Let *him* run the camera.' And that's what started his interest in filmmaking."

Was that story a fabrication? Or did it happen when Edison—or even another filmmaking outfit, its name lost to the ages—came to the ranch in search of authentic western footage? We may never know.

What we *do* know is that James Bennie Kent (the "Bennie" may have been a nickname) was a derby-wearing, cigar-chomping Englishman who'd learned the watch repair trade in his own country before immigrating to America in the late 1800s. First setting up shop in Nebraska, he later made his way to Chandler, Oklahoma, about eighty miles south of the 101 spread, and plied his trade there. He also began indulging his hobby of photography in this new place, roaming the area for suitable subjects, which included scenes of both Indian and cowboy life.

Kent's photographs soon attracted the attention of the Millers, who brought him on board to document the life and work of the ranch. Apparently, he became a full-time employee fairly quickly. "The 101 Ranch had something called the Wagon Wheel, in which a wheel was used to show the various administrative responsibilities," said Moore. "Bennie Kent was on that wheel, on one of the spokes, as the photographer for the ranch." Among his other duties, Kent put together the big souvenir booklet following the 1905 wild-west extravaganza at the 101, finding a place in it for many of the photographs he'd taken to document that historic event.

As it turned out, when Kent discovered the particular attraction of shooting pictures that moved, he began devoting much more time to filmmaking than to still photography. Acquiring his own camera from Chicago in 1908, he started shooting scenes on the ranch, soon becoming involved with some area folks in making what were probably the first Oklahoma films crafted by entirely state-produced talent. One of these pictures, 1908's *A Round-Up in Oklahoma*, used the setting of the 101 Ranch—and, undoubtedly, several of its ranch hands—to tell a cowboys-and-Indians story framed around a cattle drive.

Meanwhile, the Miller brothers decided to increase their commitment to the movie business. Or, at least, oldest brother Joe did. By the early 1910s, many of the stars of the Miller Brothers 101 Ranch Real Wild West Show had begun overwintering in warmer places, including South

America, rather than returning to Bliss and the often-bitter Oklahoma winters. California was warm year-round, and the state was drawing moviemakers to its beaches and mountains like a magnet, quickly becoming the epicenter of the still-new motion picture business. Both of those factors made it an appealing place for a group of traveling entertainers to spend the winter months.

So, in November of 1911, the troupe put on its final show of the season in Pomona, California. And instead of returning home, the performers took hotel rooms and cottages around the area and settled in to soak up some California sunshine and mingle with other show folks. According to Wallis, most of the group—including Joe Miller, who was traveling with the show—secured lodging in Venice, then a touristy spot known as "the Coney Island of the West."

As might be imagined, the flamboyant group of performers didn't just hunker down to wait out the winter. They showed up for parades and other events, and Joe indicated a desire to stay, at least for a while, by buying—according to *The Real Wild West*—a local orange grove and walnut orchard. More important, he started meeting film people. It's possible that he renewed his acquaintance then with William Selig, whose Selig Polyscope Company had moved to California from Chicago in 1909, setting up what film historian Tim Dirks (writing on the website www.filmsite.org) called "the *first* permanent film studio in the Los Angeles area." There, among other things, the Selig outfit continued its already-successful efforts to make a major cowboy star out of former 101 ranch hand Tom Mix, who surely must have visited his old Oklahoma pals during their nearby overwintering in late 1911 and early 1912.

But another collaboration between Selig and the 101 Ranch was not to be (although Selig would shoot at least one picture, the 1914 Tom Mix starrer *In the Days of the Thundering Herd*, at Pawnee Bill's Buffalo Ranch, headquarters of another Oklahoma wild-west show). Instead, Joe Miller signed up with the Bison Company, a subsidiary of the New York Motion Picture Company. As suggested by its name, the Bison Company specialized in western movies, so it was a studio that could benefit hugely from a ready-made source of cowboys, Indians, and livestock.

In *One Reel a Week*, a 1967 memoir cowritten with Arthur C. Miller, New York Motion Picture Company cofounder Fred J. Balshofer recalled Bison's initial affiliation with the wild-west show and its performers.

> [Company vice president Charles O.] Bauman learned that the Miller Brothers 101 Ranch Wild West show was in winter quarters in Venice, California, just a few miles down the coast from our location. Together we went to look over the show and the possibility of using it in our Bison pictures during the time they were wintering there. We talked out a deal with Joe Miller, who was in charge of the show. I made out a personal check for a thousand dollars, payable to the Miller Brothers 101 Ranch to bind the show. (p. 76)

For that financial outlay, Bison got the services of some 135 cowboys, cowgirls, and Indians—along with, wrote Balshofer, "the use of twenty-four oxen, some bison, and many horses complete with trappings, as well as prairie schooners and stage coaches" (p. 76). In addition to the money, the 101 Ranch also got a little moviemaking prestige, with the Bison Company changing its name to the Bison 101 Company.

The supervisor of the Bison Company was a major American movie pioneer named Thomas Harper Ince. Already a veteran of the film industry, such as it was, he moved from New York to the Los Angeles area with Bison in late 1911, around the same time as the 101's wild-west show performers and Joe Miller settled in for the winter. Ince would become most famous for creating a new way of planning and budgeting movies, figuring costs and other details via advance shooting scripts. It was a revolutionary, streamlined method of doing things that ultimately led to the departmentalized Hollywood studio system.

With the help of the 101 Ranch and its people, livestock, and props, Ince would make his first substantial mark directing western movies. And at the time he and the 101 performers began working together, there was another compelling reason to have some sharpshooting cowboys around. Back in 1908, the Edison Company—incidentally the first picture outfit to shoot at the 101—had spearheaded an attempt to control the business by gathering together eight other film companies (including Selig, which had been dragged into court by Edison on copyright infringement charges three years earlier) and creating something called the Motion Picture Patents Company. Known also as the Edison Trust, the group attempted—rather successfully at first—to limit the filmmaking activities of nonmembers by a variety of methods, including downright thuggish tactics.

According to Michael Wallis, getting out of the reach of the Edison Trust's long arm was as big a factor in eastern studios' heading for the West Coast as any other. "The whole thing with California, early on, was that it was quite a haven for filmmakers," he explained. "It provided sanctuary from the Edison interests, who could get pretty heavy-duty, right down to physical violence. They just didn't want any Edison goons breaking up their sets and equipment. It was, really, kind of an extortion thing. So that was another good thing about having the Millers around. With those Oklahoma cowboys, they had a built-in security system."

In fact, as Wallis noted in *The Real Wild West*, after the Bison 101 Company acquired nearly thirty square miles of grassland, canyons, and mountain range near Santa Monica for shooting westerns, "a group of the toughest 101 ranch riders" rolled in from Oklahoma to provide security for the area (p. 368). Of course, they were armed. And, of course, they could shoot.

While these transplanted 101 ranch hands were guarding the vast acreage—which would come to be known as Inceville—their comrades from the wild-west show were making movies with Ince. The first collaborative effort between Ince and the 101 appears to have been a two-reeler titled *War on the Plains*. Released in February of 1912, it told the story of a cowardly prospector (played by Francis Ford, whose older brother John would become one of the greatest Hollywood directors of all time) who hitches up with a wagon train after leaving his partner to die in the desert. His made-up tales of heroism beguile a young woman (Ethel Grandin) in the westward-heading party, but his true lack of mettle is revealed when the group is attacked by Indians. The prospector meets an unhappy end, and the young woman's suitor (Howard Davies) is restored to his rightful place in her affections.

Ince cowrote *War on the Plains* with its stars Davies and William Eagle Shirt, a Sioux and 101 Ranch veteran who figured prominently in Ince's early oaters. Among the picture's other players was the Stillwater, Oklahoma–born Art Acord, a big cowboy name during the silent-screen days. In interviews, Ince gave *War on the Plains* credit for starting the cowboy-and-Indian cycle of shoot-'em-up movies, although it was far from the first picture to use those two groups as antagonists. (Recall, for instance, the 101 Ranch–shot, Oklahoma-produced *A Round-Up in Oklahoma*, released more than three years earlier.)

Ince pitted the first Americans against their cowpuncher counterparts in several more two-reelers from the Bison 101 studio that year, not only because that theme had become popular with moviegoers but also because Ince had both the cowboys and the Indians—to say nothing of the horses and wagons—to do it up right. Ince's output for 1912 includes such variations on the theme as *The Indian Massacre*, *The Battle of the Red Men*, and *The Altar of Death*, the latter telling the story of a young Indian woman (Ann Little) who gives her life in order to save the staff of an Army fort. Little, along with Francis Ford, appeared in all three of those pictures, with both Acord and Eagle Shirt also acting in the first two.

The Miller Brothers 101 Ranch Real Wild West Show headed back to the road in the spring of that year, although a good number of troupers were left behind to continue making films at Inceville. But things were changing in the film industry. Within months, a new company, Universal, had absorbed the New York Motion Picture Company, the parent of Bison 101. Claiming the right to use the Bison 101 Company name, Universal shipped its own group of cowboys, Indians, and livestock to Southern California for filming purposes. The 101 Ranch sued, to no avail.

A couple of years earlier, there had been some talk about Ince moving the whole operation to the 101 itself, but that hadn't panned out. Now, although the director had left Bison 101 and started another company, taking a few of the old hands with him, things just weren't the same. Eventually, the ties between the Oklahoma ranch and the California film industry loosened and separated completely.

The 101 Ranch, however, continued to make cowboy movies, adding a department just for that purpose. Undoubtedly, the Millers saw film-making as another diversification of their empire, a relatively proven way to make some decent cash. Some documentaries were also shot on the ranch after the Buffalo 101 days, showing audiences life on a real working ranch and preserving those images—at least for a while.

Although most of the 101 Ranch efforts were shot in and around the ranch, the 101 motion picture department went on location to San Francisco in 1915 for a couple of movies, *Neola the Sioux* and *The Exposition's First Romance*. Both were lensed in conjunction with an appearance of the Miller Brothers 101 Ranch Real Wild West Show at the Panama Pacific International Exposition. A world's fair that celebrated the completion of the Panama Canal as well as the four hundredth anniversary of the Balboa expedition's first view of the Pacific Ocean—and San Francisco's recovery from the great earthquake of 1906—the exposition was big news that year, and the 101 took advantage of the recognition factor it would have with audiences. *Neola the Sioux*, a three-reeler, featured plenty of 101 Wild West Show footage in its tale of a young Indian woman (Neola Mae) who has married a white man (Duke Lee) in order to keep her real sweetheart, Red Deer (Pedro Leone), from being killed. *The Exposition's First Romance*, a five-reeler with a running time of around fifty minutes, was a western that also featured Lee and lots of wild-west show action at the exposition.

Gradually, however, the filmmaking end of the 101 operation became less and less important, although it didn't fade away until at least the mid-1920s. One of the most notable pictures shot by the ranch's motion picture unit during that time was *Trail Dust*, a pioneer epic released in 1924 and starring the Australian-born David Dunbar, who carved out a decent career as a featured player in silent action movies (mostly westerns). Posters for the film tout it as coming "DIRECT FROM THE FAMOUS MILLER BROS. 101 RANCH" and make several other boasts: "THE SEASON'S GREATEST WESTERN PICTURE . . . ALL-STAR CAST . . . OVER 2000 PEOPLE AND HORSES." Dunbar's availability as a leading man probably had a lot to do with his proximity to the ranch; that same year, he'd toiled as a secondary player in the Paramount feature *North of 36*. A follow-up to the studio's 1923 epic *The Covered Wagon*—and sharing stars Ernest Torrence and Lois Wilson and an Emerson Hough novel as source material—*North of 36* was shot, at least partially, on the 101 by the Hollywood-based studio in 1924.

According to historian Jack Spears, writing in the winter 1989–90 issue of the *Chronicles of Oklahoma*, *Trail Dust* suffered more than its share of setbacks: "The flimsy sets of a western village built on the 101 Ranch were blown down three times by strong Oklahoma winds; a tornado damaged a studio building (but left untouched $4,000 worth of electrical equipment); the star actress was seriously injured two days before filming was to begin and had to be replaced; and the cowboy hero was slightly hurt when charged by an angry bull" (p. 360).

Even given the threat of tornadoes and high winds—to say nothing of temperature extremes and other challenges—Paramount wasn't the only major studio to set up its cameras at the Miller spread during the latter days of the silent cinema. The Pathe company, which had become known for its multichapter movie serials featuring plucky heroines facing one horrendous predicament after another (including the archetypal twenty-episode *Perils of Pauline* in 1914), headed to northern Oklahoma and the ranch to make *Wild West*, a ten-chapter serial. The title of its first episode, "The Land Run," indicated its setting: in and around the massive Cherokee Strip Land Run of 1893 (in which Colonel Miller, founder of the 101, had participated). Writing in *Encyclopedia of the Great Plains* (2004, edited by David J. Wishart), Stefanie Decker described the Pathe chapterplay as "a story about a circus and medicine show traveling though Oklahoma in the 1890s and starring dozens of 101 Ranch performers" (p. 273). Other chapter titles—including "On the Show," "The Outlaw Elephant," and "Ride 'Em Cowboy!"—point toward the significant wild-west show content of this 1925 release.

As was the case with the major studio *North of 36* and the 101-generated *Trail Dust* a year earlier, Pathe's visit to the ranch apparently inspired the Millers' motion picture unit to do its own version of a Land Run film. *The Cherokee Strip*, toplining the famed Miller Brothers 101 Ranch Wild West Show performer Lucille Mulhall, also had a release date of 1925. Mulhall, whom Michael Wallis called "the world's first cowgirl" (p. 221), may well have been a performer in Pathe's *Wild West* too. (The latter starred busy Hollywood player Jack Mulhall, no relation to Lucille.)

Although there were a few years during its run when it was off the road for various reasons, the Miller Brothers 101 Ranch Real Wild West Show didn't expire for good until the summer of 1931. While it was surely cold comfort to the Millers and their cast and crew, the touring attraction had outlived hundreds of competitors before finally being done in by a number of factors, including the Great Depression and western movies—which the Miller brothers and their ranch and employees had helped popularize. As moving pictures caught on, fans of western action found they didn't have to wait until a Wild West show came to town; just about any Saturday, they could settle back in a comfortable seat at the local picture show, popcorn in hand, and experience shoot-'em-up action on the big screen. Some of the biggest stars of early sound cowboy pictures—including Ken Maynard, Buck Jones, Hoot Gibson, and western-movie stuntman supreme Yakima Canutt—had drawn paychecks from the Miller brothers at some point in their careers, either as performers in the traveling show or, later, as actors in Miller-produced movies. (Other players who appeared in Miller films included silent-screen comedienne Mabel Normand and a beautiful but minor actress named Sara Sothern—Elizabeth Taylor's mother.)

While the often inhospitable weather of Oklahoma probably precluded the 101 Ranch from ever becoming a major filmmaking center—especially early in cinematic history, when most shooting had to be done outdoors and preferably year-round—there are other reasons that the early promise of the 101 Ranch's filmmaking activities didn't pan out over the long term. The Oklahoma Historical Society's Moore theorizes that the youngest of the three Miller brothers, George—who died in a one-car wreck outside of Ponca City in 1929—loved filmmaking but could never get his siblings to completely commit to the idea, a situation that led to the eventual end of the ranch's motion picture unit.

"George was probably responsible for all of the films that were actually shot at the ranch, and there were quite a few," Moore explained. "He was really trying to set up a studio on the ranch. But I don't think the other two brothers were as excited about it as he was."

"There's a little bit of that," agreed Michael Wallis in a separate interview. "But, you know, they would've almost had to say, 'The hell with everything. Let's go into the movie business full-time.' And that just wasn't in the cards for them." Among Wallis's extensive resources for *The Real Wild West* was Zack Miller, Jr., who told the writer,

> My father and uncles and the rest of our family and outfit did a damn sight more than their share to boost the cowboy picture business at a time when not many folks even had a clue what it was all about. One hell of a lot of fine men and women who became big shots in Hollywood and household names on movie screens around the world got their start with the Hundred and One. The Miller boys and their big gang should have been acknowledged more than they were for the important part they played in keeping the great American dream alive. (p. 349)

Indeed, the ultimate legacy of the 101 Ranch and its place in filmmaking history may lie in the number of major movie cowpokes who first rode in its wild-west show or toiled in Bison 101 productions or other 101-related movies. As Wallis noted, "You've got some solid guys in Mix, Maynard, Hoot Gibson, Buck Jones, and all the rest. That's a pretty decent inventory of early western motion picture folks."

Still, it's intriguing to speculate on what might have happened had the 101 become an enduring filmmaking center, even while acknowledging all the factors that worked in Southern California's favor, and against a sprawling ranch in the Sooner State.

"Of course, Hollywood got established," said Moore. "But if the other two brothers had been as excited as George was about motion pictures, and they'd worked as hard as he did to bring them to the 101 Ranch, who knows? Maybe Hollywood would've been in Oklahoma."

TWO

Heroes and Villains, a Rough Rider, and Hollywood on the Arkansas River

How the most famous of modern bandits—a real Jean Valjean— pardoned by President Roosevelt—"Beat Back" at society until it recognized and honored him. Shows all of Al Jennings' thrilling life, including his hair-breadth escape from death at the hands of the law.

> —promotional ad for *Beating Back* (1914)

[Al Jennings's gang] robbed a post office, one or two trains, and a general store. Exactly how many robberies they pulled is still debated. Robbing was not very profitable. In one train robbery, they fled with only $3.00. Some say they also took a jug of whiskey.

> —David Dary, in the 2007 syndicated newspaper column "Oklahoma Reflections"

Every city at some time or other, tries her hand at the motion picture game, and although not many Tulsans are cognizant of the fact, Tulsa, too, once took her turn.

> —La-Vere Shoenfelt Anderson, "When Tulsa Attempted to Become a Second Hollywood," *Tulsa World* (March 9, 1930)

As the folks from the 101 Ranch blazed their cinematic trail through Oklahoma and across the country to the shores of the Pacific Ocean, they were not ignored by other would-be filmmakers, eager to get in on the action. Inspired by the visibility of the Miller brothers' movie efforts, a colorful parade of outlaws and lawmen, businesspeople, and professional entertainers came along to plunge headfirst into the nascent Sooner State scene. A U.S. president even got involved.

Before the first two decades of the twentieth century ended, much of the state's film business would coalesce around Tulsa. That city was, however, just one of the places in Oklahoma where cameras cranked and actors emoted. The 101 Ranch, having started it all, continued to devote plenty of resources to moviemaking. The most famous location for Oklahoma's earliest movies, including the pre-statehood films that Edison shot on the property, it was not the only one. It wasn't even the only wild-west show operation in the state to have a film production arm. Around 1910, at least four movies were produced by a flamboyant state-based figure, a fellow born in Illinois with the given name of Gordon Lillie. It was, however, as Pawnee Bill, head of the Pawnee Bill Wild West Show, that he achieved his fame.

He'd begun his show business career with Buffalo Bill Cody's touring western show in 1883, joining some Pawnee Indian friends who'd accepted Cody's invitation to go on the road. In 1902, Pawnee Bill purchased some Indian land and built a cabin near what is now Pawnee, Oklahoma. Pawnee Bill's holdings grew into a ranch at about the same time he got his own wild-west show up and running.

Like its 101 Ranch counterpart forty miles to the southwest, Pawnee Bill's Buffalo Ranch attracted some outside filmmakers in the early days of American cinema. As mentioned in the previous chapter, former Miller brothers ranch hand Tom Mix, by then well on his way to becoming a major cowboy-movie star, traveled to Lillie's spread to play the lead in a five-reel feature for Selig titled *In the Days of the Thundering Herd*. Released in 1914, it featured Pawnee Bill himself in a supporting role.

A year or so earlier, the Fort Lee, New Jersey–based Éclair American Company, the stateside branch of a French filmmaking outfit, had lensed five shorts around Bill's ranch. These one-reelers included three western-themed comedies (*Greasepaint Indians*, *He Could Not Lose Her*, *A Pawnee Romance*) and two adaptations of O. Henry short stories (*Hearts and Crosses* and *All on Account of an Egg*). All were helmed by William F. Haddock, a busy director of early silent pictures. It's possible that some members of the Pawnee Bill Wild West Show had roles in these productions.

In late 2007 the Autry National Center's Institute for the Study of the American West, based in Los Angeles, acquired brochures, a kinetoscope, and the four 1910 films that were shot on Pawnee Bill's Buffalo Ranch by ranch personnel. Announcing the institute's plans to digitally restore the movies, the October 2007 newsletter from the Friends of Pawnee Bill Ranch Association also published photos of the brochure covers, as well as excerpts from the text that provide insight into the psyches of that era's western-movie filmmakers and their audiences:

Why the Pawnee Bill Buffalo Ranch Feature Pictures Are the Greatest Western Pictures Yet Produced

—Because they are put on and handled by Pawnee Bill, the most romantic frontier figure and the best posted man on Western ethics the world has ever known
—Because they are made on the Buffalo ranch, located in the heart of the Indian and Buffalo country
—Because everything is genuine and true to nature. No Jersey cowboys nor painted white men for Indians.

The "Jersey cowboy" reference is obviously a swipe at the Edison folks and others who were then producing their own shoot-'em-ups back East, while at the same time a plug for the verisimilitude of Pawnee Bill's own product. (With only about five thousand people living in Hollywood in 1910, New York and New Jersey were still America's filmmaking centers—although that was changing rapidly.)

Of the four Buffalo Ranch movies, three—*The Buffalo Hunters*, *The Frontier Detective*, and *The White Chief*—star Bill himself, while a fourth, *Queen of the Buffalo Ranch*, toplines his wife, wild-west show performer May Lillie. All except *The Buffalo Hunters*, presented by "Pawnee Bill's Buffalo Ranch Film Company," carry the credit "Pawnee Bill's Buffalo Ranch Feature Films." Both names indicate that, at least for a time, a self-contained motion picture unit was operating at Bill's headquarters, even before Selig and Éclair American came through.

The painstaking restoration of these important movies in Oklahoma's filmmaking history began in 2009. Meanwhile, there are plenty of other stories to consider from the state's early moving-picture endeavors—including one that involves a famous United States president and a man who needed no weapons to vanquish a wolf.

In 1905, two years before Oklahoma's statehood, President Theodore Roosevelt stopped by the Twin Territories, following a reunion of his legendary Rough Riders, the volunteer cavalry brigade he'd led during the Spanish-American War of 1898. According to Jack Spears, in his "Hollywood's Oklahoma" piece (published in the winter 1989–90 edition of the *Chronicles of Oklahoma*), Roosevelt was taken on a five-day wolf hunt while in the area, during which he saw a man named John R. Abernathy "subdue a wolf with his bare hands." Wrote Spears: "Roosevelt was enormously impressed and urged Abernathy to record his feat on motion picture film, promising to show it at the White House" (p. 341).

"Abernathy would catch them [the wolves] and pull their jaws apart—you can see it in the film," explained Bill Moore. "That way, they couldn't bite him, and they'd eventually just wear out. The story goes that Teddy Roosevelt was just enthralled by that, and he went back to Washington and related the story to the folks in D.C., who kind of said, 'Yeah, right.' So they got to talking, and Marshal Bill Tilghman decided they did need to get it on film, so that Teddy Roosevelt could show everyone that Abernathy could really do this."

The exact genesis of the film, after Roosevelt suggested it, remains unclear. While Moore indicated that it was Tilghman, a famous U.S. marshal working the territories, who got the project under way, *Chronicles of Oklahoma* writers Spears and Leo Kelley (in his spring 1996 article, "Hoxie and Acord: 'Reel' Oklahoma Cowboys") tabbed Abernathy as the catalyst. (Kelley, in fact, wrote that "Roosevelt telegraphed Abernathy and asked him to film one of his bold captures" [p. 6].) Whichever one it was, he had the good sense to engage Bennie Kent, the official photographer at the 101 Ranch, to shoot the film.

"Tilghman was marshal of Lincoln County, where Chandler is, and that's where Bennie Kent lived," Moore noted. "I would assume they drank coffee together." Abernathy, whose apt nickname was "Catch 'em Alive Jack," was also involved in law enforcement in the area—he had become, according to Kelley, the first U.S. marshal in the new state of Oklahoma in 1907. That gig came courtesy of President Roosevelt, who was apparently so impressed by Abernathy's wolf-catching techniques that he handed Abernathy the federal job. As Moore noted, Abernathy likely knew his fellow marshal Tilghman. He surely was also acquainted with Chris Madsen, another lawman enlisted to help make the movie.

Under the newly minted name of the Oklahoma Natural Mutoscene Company, the party took to the Wichita Mountains in 1908 to find a wolf or two for Catch 'em Alive Jack to work over in front of Kent's lens. A week of shooting produced *The Wolf Hunt*, a one-reeler shipped to the White House and shown by Roosevelt to a group of notables in February 1909. In addition to Abernathy doing his stuff for the camera, the film featured a number of riders on horseback and their dogs pursuing the wolf before Abernathy stepped in to administer the coup de grace.

One of those riders was Al Jennings, a not-particularly-successful former outlaw who'd spent a stretch in prison for his crimes. At the time *The Wolf Hunt* was shot, Jennings had shifted careers and was once again practicing law, his pre-criminal profession, in Lawton, Oklahoma. He would, however, find his biggest fame in the movies and, in doing so, would greatly annoy Bill Tilghman, the Oklahoma Natural Mutoscene Company's de facto director.

Before that happened, though, Jennings would be involved in at least one other picture with Tilghman. Shot only a few days after *The Wolf Hunt* wrapped, *The Bank Robbery* was filmed on location in Cache, Oklahoma, with Jennings playing the leader of a gang that robs the local bank, only to be captured by Tilghman and his law enforcement pals. Some sources hold that *The Bank Robbery* is a re-creation of an actual Al Jennings exploit, but the Jennings bunch, in its brief career, doesn't seem to have ever held up a bank.

Although *The Bank Robbery* was wolfless, Abernathy had a part in it, as did Madsen and Comanche chief Quanah Parker, who played a tracker assisting Tilghman and the rest of the posse. Other lawmen and various Cache residents filled out the cast, the latter appearing as characters on both sides of the law.

While it must've found an audience, at least around the region, *The Bank Robbery* doesn't exactly stand as a pinnacle of the filmmaker's art, even by 1908 standards. Leo Kelley called it "ineptly made" ("Hoxie and Acord," p. 342), a far kinder, and briefer, description than that given by movie historian William K. Everson. In his *Pictorial History of the Western*

Film (1969), Everson wrote about the early "Eastern Westerns," those unauthentic pictures shot in New York and New Jersey with pretend cowboys (and referred to disparagingly in the 1910 promotional brochure for Pawnee Bill's movies). Then, he laid into Marshal Tilghman's second picture as a director:

> That authenticity of costume, locale and plot was not in itself an essential to winning public appeal was proven by a most peculiar little Western of 1908 entitled *The Bank Robbery*. . . . Its plot vaguely paralleled *The Great Train Robbery*, although it attempted to win a little sympathy for the outlaws by showing their concern for a wounded comrade, in putting their escape in jeopardy by stopping to care for him. The dusty little Oklahoma town, with the bank as its focal point, was obviously the real thing, and at two reels the film was the longest Western yet made. Its "director" was famed frontier lawman William M. Tilghman (later a good friend and advisor to [pioneering screen cowboy] William S. Hart) and its cast included train robber Al Jennings, only recently out of jail. Tilghman undoubtedly was an efficient and fearless frontier marshal, but it is fortunate indeed that he never had to make his living as a movie director. Not only did he lack knowledge of even rudiments of technique—some of the camera panning is so appallingly inept that once, when the outlaws race out of town, the camera never does catch up with more than a glimpse of the flying tail of the last horse—but he had no idea of showmanship either. One would have thought that with a "celebrity" like Al Jennings to work with, some attempt would have been made to spotlight him, either by making him the leader of the outlaws or by giving him a key scene or bit of "business." But there is not even a medium shot to give audiences the chance to recognize Jennings; he is merely one of the gang, photographed almost entirely in long shot throughout, and if one were not familiar with Jennings' face and small stature from his later starring Westerns, one wouldn't be able to pick him out from the crowd. (p. 17)

A couple of things are worth noting in that harsh assessment. First of all, Everson mentions an attempt to generate a little sympathy for the bank robbers. Chances are good that the plot twist didn't come from director Tilghman, a no-nonsense veteran lawman who had few, if any, warm feelings toward those who violated the rules. Jennings is very likely the originator of that scene, especially given the films he became involved with later on. Second, assuming that Tilghman's antipathy toward lawbreakers extended to reformed ones, perhaps his lack of filmic attention to Jennings is intentional rather than simply a missed opportunity by a clumsy filmmaker. Whether or not that's the case, Jennings would soon make up for that on-screen neglect in a big way—and inadvertently lead to one of Oklahoma's, and Tilghman's, best-known early movies in the bargain.

Alphonso J. Jennings was a man who could make a lot out of a little, especially when it came to recounting his own exploits. A Virginia native, he moved westward with his family following the Civil War, ending up in Oklahoma in the late 1800s. According to author and professor David Dary, whose "Oklahoma Reflections" articles ran in a number of state newspapers during the centennial year of 2007, the adult Jennings was initially employed in the legal profession, first as a prosecuting attorney in Canadian County and later in a law practice with his two brothers in Woodward. There the Jennings siblings quarreled with fellow attorney Temple Houston (the youngest of statesman Sam Houston's eight children and the model for Yancey Cravat, the main character in Edna Ferber's Oklahoma Land Run novel, *Cimarron*). A shoot-out with Houston resulted in the death of one of Al's brothers and an injury to the other, and Houston's subsequent acquittal of any crime seems to have been the impetus for Jennings's move to the dark side.

Whatever the reason, his life as a bad man didn't last long. After a few months of only marginally successful robberies around Oklahoma, the Jennings gang dissolved when its leader was shot, captured, and tossed in jail. Sentenced in 1899 to life in prison, but lucky enough to have a brother who was a better lawyer than Al had been an outlaw, Jennings saw his sentence cut to five years, which he served. In 1907, the year of Oklahoma's statehood, he was pardoned by President Theodore Roosevelt—the man for whom Jennings would help make *The Wolf Hunt* a year later.

After involving himself for a while in two high-profile Oklahoma vocations, evangelism and politics, Jennings met up with well-known writer and journalist Will Irwin in a New York club, and the two began putting on paper a highly romanticized version of Al's life story. A magazine piece titled "Beating Back" ran in 1913 as part of the *Saturday Evening Post's* "Human Document" series; the next year, D. Appleton and Company published a book (with illustrations by noted cowboy artist Charles M. Russell), and the Thanhouser Company of New Rochelle, New York, made a six-reel feature—both titled, like the *Post* story, *Beating Back*.

Although it is clear that Irwin wrote the book, he went to great pains in its opening chapter to explain how it was really an autobiography—and in so doing, gave some insight into what must have been one garrulous ex-outlaw. Here's an excerpt from that first chapter, titled "Introducing Mr. Jennings" (whom Irwin sometimes referred to as "The Long Rider"): "Jennings has never found time, in those full and busy years since he left prison, to learn the art of writing. . . . He is, however, a master in the art of talk, whether from the platform or from an easy-chair. That narrative gift which often freezes within him when he sits before white paper, flows limpid when he lights a cigar, crosses his feet, and engages the eye of his *vis-à-vis*" (pp. 5–6).

Both the film and the book painted Jennings in a highly flattering light, as a good and honorable man beating back at the society that had kicked him around and kept him down and finally driven him to outlawry. Despite Irwin's obvious authorship, the book's cover carries Jennings's name as sole writer (although the title page lists both names). The movie, shot in New Jersey, credits Jennings (as Al J. Jennings) with the story, Irwin with the adaptation, and in what was apparently his only produced script, actor and magician Caryl S. Fleming with the scenario. Jennings played himself, naturally.

In the *Chronicles of Oklahoma*, Jack Spears described the motion picture version of *Beating Back*:

> Like [Jennings's] episodic reminiscences [in the *Saturday Evening Post*], *Beating Back* contains many inaccuracies and outright fabrications. The life of a train robber was made to appear glamorous and exciting, and the lawmen who brought Jennings to justice are portrayed as bungling, brutal, and self-serving. Jennings is seen as the victim of circumstances which forced him into crime. The film traces his rehabilitation in prison and early release, marriage to a good woman, and a new life as a respected Oklahoma

attorney and politician. Jennings made frequent personal appearances with *Beating Back*, lecturing on the evils of crime and warning against bad companions. (p. 344)

With *Beating Back* (released under the title *Dare Devil Jennings* in Great Britain), the moviemaking bug bit Jennings hard, and for the next several years he used his celebrity as a high-profile former outlaw to work in the motion picture business, acting in a number of films and producing a couple as well. Never one to dodge the spotlight's glare, he made national news in 1945 when he sued the producers of the popular radio series *The Lone Ranger*, claiming that they had defamed him by having the Lone Ranger shoot a gun out of Al Jennings's hand in an episode of the program. According to David Dary, Jennings claimed he was the fastest gun on the range, and his reputation suffered from the contrasting characterization sent over the airwaves by the radio program. Jennings, eighty-two years old at the time of the suit, lost.

The former outlaw lived long enough to see another version of his life story hit the screen. Again based on the book *Beating Back*, 1951's *Al Jennings of Oklahoma* was a modestly budgeted Technicolor effort toplining movie tough guy Dan Duryea as Jennings, with Gale Storm and reliable veteran western-picture stars Dick Foran and Guinn "Big Boy" Williams in support. The old holdup man was eighty-eight when Columbia Pictures released *Al Jennings of Oklahoma*. He was to live another ten years, dying on December 26, 1961, in Tarzana, California.

Although the hard-bitten outlaw reputation Al Jennings brought with him to the movies was more created than earned, a couple of other lawbreaker gangs depicted in early Oklahoma movies were top-shelf bad guys. The Younger Brothers, paired up with the James Gang, had cut a decade-long swath through Missouri and neighboring states following the Civil War, regularly holding up banks, trains, and stagecoaches—and they weren't afraid to let lead fly at the slightest provocation. The Dalton Brothers Gang, out of Kansas, didn't last nearly as long, but they were well known for their attempted 1892 holdup of a couple of banks in

Coffeyville, a brazen but unsuccessful raid that led to the deaths of most of the gang members.

The movies made about these outlaws did share one thing with Jennings and *Beating Back*, however. The stories of their lives, as crafted for movie audiences, showed them as sympathetic figures shoved into crime by forces beyond their control, despite a significant body of real-life evidence to the contrary.

Take the motion picture that was shot, at least partially, in the Red Fork area around Tulsa during the early days of Sooner cinema. A short piece in the July 3, 1912, *Tulsa Daily Democrat* indicated the tone of the film with its headline: "MAKING SAINTS OF THE DALTON GANG." A reader can almost feel the headline writer's aversion to the idea in the story's subhead: "Moving Pictures to Prove That Crimes Were Highly Commendable."

The article cited the Atlas Company of St. Louis as the movie's producer, noting that the group was shooting around Red Fork that day before heading to Sand Springs, where the ill-fated attempt to rob a couple of Coffeyville, Kansas, banks was to be re-created. Then—shades of Al Jennings—came this paragraph:

> The purpose of these pictures is to show that the outlaws were a law abiding bunch of fellows before they became outlaws. They are going to try to show that it was the fault of the United States that the Daltons became bad men and not by choice. It is claimed by them that Uncle Sam refused to pay the Dalton brothers a salary that was coming to them for their services as marshals and that to get revenge the gang was organized.

The article concluded by noting that eleven cowboys from Pawhuska, Oklahoma, along with a solitary girl, were appearing in that day's shooting and that the whole thing was to wrap the next day. (The plural word "pictures" used in the piece seems to be equivalent to the singular terms "film" or "movie.")

Evidence suggests that this footage was being shot for the motion picture released later in the year as *The Last Stand of the Dalton Boys*, a three-reeler with Emmett Dalton himself supervising production. The only Dalton brother to survive the Coffeyville debacle, Emmett got involved in the film business after doing almost fifteen years in prison for his part in the botched robbery. (He claimed that, throughout it all, he had never fired a shot.) Like Al Jennings, Dalton wrote a purportedly autobiographical book, *Beyond the Law*, and starred in a 1918 movie of the same name. (In an odd bit of casting, he played his two dead brothers as well as himself.) Also like Jennings, he toured as a commentator with at least one motion picture—*On the Texas Border*, which had a run at Tulsa's Empire Theatre in January of 1912. An ad in the *Tulsa Democrat* from January 16 stated succinctly, "Emmett Dalton will make a short talk for the benefit of the boys," and also noted that Scout Younger, who was the producer of the picture, would appear along with Dalton.

According to "Hollywood-on-the-Arkansas? We Tried," an April 1, 1962, *Tulsa World* newspaper piece by Russell Gideon, "just where Scout Younger fit into the Younger outlaw family was seldom, if ever, explained." Other sources call him a cousin of Cole, Jim, John, and Bob Younger. Whatever their relationship, Scout Younger was also an early Oklahoma movie-maker with connections not only to the lone surviving Younger broth-er—Cole, the eldest of the boys—but to the Daltons as well. Gideon noted that Emmett Dalton had actually been Scout Younger's houseguest when the former came to town to appear at the screenings of *On the Texas Border*. That, of course, would make Scout Younger a Tulsa-area resident at the time—as well as a man with impressive connections to two major outlaw families.

In addition to working with the last remaining Dalton in at least one movie, Scout Younger also made a movie about his own clan. The camera began rolling only a few months after *On the Texas Border* played the Em-pire. A brief piece in the June 30, 1912, edition of the *Tulsa Daily Demo-crat*, rather clunkily titled "MAKE FILMS IN TULSA FOR MOVING PICTURES," announced, "Tulsa is to have a full-fledged moving-picture company lo-cated here," adding that Scout Younger was asking the city commission for permission to shoot "street scenes in Tulsa." A further statement by Younger that he had "connected himself with one of the largest film show companies in the business and that headquarters would soon be estab-lished in one of the suburbs" was pretty much show-biz hooey, but he did get the picture made, even though four years would pass before its release.

Nothing more about the movie can be found in the local press until

July 13, 1915, when a short article observed that Frank Patterson, the president of Longhorn Feature Film Company, was visiting from San Diego, California, and had interest in a three-reeler that Younger had recently completed, which was apparently the Younger Brothers movie. (During Patterson's visit, Younger also took him to see Pawnee Bill at the Buffalo Ranch.)

A few months later, beginning on February 28, 1916, Scout Younger was back in Tulsa, along with what the *Tulsa Democrat* called "a big display of artillery, long horns, old riding coats and everything a real sure nuf bandit once wore and used," for a two-day run of his Younger Brothers three-reeler at the Lyric Theatre. Like the Al Jennings and Dalton pictures, it put the best spin possible on the its protagonists' saga, as reported in the February 29 *Democrat*:

> The picture entitled *Younger Brothers* is interesting and educational from the first foot of the reel until the last. It shows what men can do and did and the ultimate result of their escapades. Men who can reform and then be a model example to great humanity. The picture was made in Tulsa about eighteen months ago and contains many local people in the cast with familiar Tulsa landmarks. It does not bespeak amateur work on the part of actor or camera man and is showing to a packed house from 10 A.M. to 11 P.M. People were crowded out into the street this morning when a reporter's attention was attracted to the scene by such a large crowd.

Although the article gives the film's title as *Younger Brothers*, a newspaper ad from the day before calls it *They Never Forgot Mother and Home*—another indication of the sympathetic tack taken by the filmmaker toward his subjects.

The picture was put into general release some time later by the Longhorn Company, and Scout Younger reportedly headed to San Diego to make a six-reeler with Longhorn president Patterson called *The Passing of the Longhorn*. It may be that the Longhorn studio itself passed before the picture could be released, or perhaps the film was never made or was issued under a different title. Records indicate that no film with that name ever received any significant distribution, suggesting that *The Younger Brothers/ They Never Forgot Mother and Home* was Scout Younger's last gasp as a filmmaker.

Cole Younger, meanwhile, was taking his own last gasps, even as the movie about him and his brothers played in Tulsa. The February 29 *Democrat* story concludes with these lines: "Every story has a sad part, but the sadness in this picture is not shown on the screen. Cole Younger is dying at his home in Missouri and Scout is momentarily awaiting a telegram of the event. It will not be long before the Youngers are gone, but the picture and memory will live on forever."

Cole Younger died a little less than a month later, on March 21, 1916. Forty-two years later, Allied Artists released *Cole Younger, Gunfighter*, with Frank Lovejoy in the title role. It was, unsurprisingly, a highly romanticized retelling of the eldest Younger's life and times.

Then, as now, criminals—reformed or otherwise—made for good box office. Law-abiding Americans have long seemed fascinated by those who choose to live their lives giving the Bronx cheer to polite society, and the early Oklahoma films made about (and sometimes by) outlaws found plenty of interested viewers—sometimes only locally, but often in movie houses and other venues throughout the country.

The glorification of the gunslinger lifestyle, as well as the tendency of these pictures to blame society for forcing otherwise upstanding citizens into a life of crime, did not set well with the Oklahoma Natural Mutoscene Company's erstwhile director, Bill Tilghman. He was especially incensed by the filmic activities of Al Jennings, former member of the Mutoscene stock company. As Jack Spears explained in "Hollywood's Oklahoma": "Marshal Bill Tilghman was enraged by *Beating Back*, as were his fellow peace officers in the Southwest. He felt the Jennings film made heroes of murderous outlaws, discredited brave and honest lawmen, and created an unfavorable image of Oklahoma. To counter its lies and set the record straight, Tilghman decided to produce and direct a four-reel motion picture, *The Passing of the Oklahoma Outlaws*" (p. 345).

With the Oklahoma Natural Mutoscene Company apparently having run its course after three films, Tilghman, along with his filmmaking and law-enforcing cohort Chris Masden and former U.S. marshal E. D. Nix, founded the Eagle Film Company, based in Oklahoma City. Its mission was to film an answer to *Beating Back*, told from a lawman's point of view.

"The story behind it is that Tilghman was fed up with people like Al Jennings getting all this glory for being outlaws," said Bill Moore. "He wanted everybody to know what the true life of a criminal was, and that crime didn't pay. So that was a personal motive on his part, to tell this story, to re-create all these shoot-outs in which the outlaws had died."

Tilghman himself, in a *Tulsa Democrat* interview on May 3, 1918, made his motive clear. "This picture," he said, "is calculated to discourage young men from becoming outlaws. It shows that the life of an outlaw is tawdry and it takes the glamour away from it. The law gets all of them in time."

Most of the four-reel movie, made up of six bad-guy-busting episodes, has been reconstructed, and Moore believes that only the opening titles and a few minutes from the very beginning are missing (along with the frames of film lost to splicing and deterioration). Because the reconstructed version of the film is readily available today, it's likely that more people are familiar with *Passing of the Oklahoma Outlaw* than with any of the other early Oklahoma films. Although it's undeniably crude from a filmmaking point of view—Tilghman remained a far better peace officer than director—it gets the job done, even though the heroes often seem as ruthless as the villains. (One scene especially jarring to current filmgoer sensibilities shows a pair of outlaws, Charley Pierce and George "Bitter Creek" Newcomb, ambushed and shot to death by Tilghman's forces, who outnumber their quarry by about three to one.)

Jack Spears reported that filming of *Passing of the Oklahoma Outlaw* began early in 1915 at Chandler, Bennie Kent's hometown, and spread over the next few months into Stroud, Ingalls, and Guthrie, as well as Eureka Springs, Arkansas, and the Spike S Ranch, located in the Creek Nation. As he'd done in Cache for *The Bank Robbery*, Tilghman enlisted local residents to play roles in the picture. Spears wrote that "former members" of the 101 Ranch Wild West Show were also cast ("Hollywood's Oklahoma," p. 345). Taking a page from the Al Jennings playbook, the gruff-looking, mustachioed Tilghman and several of his fellow lawmen—including his Eagle Film Company partner Nix—appeared as themselves, tracking down a slew of bad guys and a couple of teenage

THE PRESIDENT of the UNITED STATES OF AMERICA

To the Marshal of the United States for the ..Western. District of Oklahoma, and to His Deputies, or any or either of them:

WHEREAS, ...John Hixon.......... has made complaint in writing under oath, before me, the undersigned Commissioner of the District Court of the United States for the Western.........District of Oklahoma, Charging that..Bill Doolin.................... ....did on or about the ....1st..day of....September..A. D....1893..at....Ingalls in said District in violation of section........ ....of the Revised Statutes of the United States, unlawfully, willfully and feloniously ....commit the crime of murder..............

....
....

NOW, THEREFORE, You are Hereby Commanded, in the name of the President of the United States of America, to apprehend the said ....Bill Doolin.............. ....wherever found in your District and bring..him.........forthwith before me or any other Commissioner having jurisdiction of said matter, to answer to said complaint that he may be then and there dealt with according to the law for the said offense.

Given under my name and seal this....5th..day of....September....A. D....1893

J. R. Thomas [Seal]

Commissioner of the District Court of the U. S. for the........Western..Dist. of Oklahoma.

APPROVED:

C. R. Brooks United States Attorney

Approved E. D. Nix U.S. Marshal

BILL DOOLIN   BILL TILGHMAN

King of Outlaws, Captured by U. S. Marshal, Bill Tilghman

SEE THE SIX REEL PHOTO DRAMA

"Passing of the Oklahoma Outlaws"

PRESENTED BY

BILL TILGHMAN Who Will Lecture in Person.

Shown at The

— REX —

MONDAY — NOV. 25th

For years after the original 1915 release of *Passing of the Oklahoma Outlaw,* lawman Bill Tilghman toured with the picture. (Contrary to this advertisement, the film's intertitles refer to the movie as *Passing of the Oklahoma Outlaw* [singular], and most film historians agree that it was a four-reeler.) (Courtesy of the Oklahoma Historical Society) female delinquents who went by the monikers of Cattle Annie and Little Britches. (One especially memorable scene finds Tilghman swaggering into the cellar hideout of a band of desperadoes, all of whom hide under their bunks and bedclothes to keep from confronting him.)

The law officers were the real thing. The bad men—with the exception of a reformed desperado named Arkansas Tom Jones—weren't, and for a very good reason. As the *Democrat* reported: "The parts of the outlaws, of course, were taken by others, for the outlaws are all dead, with the exception of 'Arkansas Tom,' who was found after he had served a penitentiary sentence and was induced to act the part he played with the bandits in territorial days." That was a bit of an exaggeration—a few of the crooks depicted in the film were still above ground at the time—but Tilghman and his cohorts had certainly made a dent in the area's outlaw population by the time *Passing* hit the screen.

According to Michael Wallis's *The Real Wild West*, real life intruded on reel life during the filming of *Passing of the Oklahoma Outlaw* when another area lawbreaker, Henry Starr, and his gang robbed a couple of banks simultaneously in Stroud, trying to accomplish what the Youngers hadn't been able to pull off in Coffeyville, Kansas, twenty-three years earlier. Unfortunately for Starr, he and his boys didn't fare much better. They got the banks robbed all right, but as the gang attempted its getaway, a teenaged butcher-shop employee named Paul Curry began blasting at them with a sawed-off rifle he normally used on hogs. One of his shots caught Starr in the hip. By the time Tilghman and Kent arrived from their film location in Chandler, Starr was cooling his heels in the local hospital. Tilghman went out to help hunt down the rest of the robbers, while Kent, his camera always at the ready, took documentary footage of the downed lawbreaker. At least one source suggests that some of that film found its way into the final cut of *Passing of the Oklahoma Outlaw*; if that's true, it doesn't exist in the version available to us today.

Not long after the Starr incident, which occurred on March 27, 1915, filming wrapped on *Passing of the Oklahoma Outlaw*. The picture was previewed on May 25 in Chandler, followed by its official debut on June 10 in Oklahoma City. For some reason, it didn't make it to Tulsa for almost three years, after engagements all across the country. The 1918

Tulsa Democrat story noted that, in Denver, *Passing* "broke all records for moving picture films in a run of two weeks and the same has been done in other places."

Passing of the Oklahoma Outlaw was Tilghman's crowning achievement as a filmmaker, something very close to a forty-minute personal statement, and he undoubtedly knew it. For the next eight years, he toured with the picture, presenting it not only in theaters but also in churches, auditoriums, and other venues—wherever he could draw a crowd and lecture on the evils of life outside the law. Kept busy with this schedule, along with whatever lawman duties he still attended to back home in Oklahoma, Tilghman never found the time nor the inclination to make another movie.

Ironically, the man who'd done so much to try and elevate the reputations of peace officers was shot and killed outside a dance hall by a fellow lawman in the wild oil-boom town of Cromwell, Oklahoma. It happened in late 1924, not long after Tilghman had come in off the road for good and once again taken a full-time law enforcement job. The killer of the seventy-year-old Tilghman was a man from Holdenville named Wylie Lynn—a "drunken prohibition officer," according to Michael Wallis in *The Real Wild West* (p. 380). Lynn, incidentally, was tried and acquitted of the killing in a Wewoka courtroom. Several years later, in 1932, he himself died of wounds received in another shoot-out, this one on the streets of Madill.

The same spring that shooting wrapped on *Passing of the Oklahoma Outlaw*, a big newspaper story trumpeted the establishment of an honest-to-goodness motion picture studio in another Sooner State location. "TULSA TO BECOME BIG MOVIE CENTER," read the headline in the April 27, 1915, *Tulsa Democrat*, referring to a brand-new business called the Tulsa Motion Picture Company. It would produce more than a dozen features, distributed all over America and into Europe and boasting recognizable stars in many of the lead roles.

While the headline's promise was never quite fulfilled, Oklahoma's second-largest city came tantalizingly close for a few years, thanks in large part to the Tulsa Motion Picture Company, whose opening was greeted with unbridled enthusiasm by the *Democrat*'s unnamed reporter:

> The acquisition to Tulsa of the Tulsa Motion Picture company, which has recently been organized, is another stride forward in the achievement of the "Tulsa of tomorrow." There is no doubt but that it is the most stupendous project that Tulsa has landed in the past year or that will be landed in the state of Oklahoma this year. The company, under the leadership of H. A. R. Mackle, who has spent the past 15 years of his life in the business, and backed by local capital almost entirely, promises to be the grandest success of a similar undertaking that has been attempted in the United States by an independent movie concern.
>
> There are many reasons why Tulsa was chosen as the city. First the climatic conditions are even superior to those of California or Florida. The scenery is different, including the oil fields and many other features too numerous to mention. It is said and borne out by weather bureau, that there are more sunshine days in the vicinity of Tulsa than any other moving picture center in the country. There are things to be written about in Oklahoma and places to stage them that have no comparison elsewhere in the United States. This alone is a sufficient inducement for any "movie" concern to locate here.

The story went on to explain that the enterprise, which was also referred to as the Tulsa Moving Picture company, had moved into the Dry Farming Congress grounds a couple of blocks outside the city limits, next to the Frisco Railroad tracks. The Dry Farming Congress was a once-a-year event that brought farmers and other rural folks in for meetings and exhibits centered on dry farming, a technique of moisture conservation used to accelerate production of crops like wheat and sorghum. So the Dry Farming Congress area was, essentially, a fairground. Mackle saw the proximity of the railroad as a bonus, complementing the racetrack, baseball diamond, and variety of buildings around the grounds.

Apparently, Mackle and his new studio intended to make westerns, exploiting what the rapturous *Democrat* writer saw as the state's best-known resource: "Oklahoma, known the world over for the many great outlaws it has produced, will be welcomed on the moving picture screen in all parts of the country and a fortune awaits the company that can produce them." Despite the article's hyperbole, that fortune apparently wasn't in the cards for Mackle, although some sources indicate that his company produced a few western movies on the lot.

It's possible that Mackle's studio changed names or was taken over by a local concern. The most likely candidate for the latter would've been the William M. Smith Amusement Company, run by a local who'd first made his name as the manager of one of the city's early movie theaters. *Tulsa World* writer Russell Gideon remembered Smith's pioneering efforts in his 1962 piece, "Hollywood-on-the-Arkansas? We Tried": "As early as March 1912 William Smith of the Cozy Theater announced he had bought a $500 moving picture machine which he planned to put on exhibition for a few days. Then he would start a new industry in Tulsa— that of making movies in which local characters and local scenes would be featured."

It took a few years, but Smith got his studio, which he set up west of Tulsa in the area known as the Sand Springs Line, so named because of the train tracks that ran through the suburb of Sand Springs. By that time, however, Smith's ambitions had gone well beyond the local. In a lengthy *Tulsa Daily World* feature article of March 9, 1930, writer La-Vere Shoenfelt Anderson reminisced about Tulsa's attempts to become, as the headline put it, "A Second Hollywood":

> The Smith Amusement company was organized toward the close of the war for the purpose of producing motion pictures in Tulsa, incorporated and the stock sold to interested Oklahomans. Featured players from the California film colony, stars who had flickered on the then-silent silver screen and won a fan following, were brought to Tulsa to play before the Smith cameras. . . .
>
> In addition to those players imported from the west coast there were several Tulsans who found they could successfully play before the camera. Arthur S. Phillips, who had himself been in Hollywood and there acquired film experience, was scenic director, superintendent and character actor on the Smith lot. Walter Davenport served as stunt man and jumped off running horses and climbed steep cliffs all as a matter of the day's work. Norrel Woodard was the sheriff who got his man. And there were many others.
>
> For extras advertisements were run in the local newspapers, and there are doubtless those in Tulsa today who can recall answering the film company's ad and appearing in one or more of their productions in a mob scene.

During only a couple of years in the very early '20s, Smith's company cranked out sixteen movies, all featuring names that would have been familiar to many of the country's moviegoers. The first of this batch of films appears to have been one called *The Cowboy Ace*. An ad in the April 16, 1921, issue of the *Tulsa Daily World* noted, "The first showing in Tulsa of a Westart picture, made in the 'Magic City,' sponsored by local people, and already famed throughout the nation, will occur at the Rialto theatre starting tomorrow."

It's unclear whether "Magic City" was a nickname for Tulsa or Smith's studio, and *World* writer Anderson referred to Smith's company as Eight West Arts rather than Westart. What *is* clear, however, is that *The Cowboy Ace*, which featured not only cowboys and outlaws but some airplane scenes as well, was one in a run of movies from the company, all written by Smith himself, directed by Leonard Franchon (who may have been local), and featuring the British-born Hollywood actor Al Hart in the lead, with character players Jack Mower (who appeared in well over five hundred films in a career stretching to the 1960s) and Robert Conville in support. Titles like *Rustlers of the Night*, *The Range Pirate*, *Trail to Red Dog*, and *Cotton and Cattle* leave no doubt as to the genre of these pictures, while *Out of the Clouds* indicates that the company made at least one other airplane-related opus.

Smith's next set of motion pictures was even more ambitious. He brought in director Francis Ford (who had worked as an actor with the 101 Ranch players at California's Inceville a decade earlier) to helm another series of westerns featuring the popular cowboy star Franklyn Farnum. Al Hart stuck around to play second banana in these five-reel features, which bore titles like *Gold Grabbers*, *Trail's End*, *It Happened Out West* (centered around a cattle ranch whose foreman is the secret kingpin of a smuggling operation involving Chinese immigrants), and *So This Is Arizona*—which, according to the *World's* Anderson was "the one that, screened in New York City before the critics, sold the other 15 pictures the company produced." Released between late 1921 and mid-1923, these movies were all credited to William M. Smith Productions.

(Perhaps this is the place to note an odd coincidence. Sixty years later, Tulsa would again become noted for its filmmaking when *another* Francis Ford—

Francis Ford Coppola—came to town to direct a couple of pictures, a visit chronicled in detail later on in these pages. Coppola, it should be emphasized, was *not* named after the silent-film director who'd preceded him to Oklahoma by six decades.)

Naysayers had abounded when Smith launched his company, but his ability to bring in major-league talent to work on both sides of the camera, and the subsequent national release of his features, started making believers out of the local skeptics. Increasingly, there seemed to be less and less reason to bet against the Smith Amusement Company and its visionary leader.

Then came the fire.

On the afternoon of March 2, 1922, a Sunday, the studio and all it held—from its wardrobe department to its western sets, from props (including live ammo) to prints of all of its pictures—went up in flames. The *Tulsa World* reported on the conflagration the next day:

> Exploding of six electric current transformers filled with oil and hundreds of rounds of ammunition made a sensational fire near Vern station on the Sand Springs road about 2:30 o'clock yesterday afternoon, when the W. M. Smith's Motion Picture corporation's studio, located there, was completely destroyed by fire, causing a loss estimated at between $25,000 and $30,000, upon which there was no insurance. . . .
>
> The Sand Springs Electric Light & Power Co. suffered a loss of two large transformers valued at about $1,200 each, and four smaller ones valued at about $400 each. The Rayburn addition, near Vern station, is temporarily without electric lights until the damage to the lines can be repaired.

According to the article, the rebuilding and reopening of the studio would "depend on whether or not contracts are closed for the filming of pictures this summer for the Associated Exhibitors of New York, or other distributing companies," which meant that if Smith could get advance money from a national distributor who could use some new product in a hurry, he might be able to rebuild. That financing, however, was not forthcoming.

Meanwhile, members of Tulsa's police force began looking into what they saw as suspicious circumstances surrounding the blaze. They were soon joined by both private investigators and county lawmen, but a breakthrough in the case eluded them. Then, according to the May 25, 1922, edition of the *Tulsa Tribune*, the culprits confessed. It had been started by a pair of fifteen-year-olds, Marshall Dupree and Glenn Laughlin, and their twelve-year-old pal Lester Gress. Here, as reported by the *Tribune*, is how the crime went down:

> During last week in February, the boys told Mr. Welch [a Tulsa County humane agent], they were playing around in the moving picture studio, then closed [for the winter], and found a quantity of powder used for "red fire" purposes in the making of pictures. They set this powder afire, had a lot of fun watching it burn, and then searched for more. Finding none, they departed.
>
> Three days later they returned to the studio and searched again for some of the powder. Their search was again fruitless and they held a conference. It was decided that the powder they sought was kept in a small locker.
>
> The boys used a hammer and an iron bar to break into this locker. They found it filled with cans of the powder. Pouring a large quantity of the "red fire" on the floor they applied a match, "to have fun watching the powder burn." A terrific flash followed, igniting all of the powder in the locker. The disastrous fire followed.

The boys hastily beat it to a rear exit and hightailed it from the premises without being seen, swearing one another to secrecy. And they might've gotten away with it, too, had Dupree not chosen to torment young Gress while they were on an afternoon swim with friends at the Arkansas River nearly three months later.

> Marshall Dupree, it is said, began splashing little Lester Gress with water, and Lester objected. His objections were ignored.
>
> "You'd better cut it out," Lester is said to have shouted, "for I've got something on you and I'll tell."
>
> "What you got on me?" Marshall yelled back.
>
> "You burned down that picture house," Little Lester replied.
>
> "Well, you helped," Marshall replied.
>
> And there the denouement started. Another member of the swimming party told his father of the conversation that night and the father communicated with the county attorney's office.

The jig was up. The next day, the three culprits were apprehended and hauled into the Tulsa sheriff's office, where they were then turned over

SHOT IN OKLAHOMA

to A. M. Welch, the humane agent. (In that era, humane agents—appointed then, as now, by area humane societies—were often charged with protecting children as well as animals.) The two older boys were tried in county court on Saturday morning, only two days after their confession; because of his "tender age," according to the *Tribune* story, no charges were brought against little Lester Gress. Whatever penalty was leveled against the unintentional arsonists has been lost to the ages. Apparently, it wasn't much. A search of the Tulsa papers published immediately after Dupree and Laughlin's court date failed to turn up any news of their sentencing.

"Devastated" is probably too mild a word for what Bill Smith felt following the destruction of his studio. It had taken lots of money and years of relentless toil and deal-making to establish the Smith Amusement Company as a player on the national scene. Now it was gone, along with many—if not all—of the prints of the movies he'd made. All that time, effort, and cash, up in smoke.

So how much did William M. Smith love filmmaking? Enough to jump back in the saddle for a final effort called *Crossroads of Tulsa*, which was filmed in 1924. Inspired by *The Crossroads of New York*, a 1922 comedy from well-known filmmaker Mack Sennett, Smith solicited a movie script about Tulsa, offering a cash prize to the author of the scenario judged the best—which would be made into a movie.

Smith probably intended the contest to be on the up-and-up. But several years later—in the 1930 *Tulsa Daily World* retrospective article by La-Vere Shoenfelt Anderson—Smith's old lot superintendent and scenic director, the Hollywood-honed Arthur S. Phillips, spilled the beans. He had been all set to direct *Crossroads of Tulsa* for Smith, but one big thing stood in the way: not a single script they'd received was suitable for filming.

> "Nothing, in fact," says Mr. Phillips, "that we could possibly use as the basis for the picture we had to make. As the time of the prize awards grew near we were almost frantic. Then we conceived the idea, and to my knowledge this is the first time I have told this story to anyone connected with

the press, of my writing the story and sending it with an anonymous letter saying that should the story win a prize, to donate the money to the Salvation Army. So I wrote the story, had to do it, you see, and the money was presented to the Army. I believe anyone interested in this can verify the facts by consulting the news files of that period."

Bill Smith, a true Oklahoma film pioneer, died young in October of 1925, the year after *Crossroads of Tulsa* was wrapped. According to writer and actor James Vance, the film was indeed completed and shown. In a two-part article on the city's cinema history appearing in the July 22–28 and July 29–August 4, 1999, issues of *Urban Tulsa Weekly*, Vance called *Crossroads* "a purely amateur effort which was never intended to be seen outside the city limits (though it did receive a much-ballyhooed screening at Tulsa's Rialto Theater)."

And so Bill Smith's career went out with more of a whimper than a bang. But if his final on-screen effort did nothing else, it at least put a little dough in the coffers of the local Salvation Army.

If, as Vance maintained, *Crossroads of Tulsa* was an amateur production, it nevertheless had the participation of at least a couple of local filmmaking pros, Smith and his cohort Phillips. It also had a predecessor in *The Wrecker*, a homegrown production that drew overflow crowds to the Majestic Theatre during a Wednesday–Saturday run in August of 1919. Local reaction to the three-reel production was so great that the Majestic had to run an apology in its Thursday newspaper ad, stating, "We are sincerely sorry we had to keep so many standing last night waiting for seats. We strongly urge patrons to attend the matinee performances today." (The film was double-billed with the non-Tulsa production *One Woman's Experience*, starring Mary Boland.)

Billed as a "Tulsa Home Talent Railroad Photoplay," *The Wrecker* cast Tulsa mayor Charles H. Hubbard in the pivotal role of Bernard Powers, superintendent of the MN&Q Railroad and father of the heroine, essayed by "Miss Frances Riddle." A *Tulsa Daily World* piece running three days before *The Wrecker*'s premiere told readers that "men and women whose names are household words appear in the drama," including Mayor

Hubbard, oilman R. M. McFarlin (who "photographs remarkably well," according to the *World* writer), and lawyer and politician M. A. Breckenridge, as well as Charles Allen and R. C. Adler, respectively Tulsa's police chief and fire chief at the time. With those local heavyweights in the cast, it's not hard to see why an unnamed *World* scribe seemed positively ecstatic about *The Wrecker* in an August 21 review headlined, "TULSA MOVIE A HOWLING 'HIT'":

> It seemed as though everyone in Tulsa wanted to get into the Majestic theater yesterday. In spite of threatened rain, the biggest theater in Tulsa played to capacity business all day long. *The Wrecker,* a home talent photoplay, was the cause of it. . . .
>
> . . . Mayor C. R. Hubbard in one of the most important roles attracted wide attention. His acting in the feature ranks with that of professionals. His nonchalant air makes one almost believe he has appeared before the camera prior to this. R. M. Franks as the villain portrayed his part so realistically that he was given a "hand" at the end of each show, in spite of the fact that he has a part that usually gets "hisses." Albert T. Twist as the hero proved himself not only a screen Adonis, an ardent lovemaker and a good actor, but a "man" as well. In his exciting fistfight with the villain he made more than a "movie" matter out of it. It is one of the best things in the picture. The railroad wreck, auto accident, downtown fire and pistol battle are real "thrills."

Taken out of its historical context, it's difficult to understand why this group of people got together to create what was apparently a rather complex production, even given the 1910s fascination with the technology of motion pictures and the fact that the upper classes could buy the equipment needed to make their own movies. All indications are that *The Wrecker* was a giant step up from a simple amateur shoot.

Certainly, the cast and crew knew something like *The Wrecker* could be done in Oklahoma—Tilghman, Kent, and the others had shown the way. But those earlier pictures had been made in the hope of turning a profit and intended for distribution to theaters and audiences both inside and outside the state. With its roster of local notables, *The Wrecker* seems to have been aimed strictly for the local trade. In fact, that four-day screening at the Majestic may have been its only public showing.

The biggest clue to how *The Wrecker* came together is the name of the film's cameraman, who may have been the only professional on the set. The *World's* August 17 article singled him out for special praise: "One of the remarkable features about the production is the splendid photography. Usually a 'home talent' picture like this is cloudy, dim and 'rainy' on the screen, but not so with *The Wrecker*. Richard E. Norman, who photographed it, has been in the game actively for 12 years. He used one of the costliest cameras on the market and his product is all that could be asked from an artistic standpoint."

Indeed, Richard Edward Norman was a pro, one who occupies a special niche in the state's filmmaking history. Norman's shot-in-Oklahoma movies of the '20s were aimed for African American audiences, but before he did those pictures, he was involved in a specialized branch of filmmaking that could easily have led to the production of *The Wrecker*. Jill Moniz explained it in a 1984 piece posted on Indiana University Bloomington's online Black Film Center/Archive (www.indiana.edu/~bfca/): "[Norman's] early work [was] comprised mainly of contracting local events to film. Traveling the middle west, Norman invited interested local parties to act in skits which he filmed, then showed them for a price at the local theater, church, or school." *The Wrecker*, of course, was more than a skit. But then again, Norman had been at it since 1912, shooting his first feature movie—with a railroad background—in 1916, so he was certainly equipped to handle something more ambitious when the *Wrecker* opportunity came up.

The Florida-based Norman went on to film a feature in Boley, an all-black town about sixty miles southwest of Tulsa, a year or so after wrapping *The Wrecker*. Did he find out about Oklahoma's African American communities as a result of his visit to the state to shoot *The Wrecker*? Was his sales pitch to notable Tulsans the reason *The Wrecker* was made, or did they, knowing of his reputation, contact him? Is it possible that he got involved with Tulsa and the amateur actors featured in *The Wrecker* to raise funds for the film he'd shoot in Boley a year or two later?

Time long ago dropped the curtain on Norman and *The Wrecker*—which is, like so many other pictures of that era, a "lost" film—and chances are good we'll never know the exact circumstances that led to its production. All we can deduce from the evidence left us is that it was perhaps nothing more than a glorified home movie starring some of Tulsa's top citizens. Then again, maybe it was a little something more.

This chapter wraps up much the way it began, with the story of a famous lawbreaker who got the itch to tell his own life story on film. And the way the tale ends would certainly have won the approval of Marshal Bill Tilghman—who, as mentioned earlier, had to stop filming on his *Passing of the Oklahoma Outlaw* to help catch members of Henry Starr's real-life gang.

At the end of his life, Starr claimed that, in terms of sheer numbers, he'd robbed more banks than any other outlaw in the country. Committing his first misdeed in 1893, this part-Cherokee native of Fort Gibson, Indian Territory (whose aunt was the notorious Belle Starr), would spend a significant amount of his life either robbing banks or doing time in prison over the next three decades.

A few years after his unsuccessful robbery of the two Stroud institutions, a newly paroled Starr got involved with—and in fact may have helped start—a Tulsa-based studio called the Pan-American Motion Picture Company. (According to Jack Spears in "Hollywood's Oklahoma," Starr owned a quarter interest in the company.) That partnership led to the 1919 production of *A Debtor to the Law*, and—in line with what had become the custom in Oklahoma outlaw movies—Starr played himself. The cast also included Paul Curry, the young Stroud butcher who'd shot Starr, re-creating his pivotal role in the robbery drama.

But the veteran gunslinger, who was by then in his mid-forties, couldn't seem to catch a break. While his contemporaries Al Jennings and Emmett Dalton had been relatively successful in their filmmaking efforts, *A Debtor to the Law* had trouble getting off the ground. Spears detailed the problems faced by the production, including unusable footage shot inside the Stroud banks, the dissatisfaction of professional director George Reehm with the script, and the fact that "Starr, despite his striking Indian good looks, was hopelessly inept as an actor" (p. 347).

The popular western novelist, Patrick S. McGeeney, was called in to fashion a more dramatic scenario, using incidents related to him by Starr.

McGeeney also owned the well-equipped Shamrock Motion Picture Studio in San Antonio, Texas (which had been used by several New York and California companies)[,] and production of *A Debtor to the Law* resumed there. William Karl Hackett, a well-known screen actor, took over the role of Henry Starr, while the outlaw served as technical consultant. (pp. 347–48)

Even with that piebald history, the film was advertised—at least in its premiere screening—as having Starr himself in the lead role. The advance ad copy for its debut screening (at Tulsa's Royal Theater on May 9–12, 1920) read: "A story with a moral showing the utter futility of crime and its outcome, based upon the life of Henry Starr, who after thirty years, half of the time an outlaw, half of the time in prison—speaks to the world and says the law must be obeyed. This great picture will be shown in conjunction with Jack Dempsey and other pictures at the regular Royal admission price of 10 and 30c."

The Jack Dempsey reference probably indicates that the Royal was showing chapters of the 1920 serial *Daredevil Jack*, featuring the then world heavyweight champion boxer Dempsey in the title role. Like Starr, Dempsey had become famous for something other than acting; nonetheless, the nationally known pugilist fared better in his cinematic efforts than Starr did. In addition to the problems with the actual filming of *A Debtor to the Law*, Starr was apparently also aced out of his part ownership in the company. A few months before the initial screening of the picture, the Pan-American Motion Picture Company applied to the state's issues commission, as was required by law then, asking permission to sell $20,000 worth of its stock. As the August 28, 1919, *Tulsa Democrat* reported: "This is the company that Henry Starr was reported connected with when the application was first presented to the issues commission and denied. It is now explained that Starr is not now connected with the company except as to the services he may give."

It's possible that Starr simply became a silent partner in Pan-American. Sources indicate, however, that the other company principals may have used the rejection by the issues commission—which likely had to do with a convicted outlaw being a major stockholder—to force him out. According to James Vance's history of Tulsa filmmaking, Starr and Pan-American did a second picture together called *Evening Star*. "While he

SHOT IN OKLAHOMA

reckoned his share in the two releases would amount to $15,000," wrote Vance, "little cash would end up in Starr's pocket. The infamous outlaw had tried to go straight, only to be ripped off by his own business partner."

Lacking the money to fight Pan-American in court, Starr pondered what to do next. He could've followed Al Jennings's lead and headed for Hollywood, where stories about outlaws, as well as the old outlaws who told them, were doing well. But he was worried about leaving the state, believing that his crossing Oklahoma's border might give Arkansas officials the opportunity to arrest him in conjunction with an old bank robbery in Bentonville. So he stayed put and tried to get another movie going, hitting up friends and acquaintances—including the Miller Brothers at the 101 Ranch—for capital.

Further Henry Starr features, however, never got off the ground. Maybe he figured if he made one last haul, he could finally get another picture going. Or maybe he just found it too hard to change his lawless ways. Whatever Starr's reasoning was, it led to a trip via motorcar to Harrison, Arkansas, on February 18, 1921—not quite a year after the premiere of his first motion picture "showing the utter futility of crime and its outcome." He and his three compadres stopped just long enough in Harrison to hold up the People's National Bank. During the robbery, a former president of the institution who happened to be on the scene also happened to remember he'd hidden a rifle back in the vault. He retrieved it and shot Starr in the back. Four days later, the forty-seven-year-old bank robber and would-be movie star died in jail.

Dying along with Henry Starr, for all practical purposes, was Oklahoma's era of moviemaking lawmen and their outlaw counterparts, locking horns with one another not only in real life but in front of their cameras as well.

THREE

The Dusky Demon and
the Daughter of Dawn

> [I] was quite surprised when [I] met the Indian actors . . . especially
> a young man named White Parker, son of the legendary Comanche
> chief Quanah. . . . Some people in Hollywood had joked that I'd
> probably lose my scalp . . . but they would be surprised to know
> that . . . the [Indians] spoke better language than they did.
>
> > —early filmmaker Norbert Myles, from an
> > unpublished manuscript, quoted in Leo Kelley's
> > "The Daughter of Dawn," *Chronicles of Oklahoma*
> > (Fall 1999)
>
> The West is full of hardy colored pioneers who settled there years
> ago among savage Indians and founded a colored empire which
> stands as a monument to their daring and courage.
>
> > —*Black Gold* pressbook (1928)

In an interview with the author for the May 26, 1996, edition of the
Tulsa World, a pioneering African American singer and actor reflected
on his film career. "In my home town, we had integrated neighbor-
hoods of many ethnic tastes—Italians, Jews, Polish people, and some
Negro families who had migrated down from Canada," said singer and
actor Herb Jeffries, a Detroit native, who was then eighty-four years
old. "Growing up in my neighborhood, we didn't know about discrimi-
nation. Then, when I went South with [Earl 'Fatha'] Hines' band, I saw,
even in the capital of the United States, black people had to sit in the
balconies of theaters. And when we went even deeper into the South, I
saw that blacks could not go into white theaters at all, and there were
thousands and thousands and thousands of tin-roof theaters where
blacks went to watch white cowboy pictures.

"And when I saw that, I thought, 'Wait a minute. Why don't they play
black cowboy pictures?'"

The answer, to Jeffries, was simple—there *weren't* any black cowboy pictures. So he decided to try and fund his own, going to various wealthy black Americans with his idea. After two fruitless years, Jeffries, still singing with Hines's band, was ready to give it all up—when, as he recalled, he experienced a kind of epiphany in a Cincinnati alley.

"In those days, there was no air-conditioning, so the band would take its break out in the alleyway," he explained. "During our intermission, a group of children ran up the alley playing cowboys. There was one little black child trailing along after about seven or eight white children, and he was crying. So we members of the band called him over and asked, 'Did those boys hit you?'

"He said, 'No. They're my friends.'

"'Well, then, why are you crying?'

"He said, 'They won't let me play cowboy with 'em. I wanna be Tom Mix and they won't let me be Tom Mix, 'cause Tom Mix ain't black.'"

"That kind of bottomed me out," Jeffries said. "And I knew, somehow, I had to make these cowboy pictures."

And indeed he did. Beginning in 1936, Jeffries starred in a series of all-black musical westerns, donning cowboy hat and gun belt and appearing in all but one as the heroic Bob Blake, riding tall on his horse Stardusk. Not only did he become the movies' first black singing cowboy, but he was also the first black *talking* cowboy in films.

He was not, however, the screen's first black cowboy hero. Fifteen years before *Harlem on the Prairie*, the first of the Jeffries oaters, a remarkable performer with Oklahoma's 101 Ranch had starred in what was probably the first western movie to feature a cast made up entirely of African American actors and extras.

Like the Jeffries pictures, the 1921 feature *The Bull-Dogger* had an all-black cast in front of the camera and at least some white technicians behind it. Also like Jeffries's western movies, it was financed and released by a white-owned company. And finally—again, as with the Jeffries pictures—it starred a man who had become famous for something other than making movies.

Bill Pickett was that star. And by 1921, when *The Bull-Dogger* began its run in African American theaters all across the country, Pickett was a major attraction with the touring Miller Brothers 101 Ranch Real Wild West Show. A Texas native, he had joined the Millers in 1905, becoming known far and wide as Bill Pickett, the Dusky Demon. His act involved subduing a steer by jumping onto its back from atop a racing pony, seizing its horns, and wrestling it to the ground. This dangerous activity became the basis for the rodeo sport called bulldogging.

In fact, Bill Pickett has been called the inventor of bulldogging. It's of course possible that other cowboys came up with similar techniques at isolated ranches and rodeos around the country during the late 1800s, but Pickett was certainly the one who popularized bulldogging, mastered it, and brought it to the attention of America. Beginning in the early part of the last century, Pickett rode in city after city with the 101 Ranch show, and his bulldogging style, as Michael Wallis noted in *The Real Wild West*, seldom failed to bring the house down: "He would leap from his pony onto the steer's back, grab a horn in each hand, and dig his boot heels into the ground. After twisting the critter's head to bring up its nose, he chomped his teeth on the steer's tender lip and lunged backward, causing the beast to fall down. With flair, Pickett threw his hands into the air to show the audience that he no longer needed to hold the steer's horns" (p. 254).

Pickett had reportedly come up with the idea as a young boy, watching specially trained bulldogs do the same sort of thing on Texas ranches with stray calves. The dogs would immobilize the runaways by biting their lips and then would hold the calves until a cowboy could come by and take over. By the time Pickett joined the 101 operation, he'd been performing his human version of the bulldogs' feat for well over ten years, astonishing rodeo and state fair audiences in and around Texas. Pickett's affiliation with the Miller brothers only enhanced his existing reputation, bringing his breathtaking act to a far greater number of people than he'd been able to reach before. It was certainly something to see: a cowboy subduing a thousand-pound steer using nothing more than his teeth and hands.

At the same time that Pickett was becoming internationally famous for his bulldogging act, a movement was beginning in cinema that would lead to his brief shot at film stardom. Many film historians believe that the all-black film movement came along as a reaction to D. W. Griffith's three-hour epic *The Birth of a Nation*. Those historians would probably also agree with this statement by writer and TV personality Joe Franklin in his book *Classics of the Silent Screen* (1959): "Undoubtedly, *The Birth of a Nation* is the most important single film in the evolution of the screen, although not necessarily the greatest. But it is the film from which all movie grammar derives, and most important of all, it is the film which overnight won worldwide respect for the motion picture medium, and raised it from a mere novelty entertainment to the status of an art" (p. 16).

A sweeping story of the Civil War and its aftermath, *The Birth of a Nation* has received just about as much notice, however, for its negative portrayals of freed slaves and black politicians in the Reconstruction days and its romantic treatment of the Ku Klux Klan as it has for its stature as a pioneering, innovative theatrical feature. Although more recent critical appraisals of the film are especially likely to stress its denigrating depiction of African Americans, that criticism isn't anything new. Those portrayals also led to some controversy immediately following the picture's 1915 release—especially in black America. So, as historians have indicated, it probably isn't a coincidence that the first film companies specializing in movies for African American audiences sprang up a few months after *The Birth of A Nation* hit the country's screens. Whether run by whites or blacks, these companies produced films with all-black casts that refuted, overtly or covertly, the degrading images set forth in *The Birth of a Nation*. Although there were plenty of exceptions, many of these "colored" or "race" movies presented stereotype-busting and often dignified portrayals by black actors, in productions that illustrated a statement by Herb Jeffries in his 1996 interview. "All I really want to do," he said, reflecting on his films and his music, "is be, in some kind of small way, a fusion to make people understand one simple thing: forget about race, and let's realize there's only one race of people, and that's the human race."

Between 1916 and 1930, more than a hundred black-film studios came along, some for a long run, others for only a picture or two. In those segregated days, most cities of any size boasted at least one theater that catered exclusively to the African American trade, and enterprising filmmakers saw financial opportunities in aiming new pictures squarely toward those audiences. It was simply niche marketing, long before the term was invented, and the rules were simple—keep the cost of your product low enough, hit your target consumers, and you'll make a profit.

That brings us to Richard E. Norman. A native of Springfield, Florida, Norman hit the road with his movie camera in the early 1910s, when he was barely out of his teens. He must've been a pretty good salesman by then, though. Traveling mostly in the Midwest, he'd hustle up jobs in cities and towns, offering to film short but scripted motion pictures using local talent. Once a picture was done, he'd get as many area showings as the market would bear and pocket the take before moving on.

We've already seen that Norman came to Tulsa, probably under those circumstances, and shot *The Wrecker* with local amateur talent in 1919. Perhaps during that visit to Oklahoma he was first exposed to Bill Pickett, then starring with the 101 Ranch's wild-west extravaganza. He may have even traveled to northern Oklahoma and visited the ranch itself. In addition, there's a good possibility that he heard about or saw some of the state's all-black towns, settled primarily by the freed slaves who had come to Indian Territory with the Cherokees on the Trail of Tears many decades before.

In addition to his work as a traveling cinematographer, Norman had made a theatrical feature called *The Green Eyed Monster*. Released in 1916, it was a railroad melodrama that apparently also marked his only professional movie with an all-white cast. A few years later, he decided to remake the picture with black actors—Norman himself was white—and aim it toward the African American market. (Given what little we know about the plotlines of both *The Green Eyed Monster* and *The Wrecker*— that is, that they both were romances involving trains—it seems plausible that Norman could also have used or reworked the scenario of the former as a basis for the latter.)

From the beginning of his career in films for African American audiences, Norman seems to have made an effort to stay away from the stereotypes, stock characters, and low humor that some of the producers of race movies employed. A pressbook for a reissue of his all-black remake of *Green Eyed Monster* (first released in 1919) assured exhibitors that "THERE IS NOT A WHITE MAN IN THE CAST, [n]or is there depicted in the entire picture anything of the usual mimicry of the Negro. This photoplay has been indorsed by the most prominent colored people of America."

Referring to the movie as "A 100 PER CENT PICTURE IN 5 SMASHING REELS," the promotional copy went on to say: "$1,000,000 Worth of Railroad Equipment was used in the filming of this production. An $80,000.00 Train Wreck is part of the Story. The characterizations were enacted by colored people chosen from many different walks of life. The Lawyer, Doctor, Banker and Finished Actor and Actress portray this strong appeal to the highest ideals of Nature and lesson of the lowness and jealousy, The Green Eyed Monster." In support of this high-minded hype, a number of letters from African American theaters were reprinted in the pressbook, including one from the Aldridge in Oklahoma City. (A major venue on the city's Second Street, the Aldridge would be, in 1923, the place where the influential jazz band the Oklahoma City Blue Devils first came together.) The Aldridge's endorsement said simply, "Business on the Green Eyed Monster, second run, surpassed first runs on other colored company's features."

In 1919, Norman also released a second film. *The Love Bug* was a two-reel comedy he'd put together with humorous material excised from the otherwise dramatic *Green Eyed Monster*. It was advertised as a sequel to its five-reel predecessor—even though *The Love Bug* was a comedy and *Green Eyed Monster* a melodrama.

Business on both films must have been pretty good, since Norman decided to invest in his own studio in 1920. By that time, as we saw earlier, most film production had moved to the West Coast from points east. Beginning a little more than a decade earlier, however, a number of New York– and New Jersey–based studios had established branch operations in Florida, enabling them to keep shooting during winter. This activity had also spurred the rise of some local motion picture companies, particularly in the city of Jacksonville.

PAST SUCCESSES---GREATER ONES COMING

IF YOU HAVEN'T PLAYED

The Crimson Skull

You haven't cashed in on one of the greatest Box Office winners ever produced with a colored cast.

Over 6,000 paid admissions in one little Theatre seating 470. How many colored pictures have you ran that beat this?

Connect up with this money-maker. Many are running it second run and are cleaning up.

There is Only One GREEN EYED MONSTER

A 100 PER CENT PICTURE IN 5 SMASHING REELS OF THRILLS! ACTION! PUNCH!

REPEAT BUSINESS ON THE GREEN EYED MONSTER HAS SURPASSED SOME FIRST RUNS

The Bull Dogger

5 REEL WESTERN

Featuring

BILL PICKETT

World's Colored Champion

In Feats of Daring and Skill

Write for our Special Proposition

Norman Film Manufacturing Co.

52 U. S. Trust Building

JACKSONVILLE, FLORIDA

The top and bottom portions of this promotional flyer advertise two shot-in-Oklahoma features, both released in 1921 and starring famed African American cowboy Bill Pickett. (Courtesy of the Oklahoma Historical Society)

The exodus of filmmakers to Southern California, which also offered a climate conducive to year-round moviemaking, spelled trouble for Florida's cinema scene. During the 1910s, Jacksonville had been the site of much cinematic activity. By 1920, most of it was gone. (A February 4, 1999, story by *Florida Times-Union* writer Charlie Patton claimed that "the 1916 election of a reform mayor who pledged to drive the unsavory movie folk out of Jacksonville" had something to do with the situation as well.)

Florida native Norman, however, saw opportunity in the downturn. He headed into Jacksonville and made a deal to buy the Eagle Film Studios operation, a victim of the Florida moviemaking bust. From there, he launched his Norman Film Manufacturing Company, also known simply as the Norman Studios. Before it folded, Richard E. Norman would make five more all-black features—three of them lensed in Oklahoma.

The circumstances that led to Bill Pickett's doing a couple of films with Richard E. Norman are lost to time. However, Norman probably knew of Pickett well before putting him in a film. After all, by 1919, when Norman shot *The Wrecker* in Tulsa, the bulldogging Texan was an internationally known performer. And if Norman hadn't heard of Pickett before that date, it's a good bet that someone from Tulsa would have made him aware of the 101 Ranch Real Wild West Show star and perhaps even pointed him in the direction of the Miller brothers' spread.

Many Tulsans could've also pointed Norman toward Boley, one of several all-black Oklahoma towns that existed at the time. Surely, Norman—reportedly a man who strove to get the most out of every buck he spent on his pictures—would have immediately seen the advantages to filming in a town composed entirely of African American residents. There he would have at his beck and call all the extras and bit players he needed, and probably a large amount of goodwill too, since his first two black-cast films not only had been decent hits but also had offered generally positive portrayals of African Americans. Plus, the buzz and excitement of a movie company coming to a small town, even in those early days, should never be underestimated—especially when it comes to getting locals to participate for little or no money.

So, with Pickett and a cast that included New York stage actress Anita Bush and a one-legged actor named Steve "Peg" Reynolds (who appeared in every Norman black-cast production but *The Love Bug* and apparently has no other film credits), Norman headed to Boley, where he set up his cameras and shot two movies, probably back to back. They were *The Bull-Dogger*, with Pickett in the lead, and *The Crimson Skull*, which found Pickett's role reduced to supporting Bush (billed in *The Crimson Skull* as the "Little Mother of Colored Drama") and Lawrence Chenault. The latter had just starred in the all-black feature *The Symbol of the Unconquered* (1920), a melodrama crafted by pioneering filmmaker Oscar Micheaux (an African American); its story involves a Klan-like organization called the Knights of the Black Cross and a black man (Chenault) whose attempt to pass for white leads to his moral downfall.

In his *Chronicles of Oklahoma* piece, Jack Spears calls *The Bull-Dogger* "largely a compilation of [Pickett's] famous rodeo tricks in a story of lawlessness on the Mexican border" (p. 361). Why Mexico? Probably because Pickett had famously taken on a savage bull while in Mexico City with the 101 show in late 1908. The epic man-versus-beast struggle drew the wrath of the crowd, nearly took Pickett's life, and, according to *The Real Wild West*, won Joe Miller a five-thousand-peso bet.

The tale of Pickett's battle with the huge Frijoles Chiquitos ("Little Beans") had since become one of the best-known stories about the bull-dogger, and Norman undoubtedly wanted to remind audiences of it. Promotion for the picture pointed out that "[Pickett] outstunted the Mexicans at bull fighting 15 years ago in the Bull Ring in Mexico City, and his record still stands." Oddly enough, Oklahoma's Miller brothers and their 101 Ranch Real Wild West Show aren't mentioned in any of the advertising for the film. (One line simply acknowledged that Pickett was featured "as the headliner attraction with a famous Wild West Show.") In all likelihood, Norman had not reached an agreement with the Millers to use their name.

Like all 35 mm theatrical movies of its era, *The Bull-Dogger* was released on nitrate film, which was highly flammable and prone to disintegration. Nevertheless, a thirty-two-minute print, composed entirely of rodeo footage featuring Pickett and others, has improbably survived. Promotional material indicates that the original film was a five-reeler, which would make it considerably longer than a half hour; the existing print may be an incomplete print or a reissue in which the plotline is excised.

Norman's second Boley-based production was an adventure film called *The Crimson Skull*. Released not long after *The Bull-Dogger*, *The Crimson Skull* was touted in advertising as a "Baffling Western Mystery Photo-Play," featuring costars Bush and Chenault and "supported by BILL PICKETT, World's Champion Wild West Performer, the one-legged marvel STEVE REYNOLDS and 30 Colored Cowboys." The town of Boley played itself in the picture, under siege by an outlaw called the Skull. He and his minions, who've been able to get to Boley's sheriff, are terrorizing the town, robbing and rustling with impunity. With the help of Pickett's character and other cowboys from the Crown C Ranch, however, foreman Bob Calem (Chenault) infiltrates the gang and puts a stop to the cowpoke crime wave.

Surviving promotional photos from *The Crimson Skull* depict a figure dressed in a skeleton costume, complete with hooded cape. Although one would think that would be the Skull himself, it's instead Chenault's character, who dons the outfit, according to IMDb (the Internet Movie Database at www.imdb.com), to scare the gang and its superstitious leader.

"Ninety per cent will say that it is the greatest colored picture they have ever seen," enthused *The Crimson Skull*'s advertising copy. "The other ten will say that it is wonderful. And it is both."

Those two pictures marked the end of the line for Pickett's film career—but not Richard Norman's. After wrapping *The Bull-Dogger* and *The Crimson Skull* in Boley, the moviemaker returned to Florida, where he booked and promoted his pictures all across the country, concentrating much of his effort in the heavily segregated South. Two years later, another of his all-black cast films, *Regeneration*, found its way into the market. *Regeneration*'s tale of two lovers stranded on a desert island and the treasure hunters who interrupt their life indicates that it was probably shot in Florida. That picture was followed by an airplane-and-railroad

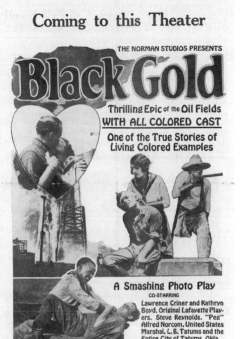

Norman Studios' final feature was shot in the Oklahoma town of Tatums and released in 1928. (Courtesy of the Oklahoma Historical Society)

adventure dubbed *The Flying Ace* (1926), which also doesn't appear to have any Oklahoma connection.

The final feature to come out of the Norman Studios, however, saw the filmmaker returning to another African American town in Oklahoma, where he shot an epic of the oil fields called *Black Gold*. This time his location was Tatums, about 160 miles southwest of Boley, near Oklahoma's Arbuckle Mountain range. Founded by its namesake, L. B. Tatums, in the late 1890s, Tatums had become one of many oil boom communities in the state, with gushers bringing wealth to a number of its residents.

In a section of the *Black Gold* pressbook entitled "A Confidential Letter to You," Norman made his pitch for the film to owners and operators of black theaters. Here is part of it, with Norman's sometimes exotic syntax and capitalization left intact:

FRIEND EXHIBITOR:—

Again, I can say that the Norman Studios has produced for your theatre, another great colored novel picture, *Black Gold*. Novel in the fact that it is the first big Oil Picture with an all-colored cast, and is a True Story of Living Colored Examples. No expense was spared, within reason, to make this picture have the proper atmosphere, and so it was made upon the location of the story, the oil fields of the Colored City of Tatums, Oklahoma. This necessitated transporting the cast of professionals, there by railroad, to within 25 miles of the locations, and then 25 miles by automobile through the mountains. The cast came from as far South as Jacksonville, Fla., and as far North as Chicago. Indeed, an ambitious undertaking, with such a few theatres for revenue. The cast need no comment. They are leaders in their profession. The story can't be beat for thrills. It's real and was staged among the proper atmosphere. Through proper connections, I was able to secure the whole-hearted co-operation of the Standard Oil Company, who were drilling several oil wells on the Tatum's property which were best to film, and through their assistance, *Black Gold*, is authentic from every drilling detail, and aside from it's thrills, is a true portrayal of the Romance of Oil towards which no oil man can point a finger of criticism.

LISTEN!

You have seen Action. But you never have seen Action in a colored picture like *Black Gold*. The Hero doesn't do all the fighting—he just pulls three different ones—but did you ever see a one-legged man fight? This same one legged man, Steve Reynolds, besides his fight, does a marvelous feat of skill on the precipitous 100 foot long roof of the derrick house on one leg that I can confidently say has never been done by a one legged man before; and in his jump, he injured himself so that he was under the Doctors care for two weeks. Have you ever seen a picture of a gas well on fire that the roar could be heard for 6 miles, the fire was so big? Well, I caught one just as she blew in and just after it had melted down the steel derrick and burned all the woodwork for a block around. It's in *Black Gold*—just one of the many thrills.

In addition to the death-defying "Peg" Reynolds and L. B. Tatums himself, who—according to the movie's pressbook—had been a U.S. marshal since the beginning of the century, *Black Gold* toplined a pair of actors named Lawrence Criner and Kathryn Boyd. The poster billed them as "Original Lafayette Players," referring to an acclaimed all-black troupe that presented plays at New York's Lafayette Theatre. (The Lafayette Players had evolved out of a prior company founded by Anita Bush, Norman's star in *The Bull-Dogger* and *The Crimson Skull*. Her costar in the latter, Lawrence Chenault, is listed in Weldon B. Durham's *American Theatre Companies, 1888–1930* as another Lafayette Player.)

Boyd, who'd also been in *The Flying Ace*, apparently returned to the Lafayette Players following her turns in *The Flying Ace* and *Black Gold*; she doesn't seem to have any other movie credits. Her costar Criner, however, after making his movie debut in *The Flying Ace*, went on to a pretty decent film career. His credits, which run through the late '40s, consist mostly of all-black features, with the occasional small part in something like Monogram's B-horror opus *King of the Zombies* (1941).

Black Gold, released in 1928, finds Criner playing the wonderfully named Ace Brand, foreman of a ranch on which oil has been discovered. When his boss is wrongly accused of robbing a bank as part of a scheme to keep him from bringing in an oil well on time, Ace, cowhand Peg Reynolds, and bank president's daughter Alice Anderson (Boyd) find themselves working against the clock, as well as outside forces, to get the well pumping.

Black Gold, according to press material from Norman Studios, was supposed to be the first in a series of "True Stories of Living Colored Examples." Norman explained what he meant by that term in a *Black Gold* pressbook story, intended to be offered to local African American papers to run as a news item—which, of course, would also help publicize the film:

> Prominent colored leaders over the United States have finally induced The Norman Studios, of Arlington, Florida, to make a series of True Stories of Living Colored Examples, showing their dramatic rise to leadership and wealth, against overwhelming odds. And it has been pointed out to The Norman Studios, that such a series of True Stories would inspire ambition in members of the colored race to accomplish the things achieved by their leaders.

Despite these stated good intentions, and the apparent endorsement of leading African Americans of the time, no further True Stories of Living

Colored Examples issued from the Jacksonville studio. And although Norman also sent out advertising material for an upcoming "Colored Serial Supreme" called *Zircon*, the fifteen-chapter photoplay was apparently never made, leaving *Black Gold* as the last movie to emerge from Norman Studios.

The picture, it must be noted, was one of a dying breed, for reasons having nothing to do with the ethnicity of its cast. In 1927, a year before *Black Gold*'s release, the Hollywood-based Warner Bros. had brought out its musical Al Jolson starrer, *The Jazz Singer*, ushering in the era of the talking picture. A few independent operators, including Norman, continued to grind out silent movies after 1927, but the writing was on the wall. Audiences demanded sound with their pictures, and African American audiences were certainly no exception. People who wanted to continue making successful movies had to get with the program and provide their audiences with real voices, not just cards with dialogue written on them.

Considering all of that, it's likely that *Black Gold*'s lack of sound had a negative impact on its box office take—which, in turn, probably contributed to Norman's decision to get out of the filmmaking business and into booking and promoting other people's films. In his *Florida Times-Union* piece, Charlie Patton indicated that Norman tried to invent a sound system himself, only to be aced out of the market by Western Electric, which quickly became the industry standard. As a result, Patton wrote, Norman was forced to declare bankruptcy.

According to Indiana University Bloomington's Jill Moniz, that wasn't enough to drive Norman from the movie business. Although he did get out of the filmmaking end, Norman became a distributor, using his familiarity with the market to secure bookings for other African American films, sometimes getting more mileage out of his own old movies by pairing them in double features with newer films. Apparently, he also distributed product to white theaters. "[Norman] showed Oscar Micheaux films as well as Hollywood serials, and lesser features," Moniz wrote on the university's online Black Film Center/Archive. "In the forties, he began distributing Joe Louis fights and Black features starring Lena Horne and others."

Norman continued using the studio as his base of operations for many years, occasionally doing a commercial or industrial film from there, but mostly employing it as a base of operations for his distribution activities. According to the *Times-Union* piece, at one point, his wife used one of the buildings as the headquarters for her dance studio. Norman died in 1960.

At this book was being written, the Norman Studios were in the midst of renovation by a Jacksonville group, with a planned reopening as the Norman Studios Silent Film Museum. At that time, Norman's *The Flying Ace* was to be screened as a part of grand opening festivities. The project's website (www.normanstudios.org) called the five-building lot "possibly the only remaining intact silent film studio complex in America."

During the period in which Richard E. Norman was producing silent feature films with all-black casts in Oklahoma, another silent film featuring a cast consisting entirely of actors from a single ethnic group—American Indians—was also shot in Oklahoma by a white filmmaker from outside the state. But there, the similarity of *The Daughter of Dawn* to the three films Norman shot in two of the state's all-black towns pretty much ends. Norman's black-cast movies had a ready-made market, with scores of theaters across the country catering to the African American trade. There was no analogue for American Indian moviegoers and certainly no niche-marketing filmmakers crafting pictures aimed for American Indian audiences.

That fact helps us understand why—unlike *The Bull-Dogger*, *The Crimson Skull*, and *Black Gold*—*The Daughter of Dawn*, with a cast of Comanches and Kiowas, seems to have never had an actual theatrical release. Leo Kelley, in his groundbreaking article on the film, "*The Daughter of Dawn*: An Original Silent Film with an Oklahoma Indian Cast" (*Chronicles of Oklahoma*, Fall 1999, p. 290), cited a "sneak preview" screening in Los Angeles in October 1920, but that was apparently it. The sepia-tinted movie (with one eerie night scene tinted blue) has remained unreleased for almost ninety years and, like most of the nitrate-stock prints from that era, was presumed lost.

A scene from the Oklahoma-shot *Daughter of Dawn* (1920), featuring a cast consisting entirely of members of the Kiowa and Comanche tribes. (Courtesy of the Oklahoma Historical Society)

As things turned out, though, it wasn't. A copy somehow survived, and in January 2007 it found its way, after much negotiating, to the Oklahoma Historical Society in Oklahoma City. "A private investigator back East had taken it as payment for a case he'd worked on," recalled the society's Bill Moore. "The word was that he'd gotten it from a descendant of the guy who'd made the film."

That filmmaker was Norbert A. Myles, a Shakespearian actor and vaudevillian, according to Kelley's article, who'd gotten into movies somewhere around 1914. He'd been a leading man for such studios as Pathe and Vitagraph, but an alleged stubborn streak had slowed his movie career to a stop. Wrote Kelley:

> By the early 1920s Myles had butted heads with several of Hollywood's top brass. Black-balled by the industry, the irrepressible director looked elsewhere for a project. Richard Banks, who had started the fledgling Texas Film Company a few years earlier, had met Myles in 1916 on a movie set in California. Impressed with the vigor and expertise of the fiery director, Banks had asked him in 1918 and again the following year to direct an adventure film for his company. (p. 291)

It was Banks who had the idea for the all-Indian film, basing it, he wrote Myles, on "an old Comanche legend—or at least it's a legend from one of the tribes around there such as the Apache," he added (p. 291). Kelley, who dug up original correspondence between the two filmmakers, gave the date of that letter as August 20, 1919. Some short time after that, Myles took a train from Hollywood to Lawton, Oklahoma, and from there headed to the Wichita Mountains Wildlife Refuge outside of town, where Banks had arranged for the shooting. In addition to the picturesque terrain, the refuge was home to a sizable buffalo herd, which would be used in the movie.

It's unclear when Myles started production on *The Daughter of Dawn* or exactly how long it took him to complete it. What we do know is that it was a six-reeler that ran somewhere around eighty minutes. (Although a reel held around ten minutes of film in those days, it might run a few minutes more if it was exceptionally full. It could also run a little less.) When the Oklahoma Historical Society received the print of *The Daughter of Dawn*, however, there were only five reels.

"It was a mystery," noted Moore. "When I sent it to the lab in California, Hollywood Film Technology, to have it restored, they found it didn't have any opening credits, which accounted for part of the missing reel. But that wasn't all of it.

"Then, one day, I got a call from someone working in the lab, and he said, 'We've solved the mystery.' As it turned out, the guy who'd been working on the intertitles [the printed words that indicate action or dialogue in silent movies] said, 'Well, by the time I restore all of these, it'll add another thousand feet of film.' That's just about another reel."

The version of the movie received by the Oklahoma Historical Society, explained Moore, had apparently been a prerelease print, something for the filmmaker to work with and fine-tune, and not the version intended for theaters. So there were only three or four frames of each of the intertitles on that print, rather than the usual several feet. And thus the mystery of *The Daughter of Dawn*'s missing reel was solved.

After having the restored version converted to a DVD format, the Oklahoma Historical Society then asked David Yeagley to write a classical music score for the film—marking, Yeagley believes, the first time an American Indian composer had been commissioned to write all the music for a feature-length movie. "Dr. Bob Blackburn [the society's executive director] called me in for an interview," recalled Yeagley. "He was really a visionary in this. He wanted the highest quality of music he could get. I happened to be a classical symphonic composer, and I happened to be an Oklahoman, and I happened to be Comanche. I was tailor-made for what he wanted."

In June 2008, Yeagley delivered a score consisting of "eighty minutes of nonstop, nonrepetitive, not sectionalized, beginning-to-end classical music." At this writing, efforts were under way to raise funding for a symphonic orchestra recording of the score. After that, *The Daughter of Dawn*, with its new sound track, was to be made available to the public for purchase.

In addition to breaking new ground by having a Comanche composer create its sound track—albeit some eighty-seven years after the picture was wrapped—*The Daughter of Dawn* was also revolutionary in its casting of American Indians for the leads. The film features a raid on the Kiowa camp by Comanches, followed by a battle between the Comanches and the Kiowas. Some of the Kiowa actors play Comanches in the film, and vice versa. As Moore noted, "Considering that, we wonder if they were just having a little fun there."

Two of the pivotal roles went to a brother and sister, White and Wanada Parker, the children of Comanche chief Quanah Parker (who had done his own emoting in an Oklahoma film a dozen years earlier as a member of the cast of Bill Tilghman's *The Bank Robbery*). Both were cast as Kiowas, with White Parker playing the warrior White Eagle and his sister taking the role of Red Wing, a Kiowa maiden. Other major roles went to a Kiowa actor named Hunting Horse, who played the Comanche chief; Jack Sankadoty as the Kiowa Black Wolf, who later in the film joins the Comanche tribe in order to try to take the Daughter of Dawn for his own; and Esther LeBarre (spelled "Ester Lebarr" in some sources) as the title character—so named, as an intertitle states, "because she was ushered into the world as the sun rose." (The titles also give unanglicized names to the actors, which are either their American Indian names or monikers dreamed up by the producers in an attempt to make the cast seem more exotic to audiences. So Jack Sankadoty is billed as "Sanka Dota" on-screen, and LeBarre as "Princess Peka.")

Although allegedly based on an American Indian legend, the basic plot essentials are standard escapist-literature fare. Dawn loves White Eagle, but Black Wolf loves her, and he's a lot richer than White Eagle. ("Do not forget," Black Wolf tells Dawn via an intertitle, "I have many ponies to give.") The two ultimately have a competition for her hand, ordained by the chief, which involves jumping off a huge cliff.

Playing by the rules, the noble White Eagle sails into space and crashes to the ground. Black Wolf, however, manages to grab an outcropping on the side of the cliff that breaks his fall after only a few feet. Drummed out of the tribe for his cowardice, Black Wolf forges an alliance with the Comanches, leading that group to a climactic battle with the Kiowas. Death, as it is wont to do in movies, conveniently wraps up the plot.

As composer Yeagley pointed out, however, there's a little more going on here than there might be in a garden-variety melodrama. "It's a typical love story, but it's ingeniously put together," he observed. "I say that because it's actually a complex plot. There's the love story. There are the tribal struggles of a group. There's an intertribal war between Comanche and Kiowa. And there's a big buffalo hunt. [An intertitle] in the film refers to the archetypal love triangle, but that's a mistake. It's a quartet. The other girl, Red Wing, is in love with Black Wolf, and she's like an extended version of Liu, in [the Puccini opera] *Turandot*, who gets the short end of the stick all the way around. It's unrequited love that ends tragically for a person who's absolutely innocent.

"Personally," he added, "that's what got my attention. This woman. This woman's situation. I picked up on that, and every time she appears I have a solo piano [on the sound track]."

The picture begins with White Eagle's spotting a herd of buffalo, which is good news for the hungry Kiowas. They make plans for a big buffalo hunt, ride out in full force, and return triumphant. The actual attack on the herd, however, isn't seen in the film. Perhaps director Myles and his cast were discouraged from disturbing the buffalo in the Wichita Mountains Wildlife Refuge, which were just beginning to make a comeback. "The herd had been reintroduced in 1907," said Bill Moore. "They started it with twelve or thirteen buffalo, brought in from the Bronx Zoo."

One of the major reasons *The Daughter of Dawn* will be of interest to audiences today, Moore added, lies in its depiction of the Comanche and Kiowa people in that place and time, right down to the ornamentation they wore and displayed in their teepees. With the possible exception of a medallion worn by the Kiowa chief, which some historians believe is too outsized to be authentic, the camp settings, clothing, and accoutrements are all completely true to life.

"That's what's wonderful about this film," Moore noted. "Besides its historical significance, there are all these artifacts of the era, which has excited folks from the tribes as well as our historians here. This movie shows life as it was then. There are no props. It's all real."

Why *The Daughter of Dawn* was never seen beyond its Los Angeles preview showing—Moore said he can't even find evidence of a screening in Lawton—remains something of a puzzler. As the story of a way of life unfamiliar and even exotic to most Americans, the picture should've had enough curiosity value to land at least a few bookings. Evidence, however, points in the other direction.

After traveling to Oklahoma to produce the film, director-writer Myles resumed his career in Hollywood as an actor, director, and writer, although he doesn't seem to have any credits for about a four-year stretch following *The Daughter of Dawn*. As happened with so many other silent-film personnel, his movie career withered away with the advent of sound; Myles's final credit came as an actor in a low-budget Tinseltown melodrama called *Secrets of Hollywood*, released in 1933. He was still a resident of Los Angeles when he died in 1966.

FOUR

Roy and Dale in (Hereford) Heaven, Jesus in the Wichitas

Oklahoma was still a relatively young state in 1935, playing catch-up with the other states in many areas. But Oklahoma was ahead of most when it came to motion picture coverage of its historical moments. Some of the film shown in the world's theaters was shot by Oklahoma photographers who . . . had the "newsreel habit."

—Bill Moore, "Lights, Camera, Action!" *Chronicles of Oklahoma* (Fall 1993)

As the Depression took hold, pros and amateurs alike concentrated on simple survival, and that had nothing to do with making movies. For a generation after the advent of sound, the rest was silence. Outside of newsreel and home movie photography, motion picture cameras rarely rolled anywhere in the state.

—James Vance, "Rewind to Fast Forward," *Urban Tulsa Weekly* (July 22–28, 1999)

Every Easter season, in the late forties, the citizens of Lawton, a town of eighty thousand people in southwest Oklahoma, staged a Passion play—a regular Okie Oberammergau. The spectacle attracted several thousand pious southwesterners, but [was] not otherwise widely heralded. . . . [S]oon enough, the film industry discovered the event through ads in *Boxoffice.* Kroger Babb's newest and greatest accomplishment in his lifelong crusade for America's uplift was an inspirational film of pageantry and reverence bearing a prosaic, un-Babb-like title, *The Lawton Story.*

—David F. Friedman, *A Youth in Babylon* (1990)

After the boom of the 1910s and '20s, made-in-Oklahoma features went into a long eclipse, a development that coincided roughly with the onset of the Great Depression. The dry spell lasted through the World War II years before ending with a bang, or at least a thundering of hoofbeats. Whatever the sound, it signaled a new era of Sooner State filmmaking, helped along by a governor who loved the movies as well as by a couple of exploitation-film characters and others who saw the state as fertile ground for their cinematic schemes.

Until that time, however, the state's filmmakers turned their energies largely toward the nonfiction, or newsreel, side of the business. There were several reasons for this. One was that the ground rules had gotten tougher. It cost a great deal of money to convert to sound, especially in the first few years of talking pictures, and a lot of would-be moguls simply didn't have the capital. Also, the big Hollywood studios were solidifying their hold on America's filmgoers, actually owning many of the theaters that played their movies (until 1948, when the Supreme Court put an end to that practice), and that made it increasingly hard for independent distributors to get significant bookings. Then, of course, there was the Great Depression, compounded in and around Oklahoma by the Dust Bowl, flailing the state with a one-two economic punch that would stagger it for years.

Still, there were people, including the pioneering 101 Ranch photographer Bennie Kent, who found ways to continue shooting films and sometimes actually make some money at it. In addition to his work on early Oklahoma movies like *Passing of the Oklahoma Outlaw* and *The Bank Robbery*, Kent used his camera to record events not only on the 101, which employed him as its resident photographer, but all across Oklahoma. Kent and his omnipresent camera rambled around the state, always ready to film some interesting or important event for posterity. And while much of his work proved to be transitory, thanks to the unstable nitrate film used in those days, some of his footage does survive. We know, for instance, that he was on the scene of Tulsa's infamous 1921 race riot, and it just may be Kent-lensed material that James Vance referred to in this excerpt from his "Rewind to Fast Forward" article in the July 22–28 issue of *Urban Tulsa Weekly*: "One remarkable if grim example [of Oklahoma-lensed newsreel footage] that survives is a film of a Ku Klux Klan parade down Main Street the year following the Tulsa race riot; for a dime, local patrons could view scenes of their neighbors marching around in sheets, and shots of an airplane soaring above the city with a glowing cross attached to the underside of its fuselage."

Although they haven't been a part of the moviegoing experience in the United States since the early 1960s, newsreels—like cartoons and short subjects of various kinds—were once expected by audiences, right along with the main attraction, which was usually not one but two feature films. Writing in *Movietone Presents the 20th Century* (1976), a pictorial history of one of the biggest supplier of newsreels, Lawrence Cohn explained the phenomenon in this way:

> Though perhaps difficult to imagine today, there was a time in the not-too-distant past when no movie program was complete without a newsreel. Before the onslaught of television, the standard movie theater program was comprised of two features, previews of coming attractions, possibly a short subject and/or a cartoon and always, the newsreel. With the advent of the newsreel, all of the activities of 20th Century man were presented visually via the medium of the motion picture. The subjects covered were all-encompassing: politics and politicians of the day, kings and king-makers, dictators and demagogues, sports, transportation, technology, science, disasters, conflagrations, news events, not-so-newsworthy event, persons and personalities, planes and trains, fashions of the day and yesterday. Fads and follies, crazes and crazies, the interesting as well as the banal, public works, some entertainment, and always, war—the last being the constant item throughout both the history of newsreels and apparently, the behavior of modern man. (p. 4)

Shipped to movie houses weekly, newsreels (which usually had a running time of ten to twelve minutes, or one reel) became so popular in the '30s and '40s that theaters specializing in them—detached from the feature-film programs they were intended to support—began popping up in major cities across the country. In a time well before television, people who wanted moving pictures to illustrate what they heard on the radio or read in the newspapers had to leave their homes to get them.

At least a little bit of what those news aficionados got, no matter where they lived, was footage shot by a couple of Oklahomans. The first was Bennie Kent, the British-born amateur photographer who had become excited about the possibility of moving pictures very early in Oklahoma's film history. The second was a man named Arthur B. Ramsey—who, in the midst of the Great Depression and the Dust Bowl, set up a successful filmmaking concern in Oklahoma's capital city.

By 1911, when the Pathe company began releasing newsreels to America's theaters, Bennie Kent was already a veteran cinematographer, having shot whole narrative films as well as scenes around the 101 Ranch and his hometown of Chandler, among other sites. When some of his footage was accepted by Pathe for incorporation into its newsreels, he began a relationship with the company that lasted for several years. Over that period, material shot by Kent was shown to audiences all over the world. Sometimes it depicted an event as important as the massive Tulsa race riot of 1921; other times, he used his cameras to record state leaders, from governors to important Native Americans, as well as everyday Oklahomans, such as a group of cotton pickers at work.

The checks Kent received from Pathe, however, were only part of his motivation for shooting all that film in his adopted home state. According to Bill Moore's "Lights, Camera, Action!" (in the Fall 1993 issue of the *Chronicles of Oklahoma*), Kent's overriding ambition was to preserve Oklahoma's early history for the generations to come. In fact, he wanted to put together his own feature-length documentary film, incorporating the best and most important scenes he'd shot over the years.

Kent, never realized this dream. Needing money toward the end of his life (he died at the age of eighty in 1945), he was even forced to sell off some of his footage. It was on nitrate stock, the only 35 mm film available at the time, so much of what he intended as historical documentation no longer exists. However, as Moore noted, some of his films went to a wealthy Ponca City resident named Lew Wentz, who in turn donated the reels to Oklahoma A&M College, the predecessor of Oklahoma State University. Before it decomposed or caught fire, Wentz's donation was transferred to 16 mm safety film and edited into a group of documentaries collectively known as *The Oklahoma Heritage Series*. They are now a part of the film collection at Oklahoma State.

The other major figure in Oklahoma's newsreel scene, Arthur Ramsey, was the son of Oklahoma City banker and oilman Walter R. Ramsey. The elder Ramsey was a millionaire and thus was in a position to help when his son showed an early interest in motion pictures. It was an uncle, however, who triggered that interest by giving Arthur his first movie camera in 1927, the same year that *The Jazz Singer* ushered in the talkie era. Thirteen years old at the time, Arthur took to filming immediately.

An Oklahoma teen who owned and operated state-of-the-art movie-making equipment was unusual enough to merit the attention of the *Daily Oklahoman*—which was also, of course, very aware of Arthur's dad—and it was someone at that Oklahoma City newspaper who gave Pathe young Ramsey's name when it called to inquire about filmmakers in the area. Although he was still in his teens, Ramsey was hired to travel more than 1,200 miles northwest to Yellowstone Park, where he would shoot the president of the United States, Calvin Coolidge, standing by a geyser. (It's unclear why Pathe didn't hire a cameraman who lived a little closer to the event.)

History doesn't record Arthur Ramsey's mental state once he agreed to this assignment, but one has to admire the pluck of a youngster who had the self-confidence to give orders to a U.S. president. In a 1989 interview, done for the Oklahoma Historical Society and quoted in Bill Moore's story, Ramsey recalled telling Coolidge, "Stand here because this thing will go off in a minute and I want to get the scene and get you out of the water" (p. 307). He also still seemed amazed, some sixty years after the fact, that the president not only stood under the geyser until Ramsey could finish the scene, but stayed for a considerable time, getting progressively more drenched, after Ramsey had finished shooting.

"A New York newsreel company had sent a teenaged boy from Oklahoma City to Yellowstone Park to film the president of the United States," wrote Moore. "It was quite a beginning to what would be an accomplished film career" (p. 307).

Thanks to backing from his dad, young Ramsey became the first Oklahoma filmmaker to begin shooting with sound equipment. That was in 1929, and by that time the teen had become a busy newsreel photographer, missing many of his high school classes in favor of fulfilling assignments for Pathe and, increasingly, Paramount. He first cracked the sound newsreels a couple of years later, when he shot Oklahoma governor "Alfalfa Bill" Murray taking the oath of office—sworn in by his ninety-one-year-old father.

Before he'd even reached college age, Ramsey had his own plane, which he used to fly himself and his equipment to newsreel assignments. Over the next several years, Ramsey was on the scene for some of the state's most intriguing events, from oil field fires to Governor Murray's war on toll bridge owners at the Texas border. In addition to filming Governor Murray, a man who reportedly enjoyed his publicity, Ramsey's cameras caught famous Oklahomans like Will Rogers and professional base-ball star Pepper Martin. And as his predecessor Bennie Kent had done, Ramsey shot scenes of ranch life, traveling to both the Miller Brothers' 101 Ranch and Pawnee Bill's spread in search of material. Perhaps his biggest story came in 1933, when he and his film crew were allowed inside an Oklahoma City courtroom where the notorious gangster George "Machine Gun" Kelly was being tried on kidnapping charges.

At its peak, the Ramsey Picture Corporation boasted two offices in Oklahoma City, one with a complete sound stage. These weren't only the bases of his newsreel operations; he and his staff also shot political campaign films, musical performances, promotional films for various causes, and industrial films (which are, generally speaking, movies shot on assignment for specific companies). For a short time, he worked in Hollywood, with Moore listing the 1936 Mae West vehicle *Klondike Annie* and 1939's *Man about Town*, a musical comedy with Jack Benny and Dorothy Lamour, as Ramsey's two major-studio credits. Both those features were released by Paramount Pictures, whose newsreel division had been buying footage from Ramsey for a few years by then.

One of the major players in the Ramsey Picture Corporation began his own significant Hollywood career a couple of decades after Ramsey's brief Tinseltown tenure, also making his entrée into the big-time movie business with Paramount. Cinematographer Haskell Boggs, a native of Jones, Oklahoma, and a high school friend of Ramsey's, is perhaps best known for shooting Paramount's Jerry Lewis comedies, beginning with 1957's *The Delicate Delinquent*—the first film Lewis made after splitting with his longtime partner Dean Martin. The notoriously finicky Lewis must've liked Boggs's work, because the cameraman shot several more of his vehicles over the next few years.

Boggs, working mostly for Paramount, was also the cinematographer on the fact-based baseball movie *Fear Strikes Out* (1957) and the science fiction cult favorite *I Married a Monster from Outer Space* (1958), among several other features. Beginning in the late '50s, he gradually moved into television, finding especially lasting employment in series starring popular TV actor Michael Landon. According to IMDb.com, Boggs shot eighty-eight episodes of *Bonanza*, eighty-one of *Little House on the Prairie*, and several installments of Landon's final television show, *Highway to Heaven*. Boggs's last credit was the 1993 TV movie *Bonanza: The Return*, which aired ten years before his death.

Unlike Boggs, Ramsey didn't take to Hollywood. He returned to Oklahoma City in the late '30s and continued to work there, with newsreels becoming an increasingly smaller part of his operation. According to records cited by Bill Moore, the Ramsey company shot its last newsreel footage—of a grisly crash of a passenger plane in Oklahoma City—during March 1939.

Ramsey continued to work out of his hometown until the Japanese attack on Pearl Harbor precipitated America's entry into the war. He joined the army and rose to the rank of captain, first making training films for the troops and later becoming the head of the Combat Film Office in New York, where he helped other government officials collect and analyze war-related footage shot by filmmakers all over the globe.

When World War II ended, so did Ramsey's career in film. Like his father, he became an oilman, pursuing that business for the rest of his life. In the early '90s, however, he agreed to sit down for an interview with Bill Moore at the OETA studios in Oklahoma City. A subsequent documentary, blending interview material with films and photos from Ramsey's newsreel days, first aired on the network in 1994 under the title *Oklahoma Newsreel Cameraman*.

Ramsey died six years later in Albuquerque, New Mexico. Although he'd been out of the movie business for more than sixty years by that time, his place in Oklahoma's movie history had been secured long before. Put simply, what Bennie Kent did with silent film, Arthur Ramsey did with sound.

Once one gets past the substantial work of the documentarians, Oklahoma's filmic output in the '30s and most of the '40s is a mixed, and not very full, bag. Continuing a practice that began with the Selig Polyscope Company's spring 1909 visit to the 101 Ranch, a couple of major studios sent crews into the state to film background scenes in the late '30s. The first was Paramount, in conjunction with director Cecil B. DeMille's epic tale of the building of the transcontinental railroad, *Union Pacific*. Starring Joel McCrea, Barbara Stanwyck, and Robert Preston (who would figure in a major Oklahoma movie a decade later) and released by Paramount in 1939 with the advertising tagline "The Greatest American Epic of Them All!" it featured some secondary footage shot around the railroad tracks near the southwestern Oklahoma town of Cache.

Then there was *The Grapes of Wrath*, Twentieth Century-Fox's 1940 adaptation of John Steinbeck's brilliant, powerful, and then-controversial novel. By the time cameras started rolling on the film version, helmed by top director John Ford and featuring a knowing and empathetic script by Nunnally Johnson, the book had been excoriated in certain quarters for its unflinching depiction of the plight of the tenant farmers and other agricultural workers of the time. Usually referred to as "Okies," even though they came from surrounding states as well, they had been driven off their lands by the Great Depression and the Dust Bowl and both shunned and exploited by those they met along the way.

Unsurprisingly, Steinbeck's sympathetic portrait of the migrants and his anger at those who took advantage of them had riled many of Oklahoma's politicians and civic leaders. U.S. representative Lyle Boren, for instance, famously took to the floor of the House for a 1940 speech in which he called the book "a lie, a damnable lie, a black, infernal creation of a twisted, distorted mind" and noted, "As a citizen of Oklahoma, I would have it known that I resent, for the great State of Oklahoma, the implications of this book." Also, the August 7, 1939, issue of the *Oklahoma City Times* carried a story indicating that officers of the Oklahoma City Chamber of Commerce thought that "someone should protest the inaccurate and unfair treatment the state seems to be about to receive in the filming of the picture," and they planned to talk to the governor, among others, about doing just that.

But even with all of the brouhaha about the upcoming movie, a crew managed to roll into the state and take some shots—mostly around what was then U.S. Highway 66, the fabled "Main Street of America." Reportedly, in order to keep away from controversy, Twentieth Century-Fox put the word out that the filming was not for any *Grapes of Wrath* picture at all but for a feature to be titled *Route 66*.

Very little Oklahoma-lensed footage made it into the final cut of *The Grapes of Wrath*, which—like its source novel—became an American classic. However, those familiar with Sooner State landmarks can spot the distinctive Beckham County Courthouse in Sayre as a part of the montage depicting the flight of the Joad family out of their home state.

Besides those two small moments in big pictures and some newsreel and other documentary efforts, there just wasn't much going on movie-wise in 1930s Oklahoma. One effort that does deserve a mention was a modest little one-reeler created by the state's Cal Tinney. Tinney was a kind of Will Rogers lite, a characterization not intended as unduly negative. *Tulsa World* writer Gene Curtis pointed out the similarities between Rogers and Tinny in his August 22, 2007, "Only in Oklahoma" column:

> Cal Tinney sang, wrote newspaper columns, acted on stage, in the movies, on radio and television, ran businesses and developed land—always with humor. . . .
>
> Tinney's life was crammed with material suitable for story-telling, and he delighted in recalling the events in his "home-spun" humor.
>
> It was inevitable that Tinney would be compared to Will Rogers, a comparison he never resisted. Tinney had met Rogers in the late 1920s, had begun emulating him and was writing a biography about him. . . . After Rogers' death in a plane crash in Alaska, NBC hired Tinney to portray him in a radio tribute. Tinney later portrayed Rogers on Eddie Cantor's Sunday night television show.

Tinney also had a *Tulsa World* column, beginning in 1973, called "Will Said and Cal Says," It further cemented the relationship between the two humorists by presenting quotes from the late Rogers in concert with new observations from Tinney.

It's not known whether Will Rogers was referenced in *Oklahoma As Is*, a 1937 Warner Bros. short subject from Tinney that specifically poked fun at the northeastern Oklahoma town of Oologah. Given Tinney's fascination with Rogers, however, the chances are good, especially since the movie star, humorous commentator, and columnist was born on a ranch near Oologah in 1879. (Tinney, born under similar circumstances in Pontotoc County in south-central Oklahoma forty-one years after Rogers's birth, was a resident of Oologah for a time as well.)

The one-reel *Oklahoma As Is* didn't seem to make much of an impact in the state or anywhere else; although it was released under the auspices of a major studio, it is not found in any standard movie reference and is unavailable for viewing today. In fact, just about the only thing we know about it comes from a March 2, 1937, *Tulsa Tribune* piece (in which the unnamed writer consistently misspelled the town's name):

> Oklahomans will join easterners in laughter at Cal Tinney's movie short, *Oklahoma As Is*, despite its uncomplimentary satire.
>
> Cal, Tulsa syndicate humorist and in demand in the east for lectures and dinner speaking, had [*sic*] made a highly amusing Warner Brothers Vitaphone short that will show a week at the Orpheum theater beginning Friday.
>
> The movie was filmed in Oolagah and shows the drabbest, shabbiest spots of that community. Cal carries on a dialogue explaining what the shots are. However, he calls his home town "Oolala."
>
> All the Oolagah old-timers appear in the short as does Tinney and his father, David Tinney, who lives on a rural route out of West Tulsa.
>
> Cal takes one amusing crack after another at the expense of "Oolala" and Oklahoma in general. He described "Oolala" as being so small that the "Welcome to Oolala" and "Come Again" signs are on the same board.

The writer concluded, "Whether the citizens of Oolagah will enjoy it depends upon how broad their sense of humor is."

The number of moviemakers—in Oklahoma as well as everywhere else in the country—exploded in the late 1980s, when technology put videotape capabilities in the hands of anyone who had enough cash to buy a camera, or a good enough story to borrow one for a while. By the turn of the twenty-first century, an editor could sit at a computer and digitally put together a movie in ways so sophisticated that they would've taken a roomful of equipment to achieve only a few years before.

Given those circumstances, it may be hard for today's film audiences to imagine that just about *any* sort of movie being made in Oklahoma in the '30s and '40s was novel enough to attract major attention. If you had a camera, some actors, and a script, you could usually attract interest from the local press—as was the case with a cowboy movie called *Death Rides the Range*. An Oklahoma City feature film shot and acted by amateurs, it was the subject of a story-and-picture layout in the August 10, 1942, issue of the *Daily Oklahoman*. If the unbylined story is to be believed, the film also drew notice of a different sort: "There is a saloon scene, filmed in the basement studio of the producers on North Broadway, and it is a lulu. Everything except the plaster on the wall is smashed. Police heard the noise, the shooting and the wild goings-on. They hurried in. The raiders found the battle was all sham. They found no gambling, and the 'whisky' turned out to be orange juice."

Shot in Technicolor by city residents Fritz Holzberlein and Eugene Heflin, the film starred a number of locals who apparently weren't afraid to suffer for their art (and in an indication of how different things were then, the article lists all of their home addresses). The writer of the piece pointed out that since there were no stand-ins, all the cast members had to do their own stunts, including a leap from train tracks by the hero and heroine just before a locomotive (whose engineer hadn't been notified of the filming) hit them, the hero's riding a horse into a lake whose waters suddenly swallowed both horse and rider, and the heroine's fall onto a steel rail, which knocked her unconscious. ("But the injury was not serious," noted the writer.)

Holzberlein and Heflin planned to enter *Death Rides the Range* in something referred to in the article as "the Lloyd Bacon trophy contest for amateur producers." At the time, Bacon was a top-line director for Warner Bros., with credits that included 1939's *The Oklahoma Kid*, a western featuring Warner stars James Cagney and Humphrey Bogart in a departure from the gangster roles that had made them famous. Although none of *The Oklahoma Kid* had actually been shot in Oklahoma, it received a pair of gala world premieres, more or less simultaneously, in Oklahoma City and Tulsa.

Death Rides the Range was to have its own premiere in mid-August, at Oklahoma City's McKinley Park. That event, assuming it came off as planned, was no doubt far more modest than the one held in the city for Bacon's big-studio epic. But then again, the film's budget was a lot more modest too. According to the story, the producers brought *Death Rides the Range* in for exactly $63.21.

The long dry spell for feature filmmaking in Oklahoma finally was broken in the late 1940s. In fact, the last three years of the decade not only brought a minor flurry of movie activity in the state but also saw two of the most popular players in western movies wed on a ranch near the south-central Oklahoma town of Davis.

Republic Pictures—a studio that occupied a place in the Hollywood hierarchy somewhere between the low-budget Poverty Row outfits and majors like MGM and Paramount—first put Roy Rogers and Dale Evans together in the 1944 feature *Cowboy and the Senorita*. Their on-screen chemistry was evident from the beginning, and by the time 1946's *Home in Oklahoma* rolled around, they had costarred in fifteen more western pictures. But *Home in Oklahoma* differed from the others in one important way—as its title suggests, it was shot on location in the Sooner State.

The reason that a unit from Republic came halfway across the country with two of its biggest stars to make a movie in Oklahoma, when the studio had everything it needed on its own backlots and in California locations, had to do primarily with a couple of Oklahomans named L. C. Griffith and Roy J. Turner. Griffith and Turner knew one another, serving as directors of the Oklahoma City Chamber of Commerce in the mid-'40s, among other connections. But another man, Bill Likins, who owned a substantial ranch near Turner's equally impressive cattle operation in south-central Oklahoma, probably helped bring the Republic production to the Sooner State too.

At the time, Griffith was the head of a large chain of theaters bearing his name, and he played a lot of product from Republic, which, unlike several of its major-studio brethren of the time, didn't own its own movie houses. Also, much of what Republic put out, including its westerns and

Sheet music cover for a song that celebrated the cattle operations in the Arbuckle Mountains and may have led to the filming of a Roy Rogers western in the area. (John Wooley Archives)

countrified musicals, was especially welcome in the less urban areas of the country, including Oklahoma. So when the owner of a major theater chain in the hinterlands spoke, the studio had a tendency to listen. And that's just what happened, according to an article penned by Imogene Patrick in the June 14, 1946, *Daily Oklahoman* while shooting on *Home in Oklahoma* was still under way in the state. "Griffith Theaters sold Republic on the Oklahoma location trip," Patrick wrote, "and crew officials, sold on Hereford Heaven's special brand of scenery and ideal shooting weather, were not sorry."

"Hereford Heaven" was a well-known nickname referring to the area around the Arbuckle Mountains where Roy J. Turner, Bill Likins, and others had their massive cattle spreads, raising some of the top Hereford cattle in the world. Turner was so bullish on that particular breed that he not only served as the president of the National Hereford Association in 1946 but also penned a song called "Hereford Heaven," extolling the virtues of both the breed and the area around the Arbuckle Mountains where the cattle were raised—and the movie's Oklahoma scenes were lensed. Although theater chain owner Griffith indeed carried weight with a studio like Republic, Turner's "Hereford Heaven" ditty might have had something to do with the location shooting as well.

That was the theory proposed by the *Daily Oklahoman*'s Ray Park in a January 13, 1947, piece. By then, Turner had been elected Oklahoma's new governor, his inauguration filmed by a crew commissioned by L. C. Griffith for showing in Griffith's theaters. (One of the things Turner would do in his first year would be to appoint Bill Likins—the third leg of this particular stool—special ambassador to Hollywood, where Likins would be in charge of rustling up more movie-studio business for Oklahoma.) Wrote Park:

> Roy J. Turner, the incoming governor, is a modest, unassuming man at heart, and for a long time few of his friends knew that he had sat himself down and composed a song, entitled, of course, "Hereford Heaven."
> Then Bill Likins got hold of it, and it was no longer a secret. Bill, who also loves Herefords, thought this was the greatest song he ever heard.
> He even went out and organized himself a quartet—"The Flying L Boys"—to sing it. Carried away with sentimental exuberance, he often

Home in Oklahoma, a 1946 western, was shot in Oklahoma's "Hereford Heaven." (John Wooley Archives)

called friends by long-distance phone, in various sections of the state and at unexpected hours to have them listen to the quartet singing of those beloved White Faces.

As time went on, "Hereford Heaven" became right well known, and nobody was prouder than the beaming author, who never really thought he could do it when he first sat down to compose.

Then came a thrilling moment—Roy Rogers sang the song over his national radio broadcast. Likins and the author were so overwhelmed they offered to put both of their Murray county ranches at Hollywood's disposal if anybody would like to make a movie there.

Most of *Home in Oklahoma*, in fact, would be shot on Likins's Flying L Ranch, although the cast spent a few days in front of the cameras at the Turner spread as well. Patrick's *Daily Oklahoman* story noted that some 250 head of Likins's prize-winning Herefords, valued at $250,000, were used in a big climactic scene that also featured dozens of horsemen from around the state. "According to producer [Edward J.] White," she wrote, "it was the most valuable bunch of cattle ever used in a Hollywood shot."

As far as Oklahoma *people* were concerned, 35 horsemen from Oklahoma City's Ranger Club and "another 15 expert riders from this area," in Patrick's words, supported Roy and Dale and his other regular costars, grizzled funnyman George "Gabby" Hayes; Roy's palomino horse, Trigger; and Bob Nolan and the Sons of the Pioneers, who were joined by an aggregation known as the Flying L Ranch Quartette—probably the same singing group mentioned in the Ray Park story. Action specialist William Witney was on hand to direct the tale, which featured the blend of action and music that Rogers fans had come to expect. Roy played the part of a small-town newspaper editor investigating the suspicious death of the owner of the Flying T Ranch, while Dale was a big-city reporter on the trail of a possible story revolving around the same incident.

"We were real, real excited when Roy Rogers and Dale Evans came to Murray County to make a movie," recalled Charlene Howe Gilliam in a 2004 telephone interview with Butch Bridges on the OklahomaHistory. net website. "Everybody in town just thought they were great. They were just the nicest people."

Gilliam also remembered that someone had cut off Trigger's tail, a story confirmed by Imogene Patrick's *Daily Oklahoman* piece, which explained that the horse's "long, flowing blond tail [had fallen] victim to a souvenir hunter when he was enroute from California."

"That was one of the most interesting things that happened during the making of that movie," noted Gilliam. "Roy Rogers had a false tail flown out for him, so when you watch the movie, try and figure out when the tail changed. I think I know, but I'm not sure."

Home in Oklahoma had twin premieres on October 30, 1946, in the towns of Ardmore—where many of the cast and crew had stayed during filming—and Ada. Rogers, Evans, and Hayes were on hand for both events, even though Evans had a sprained ankle and Rogers's wife, Arlene, had given birth to a son two days earlier.

Then, only a few days after the premieres, Arlene suddenly died of an embolism. Following the shock of becoming a widower with three small children, Rogers looked to his costar for solace, and soon their romance wasn't just being played out on America's screens.

A little more than a year after his wife's death, Roy and Dale returned to the Flying L near Davis, this time to tie the knot—on the afternoon of New Year's Eve 1947. Apparently, the decision to be married there was made earlier in the month and then officially announced by Governor Turner's Hollywood ambassador. As the Associated Press reported on December 4:

> V. B. Likins telephoned Gov. Roy J. Turner from Los Angeles today that Roy Rogers, western film star, and Dale Evans, his leading lady, would be married at Davis, Ok., December 31.
>
> The wedding will be at Likins' Flying L ranch. Rogers and Miss Evans will arrive at the ranch December 27.
>
> Governor and Mrs. Turner will be among the wedding guests.

In a story filed the same day as the wedding, an AP reporter noted that the governor and his wife were indeed among the "approximately 80 persons" (including actor Wayne Morris, a houseguest of the governor at the time) in attendance watching as "the vows were read by the Rev. W. H. Alexander, pastor of the First Christian church of Oklahoma City, before the mantel in the living room of the sprawling ranchhouse as sleet and snow fell outside." Roy's best man was Art Rush, his manager. Rush's wife, Mary Jo, was matron of honor. Songs performed at the wedding, according to an Imogene Patrick *Oklahoman* piece on January 1, 1949, of course included "Hereford Heaven," performed by the Flying L Quartet.

"They took the license out at the Murray County Courthouse in Sulphur, and I understand from other people . . . that it snowed so much [on the day of the wedding] that the preacher had to come in on horseback," said Gilliam. "Then, for their honeymoon, he took her coon hunting at Nebo [a town south of Sulphur]. He had met [local resident] Paul Thompson when he was there making the movie, and they'd become coon-huntin' buddies. And Roy Rogers was a real coon hunter."

Although it's certainly possible that Rogers returned to the area over the years to visit with the friends he'd made and chase down a few ring-tailed mammals, he never made another film in the state. The closest he got was in 1955, when he sent a letter to the state's Planning and Resources

Rock Island Trail star Forrest Tucker in a publicity shot from the 1950 release. (John Wooley Archives)

Board in Oklahoma City, announcing his idea to shoot the next season's episodes of *Brave Eagle*, a TV series produced by Roy Rogers Enterprises, in the Wichita Mountains around Cache and Lawton. But the unusual series—which featured stories told from an American Indian point of view—expired before that could happen, running only a single season on CBS.

Although Roy and Dale returned to Oklahoma only to get married, not to make another film, their home studio sent another cast and crew to Oklahoma a couple of years later to shoot outdoor scenes for a railroad-themed feature titled *Rock Island Trail*. The story of a young railroad man (played by Forrest Tucker) trying to expand his operations in the face of opposition by a stagecoach and steamship magnate (Bruce Cabot), the screenplay was derived from Frank J. Nevins's fact-based historical novel *A Yankee Dared: A Romance of Our Railroads*. Published in 1933, the novel dealt with the expansion of one of the most famous names in railroad lore, the Rock Island Line.

Much of the feature was shot at Republic's base of operations in Hollywood. But enough of it was lensed in Oklahoma to require the presence of the two male leads and featured player Grant Withers, as well as director Joe Kane and associate producer Paul Malvern. A photo accompanying a September 10, 1949, *Tulsa Tribune* article by Roger V. Devlin shows the three actors arriving via train in McAlester, near the outdoor locations of the shoot.

Although Republic released both the Rogers vehicle *Home in Oklahoma* and *Rock Island Trail*, there doesn't seem to a strong connection between the two, at least in terms of why they were filmed in the Sooner State (not to discount Bill Likins's Hollywood-ambassador work, which likely played a part). According to Devlin's *Tribune* piece, Oklahoma was chosen as a location for the latter on the recommendation of personnel from the Rock Island Railroad, the company whose origins had given rise to the book and subsequent movie. Devlin described the railroad's participation in the filming: "The picture is being shot in a rural section of eastern Oklahoma because western Illinois, locale of the story, today is too highly developed and modern. The Rock Island railroad searched its 8,000 miles of tracks to find a spot which still looked as Illinois did a century ago. It found it along an abandoned stretch of rail between Haileyville and Pittsburg, southeast of McAlester."

Even that area, Devlin noted, had to be de-modernized a bit before shooting could commence. And apparently the film crew got plenty of advice on how to do it. An authentic old locomotive, on loan from the Western Historical Museum in Denver, was going to be equipped with a hose that would belch out steam, giving a little extra cinematic color to the proceedings. But the assistant director who'd come up with the idea, reported Devlin, was stopped by a Rock Island representative who happened to be on the scene.

"Whoa," William E. Hayes, executive assistant to the president of the Rock Island railroad, shook his head. "You can't do that. There were no steam lines through passenger cars in 1850."

A road along which a six-horse stage coach will race the locomotive in another scene also had to be altered. A few days ago it was a well-graded, graveled Oklahoma state highway between Haileyville and Pittsburg.

Before the scene was shot, it was swept carefully so no automobile tire marks would show. Bushes and shrubs were moved from adjoining fields to line its right-of-way, making it a narrow lane. Other bushes were placed to hide fence posts.

And a 30-foot cottonwood tree was moved bodily to a spot immediately in front of a tall—and obviously modern—telephone pole.

Devlin further noted that all of the Oklahoma footage—including the dynamiting of a trestle bridge and a major battle between Indians on horseback and railroad construction workers—would be recorded without sound equipment: "Practically all the scenes being shot near here are long-range views, so it isn't even necessary to record dialogue. That also will be 'dubbed' in at the Republic studios. The director himself can use a loud speaker public address system to maneuver his mobs of Indians or his cordons of track workers."

One other reason for the choice of Oklahoma as a location might have to do with Trucolor, the process Republic used for its color films. Back in 1946, the then governor-elect Roy J. Turner had announced—after a visit to the West Coast—that he was hoping to convince producers that the state was a good place to shoot in Trucolor. An un-bylined *Daily Oklahoman* piece from December 24, 1946, gave further details:

> Turner said studio officials told him "true color" [sic] production is handicapped in California and Nevada because of seasonal overcast which is causing the loss of a great deal of "shooting time" and a resultant loss of thousands of dollars on each film.
>
> "I was told that filming has been held up as long as nine consecutive days," Turner said. "That would never happen to them in Oklahoma. I'm going to try to sell the studios on some of our Oklahoma winter sunshine as one phase of the program of bringing new industries into the state.
>
> "The studios are particularly interested in the landscape color available in Oklahoma. Color photography requires direct sunlight, unobscured by

haze, which is prevalent in California. Oklahoma offers the kind of sunlight required by this photography."

Rock Island Trail was shot in Trucolor, and Republic continued to use the process for many years afterward. Despite Turner's efforts, however, the studio never made any other significant filmmaking forays into the state. Oklahoma's part in *Rock Island Trail*, meanwhile, was soon concluded, and Kane and company returned to Hollywood for dubbing and other finishing touches. The ninety-minute feature was released on May 18, 1950.

At the time the *Rock Island Trail* crew arrived in Oklahoma, another, unrelated assemblage had just wrapped its own western-themed production in the state. Like *Rock Island Trail*, *Osage* had a cast full of recognizable B-picture names, including western star Smith Ballew, character actors Lon Chaney, Jr., and Lee "Lasses" White, veteran leading man Edward Norris, and busy movie heroine Noel Neill, a few years away from becoming Lois Lane on the *Superman* TV series. Western-swing bandleaders Spade Cooley (from Los Angeles) and Johnnie Lee Wills (from Tulsa) also reportedly had roles in the film.

Director Oliver Drake was also, like *Rock Island Trail*'s Joe Kane, a veteran western director. Most recently Drake been helming the Jimmy Wakely singing-cowboy movies for Monogram Pictures, a Republic rival. Drake even had a Southern California ranch where he sometimes filmed his pictures.

But there was one big difference between the two westerns. The first one got a legitimate theatrical release and played in scores of movie houses. The second one, from all indications, didn't.

The key figure in getting *Osage* off the ground appears to have been a Tulsa native named Bob Gilbert, who had attended the University of Tulsa before heading west to take his shot at a film career. By August 1949, when the *Osage* cast and crew traveled to Pawhuska—sixty miles northwest of Tulsa—to begin filming, Gilbert had amassed a handful of legitimate credits, including a supporting part in the 1947 Wakely starrer

Rainbow over the Rockies, which was produced, written, and directed by Oliver Drake. Gilbert had also started his own filmmaking enterprise, the Hollywood-based Ranger Production Company, and had apparently gotten noted Tulsa businessman John Zink interested enough for Zink to form his own movie company as well—Sooner Pictures, based in Zink's (and Gilbert's) hometown. In an August 7, 1949, *Tulsa Tribune* article, Sooner Pictures vice president Ferne King explained the mission of the new company, saying, "We want to do movies on Oklahoma that will show it as the wealthy and beautiful state it is. Bob Gilbert, a Tulsa boy himself, agreed with us that such a series of pictures would aid in overcoming false opinions some people have about our state."

The *Tribune* piece noted that the movie had been in the planning stages for three years. Once it actually got going, however, shooting wrapped in only a couple of weeks. (In stories from August 10 and August 20, the *Tulsa World* reported that Drake was scouting Oklahoma locations for an Old West–style town to represent Pawhuska in the 1880s. The latter article indicated that he'd been unable to find one "without paving on the main street," so he was going to have to wait until the cast and crew returned to California, where they would "build and shoot that scene.")

Filmed in and around Pawhuska, *Osage* used as its primary location Gene Mullendore's Cross Bell Ranch. In an article published in the August 28, 1949, *Tulsa Tribune*, the director and his costar reminisced about the just-wrapped shooting.

> Some of the highlights of the filming, recalled by Drake and Gilbert, included a stampede of hundred of horses, rounded up by Mullendore ranch cowboys; pictures of some of the largest herds of cattle in the world; a death scene during the stampede involving Kay Mullendore, 9-year-old daughter of the ranch owner; a fight in and around a blazing log cabin, filmed on the John Zink ranch near Skiatook, and an early-day wagon train school scene. Pawhuska children took part in the school scene and the teachers were Thressa Dean of Ada and Virginia King, in real life actually a Tulsa teacher.

The unnamed writer had begun the piece by noting, "Hollywood-in-the-Osage was a thing of the past, for the time being at least, [on] Saturday with the last of the movie contingent on their way to California after completing production of the color movie, *Osage*, in the cattle country around Pawhuska." That sentence turned out to be prescient. Hollywood-in-the-Osage was indeed a thing of the past, as there is no record of the movie ever being shown or even completed. A premiere, scheduled for a Pawhuska theater later in the year, doesn't seem to have happened; neither does even one of the "five other pictures" planned by the Sooner Pictures/Ranger Production Company tandem.

For several years after the filming of *Osage*, neither Drake nor Gilbert appears to have any movie credits. (Gilbert acted in and wrote a couple of pictures starring Spade Cooley that were released in 1950, but they had been completed years earlier.) Drake found a second coming as a TV director in the mid-'50s, but Gilbert's only significant credit in his post-*Osage* days came with the strange Columbia Pictures western *The Parson and the Outlaw*. Released in 1957, its cast consisted of old-timers and reliable B-movie players (including Charles "Buddy" Rogers, Sonny Tufts, Marie Windsor, Jean Parker, Robert Lowery, Bob Steele, and Kenne Duncan) to tell the story of Billy the Kid (Anthony Dexter) returning from his alleged death to defend a town against a villainous landowner. Gilbert was the executive producer and played a small role. The film was cowritten and directed by Oliver Drake. An online review of the film, written in 2004 by John Seal for IMDb.com, noted the "stock footage" of fires and wagon trains "shoehorned into the feature." Considering the filming "highlights" that Drake and Gilbert recalled for the *Tribune* writer, it's possible that some of the scenes from *Osage* ended up being recycled, eight years later, into *The Parson and the Outlaw*.

In 1970, E. C. Mullendore III, heir apparent to the Cross Bell Ranch, was murdered on its premises, and the still-unsolved crime has given the ranch a lasting notoriety. *Osage*'s falling off the edge of the world is hardly in that league, but it remains another mystery associated with the Mullendore spread.

What could bring a crowd of well over a hundred thousand souls to downtown Tulsa on April 13, 1949? The answer: all the hoopla surrounding the premiere of that city's namesake movie, *Tulsa*, starring Robert

The world premiere of *Tulsa* (1949) followed a major celebration in its name-sake city. (John Wooley Archives)

Preston, Susan Hayward, and Chill Wills. First, the top-billed stars, along with director Stuart Heisler and producer Walter Wanger, shared space in a huge, two-hour-plus parade with floats, high school and college bands, and more than $10 million worth of oil field equipment. Then the picture, released by Eagle-Lion Films, made its simultaneous debut at four of the city's biggest downtown movie houses—the Ritz, the Orpheum, the Majestic, and the Rialto. According to a *Tulsa World* article from March 27, a couple of weeks before the event, the parade celebrating the movie was to become the subject of a motion picture itself, "filmed and shown as a two-reel feature in 15,000 theaters over the nation."

There's some question as to whether that two-reeler was actually completed and distributed, but its existence, or lack thereof, in no way diminishes the event that unfolded on that April day in the city then known as "the Oil Capital of the World." A VHS version of *Tulsa,* distributed in the late '90s by the Tulsa-based Vintage Films, included added footage of the massive parade, along with interviews of eyewitnesses, all compiled by noted local historian and filmmaker Jack Frank. In one of the interviews, Sadie Adwan, a radio station salesperson at the time of the premiere, remembered the big event as "the greatest thing that happened in Tulsa in years and years and years." Eunice McDaniel, who did promotions for the city's theaters in the '40s, agreed. "The schools were out, the offices closed," she recalled, "and it was reported that there were between 125 and 150 thousand people in downtown Tulsa that day."

The *Tulsa* crew had begun production in June 1948, coming in almost exactly a year after Roy Rogers and his film crew had arrived in the state to make *Home in Oklahoma.* As with that movie, filming locales included the ranch of Governor Roy J. Turner, deep in the heart of south-central Oklahoma's Hereford Heaven.

In a February 2, 1979, column concerning a thirty-year-anniversary showing of *Tulsa* on the University of Tulsa campus, the *Tulsa Tribune*'s Bill Donaldson told the kind of story about the film that can easily pass into legend, regardless of a certain infidelity to the truth:

> While the movie used exterior photographs of many of the city of Tulsa's landmarks—and there was a painstakingly accurate soundstage re-creation of the lobby of the Hotel Tulsa—its producer, Walter Wanger, found himself in the middle of a friendly state feud—the one between Tulsa and Oklahoma City.
>
> When Wanger sent director Stuart Heisler to the Sooner State for location scouting, the original press book for the film says, Heisler discovered the most picturesque pasturelands in Oklahoma are not located in the vicinity of Tulsa.
>
> To the consternation of Tulsa's civic leaders, he found the suitable spots nearer Oklahoma City.
>
> As a result, practically all the cattle ranch scenes were shot on the outskirts of Oklahoma City, much to the chagrin of loyal residents of Tulsa and environs.

Technically, Donaldson was correct. The Hereford Heaven area around the Arbuckle Mountains is closer to Oklahoma City than to Tulsa by about seventy-five miles, although it's hardly on the capital city's "outskirts," given that it lies some eighty-five miles southeast. The point here is not to disparage Donaldson, one of Tulsa's best-known columnists for decades and a tireless advocate for the arts. Instead, a couple of things should be noted. First, motion-picture pressbooks—the publications sent to theaters to help in promoting upcoming movies—were notorious for playing fast and loose with the truth. Second, the Turner ranch location was in all likelihood a fait accompli from the very beginning. As Jack Frank, an unabashed lover of his hometown, observed in an interview with the author for the September 17, 1997, entertainment section of the *Tulsa World*, "Most of it was not filmed here. If there's a downside to the movie, I guess that's it. What happened was that the company came to the governor of the state at that time, Governor Turner, and showed him the script, and he liked it so much that he told them they could shoot it at his ranch. So most of it was shot down in southern Oklahoma. That's Oklahoma cattle country. To an outsider, it looks like Tulsa. But it portrays Tulsa as this landscape of oil derricks, this rough and tough landscape, and it wasn't that way at all."

In her 2004 interview on OklahomaHistory.net, Charlene Howe Gilliam remembered the cast showing up in and around her hometown of Sulphur, with star Susan Hayward riding a horse in the annual Hereford Heaven rodeo parade. "They gave several local people parts in that movie," she added. "The man who played Steve [the main ranch hand on the spread run by Susan Hayward's character, Cherokee Lansing] was a man named Roland Jack, who was from Sulphur, and they offered to take him to Hollywood and make him famous. And he said, 'No, I believe I'll just stay here.'"

If the invitation came from someone affiliated with the film's releasing company, Jack made a good choice. Despite some successes—including an upcoming Academy Award nomination for *Tulsa*'s special effects—Eagle-Lion Films would never quite establish itself as a major studio, dying out in 1951 when United Artists took over distribution of its features. It had been born only a few years earlier, in 1948, when the British-based

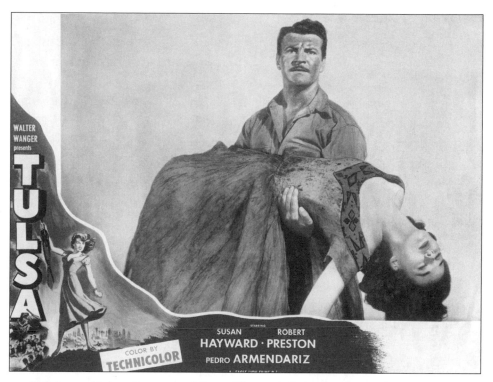

Tulsa's stars, Robert Preston and Susan Hayward. (John Wooley Archives)

Eagle-Lion had merged with Hollywood's Producers Releasing Corporation (PRC), one of the most fondly remembered of the low-budget Poverty Row studios of the '40s. Perhaps its humble origins on this side of the Atlantic had something to do with the uphill struggle the new Eagle-Lion never quite overcame.

Tulsa may have come in on the back end of Eagle-Lion's run at the majors, but it was nonetheless a good-looking Technicolor picture (with a reported budget of $2 million) and boasted some decent star power in principals Hayward and Preston as well as reliable performances from familiar character actors like Pedro Armendáriz, Ed Begley, and Chill Wills—who, as the happy-go-lucky entertainer Pinky Jimpson, narrated the film.

Based pretty loosely on the early days of the oil industry in Oklahoma, *Tulsa* begins with a bit of Wills narration, including a line affirming that "any oilman" will tell you that "the oil capital of the world is Tulsa." From there unfolds the story of Cherokee Lansing (Hayward), a rancher who gets into the oil game in the early '20s, following the death of her father in an oil rig accident. Initially motivated by revenge and knowing little about the business, she takes on a geologist named Brad Brady (Preston) as a partner, and as a romance blossoms, they together try to outwit tycoon Bruce Tanner (Lloyd Gough), who's angling for the same leases. Meanwhile, Native American landowner Jim Redbird (Armendáriz), preferring to continue raising animals and live in harmony with the land, finally resists Cherokee's requests to drill more on his property, even though he has long carried a torch for her. The film's denouement comes with a massive, protracted oil field fire, which helped earn *Tulsa* its special-effects Oscar nomination.

Viewed now, *Tulsa* seems well ahead of its time, environmentally speaking, in its treatment of the animal and human life affected by oil exploration. As Frank noted, "One of the things I really like is that the people who made it seemed to really want to show the conflict between ranchers and oilmen, and show that oil didn't have to destroy and pollute if both sides could work together. It was a real political statement, woven into the story of this big love affair."

On April 13, 1949, that "big love affair" designation could've also applied to the warm feeling the people of Tulsa had for the film and its stars. In two stories filed the day after the huge blowout, the *Tulsa Tribune*'s Roger V. Devlin and the *Tulsa World*'s Yvonne Litchfield both riffed on the same idea: "Tulsans loved *Tulsa*," Litchfield wrote in her lead. She continued:

> When the world premiere of *Tulsa* opened at four downtown theaters Wednesday night everyone was saying nice things about everyone else.
>
> Visiting reporters from over the nation acclaimed Tulsa Day festivities as the biggest they had ever seen. The city itself bowed to Hollywood for its exciting story of the building of a city and an industry. . . .
>
> Terry Coleman of *Time* magazine and Earl Wilson of *The New York Post* told listeners they had never seen anything like Tulsa's welcome to its namesake picture, even on 5th Avenue.

For his part, Devlin—under the headline of "Tulsa Basks in the Lime-light—And Do We Like It!"—called the celebration "Tulsa's wildest, most enthusiastic and most Hollywoodish four-day civic party," noting:

> It had started Monday. It reached a spectacular crescendo Wednesday morning in an oil industry parade and pageant, which snaked through the downtown area for a full two and one-half hours.
>
> Then, as if one climax weren't enough, the celebration reached another—a glittering, star-studded, glamorous party—in the world premiere of the motion picture *Tulsa*, held simultaneously at four downtown theaters.

On the day the story ran, Devlin further reported, producer Wanger was to receive an honorary degree from the University of Tulsa, followed by a Tulsa Chamber of Commerce luncheon, where Wanger would be joined by the stars of the picture. "Then," Devlin concluded, "at 2 P.M. they were to leave for the state capital, where they will appear at the Oklahoma City premiere of *Tulsa*. They will return to Los Angeles Friday."

Of course, Governor Roy J. Turner was right in the big middle of all of this, proclaiming April 13 "Tulsa Day" in the state and, according to Litchfield, telling the premiere-night crowd that "the picture will do more to tell the world about Oklahoma than the stage play *Oklahoma!* was able to do." He was even thanked in the opening of the movie, with a full-screen dedication that read: "TO THE GOVERNOR AND THE PEOPLE OF OKLAHOMA OUR GRATEFUL APPRECIATION FOR THEIR SPLENDID COOPERATION IN THE PRODUCTION OF THIS MOTION PICTURE." But on that Friday, after the producer and the stars flew back to the West Coast to resume their daily lives, the little flurry of filmmaking activity in his state—which the governor had undeniably helped start—was over, and it would stay that way for a good long time.

One other theatrical feature filmed in Oklahoma at the end of the '40s may have been the strangest one of the decade, revolving around a true character, a pioneer in the art of the cinema road show.

His name was Kroger Babb. He made and relentlessly promoted a famous "hygiene film" called *Mom and Dad*, which was so shocking to 1940s audiences that he held separate shows for female and male patrons, complete with lecturers who addressed matters that weren't spoken of in polite company—and, not coincidentally, hawked books on the same subjects. Then, somehow, Kroger Babb found Jesus in the Wichita Mountains.

"Babb—the definitive hearty, jovial demi-capitalist and one of exploitation's true titans—proclaimed himself 'America's Fearless Young Showman' and, on the strength of his flair for Barnumesque ballyhoo, enjoyed a few years of remarkable prosperity during the late 1940s" wrote Felicia Feaster and Bret Wood in their book *Forbidden Fruit: The Golden Age of the Exploitation Film* (Midnight Marquee Press, 1999, p. 109). That's as good an introduction as any to the man who, during his heyday in the late '40s, would come across a film of the Lawton passion play and end up exploiting it with the same skill and panache as his cash-cow drama about the pitfalls of sexual ignorance, *Mom and Dad.*

Born in Lees Creek, Ohio, Babb had been a sportswriter and a basketball and football referee before the lure of show business, even—or perhaps *especially*—at the edges of legitimacy, proved irresistible. Feaster and Wood noted Babb's early success with promoting a macabre attraction called "Digger" O'Dell. "As often as Babb could find a virgin town and a vacant lot suitable for banners and streamers and a portable ticket booth," they wrote, "'Digger' would be ceremoniously interred and dramatically resurrected after six days of staring up a narrow airshaft into the eyes of the curious" (p. 109).

Perhaps this was where Babb first learned about the surefire attraction of the unseemly, something he would exploit to great advantage with a variety of movies. He began with the incredibly successful *Mom and Dad*—which, according to the Arkansas-based pop culture writer and historian Dale Ingram, as well as other sources—had its world premiere at the Warner movie theater in Oklahoma City on January 2, 1945. Wrote Feaster and Wood:

> With the help of J. S. "Jack" Jossey, Babb raised enough cash to form Hygienic Productions. With their $62,000, they hired former Hollywood director William Beaudine, a cast of struggling actors and a handful of

Stupid 'Jerks' Always Try to Outsmart the Proven Facts!

The art of properly exploiting, advertising and selling an attraction is like baking a cake. Two housewives can use the same recipe, yet get entirely different results.

Showmen hit the same snags. To achieve the finest results with a campaign formula that has been tested and proven a "perfect recipe" for record grosses, a theatre man needs follow it thru 100 percent, without attempting to change or improve it. Like the woman whose cake doesn't turn out good, the theatre manager who doesn't put in all the ingredients...who doesn't use them in exactly the same ratio already proven correct...is a darn fool, too — because his box office won't hum, either.

In this Press Book we are providing you with a tested, proven, useable campaign.

Thousands of dollars, many months, much sweat and blood, went into the tremendous job of creating, developing, testing and proving each of its punches, *for you!*

When a stupid jerk tries to outsmart proven facts, he should be in an asylum—not a theatre.

Today, business is tough to get. It's a He-man's job to knock out competition and bring them in by the thousands. When you leave out window cards you eliminate a very important left hook. When you don't use enough window cards, or don't get them out, up and displayed "on schedule," you hit a glancing blow instead of a solid one to the jaw. When you try to pinch pennies and reduce the necessary newspaper space, radio plugs or tab herald distribution, you simply eliminate belly-punches. So you end up worn out from the long, 15-round battle and still you're not a winner. Maybe you get out with a draw — maybe you lose on points.

What's wrong with being champion? What's bad about delivering left hooks, right jabs, crashing punches to the waistline and knocking television, ball parks, swimming pools, bridge games and everything else that is keeping folks away from your theatre, for the proverbial loop.

Kroger Babb

THE SID GRAUMAN SHOWMANSHIP AWARD

PRESENTED TO

KROGER BABB

BY THE
HOLLYWOOD ROTARY CLUB

★ *The Coveted*
SID GRAUMAN
SHOWMANSHIP
AWARD

To perpetuate the name and great showmanship of its faithful entertainment chairman, the late Sid Grauman, Hollywood Rotary voted in 1950 following Sid's death, to make an annual SID GRAUMAN SHOWMANSHIP AWARD.

—3—

Kroger Babb, the man who put Ginger Prince and Jesus together in a movie. From a circa-1957 pressbook for the double feature *Mom and Dad* and *She Shoulda Said "No"!* (Courtesy of the Dale Ingram Collection) musical variety acts to give the picture a touch of class—1940s dinner-club style—so that it rose above the common exploitation film by "passing" as a respectable feature.

From Babb's mistress, Indianapolis film critic Mildred A. Horn, a competent screenplay was coaxed. Ms. Horn would also compose the sex-education booklets sold during each "performance" of the film. A few reels of birth and VD footage from a medical supply company completed the package. (p. 109)

In fact, that package was *really* completed at each stop with the live appearance of a lecturer, whose job involved a frank little talk on what was then euphemistically know as "hygiene," winding up with a pitch for booklets that explained sex-related topics in easy-to-understand terms. The newspaper ad for the Oklahoma City premiere of *Mom and Dad* noted that the lecture topic was "Secrets of Sensible Sex," to be given at each performance of the movie by "Radio's Hygiene Commentator Elliot Forbes."

There were, of course, dozens of Elliot Forbeses hotfooting it around the countryside, giving their talks and selling their educational wares. Later, according to *Forbidden Fruit*, women lecturers were added to better address (and move books to) the female-only audiences. (In the initial Oklahoma City run, "women only" shows were at 2 and 7 P.M. and "men only" at 9 P.M., a typical pattern for subsequent *Mom and Dad* screenings.)

Mom and Dad was an immediate moneymaker. It remains one of the great examples of the "road show" film—a movie, usually featuring elements not found in mainstream Hollywood products—peddled from town to town, theater to theater, rather than getting widespread, multiprint distribution from a major studio.

While *Mom and Dad* and any number of Elliot Forbeses were busy racking up box office receipts for Babb and his partner, Jack Jossey, something totally unrelated was happening in the Wichita Mountains around Lawton. Sixty years down the road, *Mom and Dad's* creator and Lawton's annual Easter pageant seem a highly unlikely combination. Somehow, though, the ever-alert Babb found out about the annual play—and apparently saw as many potential exploitation possibilities in the story of

Christ's death and resurrection as he'd found in unwed motherhood and venereal disease.

A Congregational minister, the Reverend Anthony Mark Wallock, had originated the Lawton passion play in 1926, staging it alfresco in the nearby Wichitas. From a modest one-scene, five-character beginning, the pageant had grown to an extravaganza with dozens of scenes, drawing hundreds of thousands of viewers from all over. A February 25, 1949, *Tulsa Tribune* story called it "the largest Easter service in the world . . . [requiring] the time, efforts and talents of hundreds of Lawtonians as well as of many men and women outside that city."

Among the multitudes inspired by the play was a Tulsa attorney and building-materials dealer named Neil Bogan. He was so inspired, in fact, that he formed a company called Principle Films, with the intention of filming a feature-length movie of the play.

Even though contemporary accounts—including the February 1949 *Tribune* story—indicated that color filming of the pageant was begun in 1948 but never completed, the existence of a feature-length version of Wallock's outdoor event suggests otherwise. So does a *Time* magazine piece from April 18, 1949, following the release of Babb's Easter pageant-inspired picture: "The producers [of the movie] decided to try religion when they got hold of a four-hour Cinecolor film of the annual Easter sunrise passion play put on as an Oklahoma hillside Oberammergau by citizens of Lawton, Okla. Babb & Jossey trimmed the film and added some homey fictional sequences fore & aft, starring a six-year-old 'find' from Atlanta named Ginger Prince ('42 inches and 42 pounds of Southern charm')."

Bogan and Principle Films may indeed have shot four hours of footage, but the only *Prince of Peace* that currently exists is what appears to be a feature that was completed before Babb ever came on board, running a full 72 minutes. It begins with "OKLAHOMA U.S.A." lettered over an American flag waving above a flagpole, just before veteran radio announcer Knox Manning gives us the backstory over shots of cars rolling down Lawton's main street on the way to the event. It's "a typical American small town," Manning intones, "nearly all of whose citizens, from the mayor on down, take some part in the Wichita Mountain Easter Pageant."

From there we see the Little Rock Church, the late Wallock's place of worship. Then we're introduced to some of the townspeople with major roles in the pageant. Sure enough, they include the mayor, along with a major from the nearby Fort Sill army base, telephone operators, salesmen, barbers, and a local bank employee named Millard Coody, who stars as Jesus.

Before the play gets going, this version of *Prince of Peace* offers a kind of warning, given over scenes of people camped out in the mountains, waiting for the event to begin. "The great story will be told again," narrates Manning, "the eternal story told once more in the native accents of a plain and reverent people, against the background of the brown Oklahoma hills." This little caveat was probably meant for viewers outside of the South and Southwest, who might find the line readings of some of the principals more reminiscent of the then-popular Ma and Pa Kettle movies than, say, one of C. B. DeMille's biblical epics.

Although the actors are all locals, the credits for this *Prince of Peace* feature all kinds of industry pros. They include the writer of the "screen narration," DeVallon Scott, and the producer and director, Henry Daniels, both of whom had legitimate Hollywood credits in features as well as theatrical shorts. In addition, director of photography and associate producer Henry Sharp was well known as a top-notch color cinematographer of the time. (There are some cinematic effects, such as miniatures, lighting, and rear-screen projection, that make this feature more than just a straight filming of the pageant and further indicate the hands of Hollywood veterans.)

All of this suggests that the surviving version of *Prince of Peace* was its first incarnation. How many places this *Prince of Peace* actually played, or even the kinds of venues it played, is a matter of conjecture, as is the reason for Babb's subsequent involvement. Perhaps one of the professionals associated with this version sought Babb's advice on how to promote it or actually showed it to the exploitation master. Maybe Babb ran onto it himself somehow and realized that, with some new wraparound scenes added and a little tweaking here and there, this beautiful color movie about Jesus Christ had the potential to do boffo business in the Bible Belt.

The souvenir program for Kroger Babb's version of *The Prince of Peace* (1949) featured Lawton's Millard Coody as Jesus on the front cover. Ginger Prince (as Ginger) was featured on the back of the program. (Courtesy of the Dale Ingram Collection)

The question of how America's Fearless Young Showman and the Wichita Mountain Easter pageant connected begs another question. What did Babb tell the folks at Principle—by all accounts, a traditionally religious group—when they first met? How much did any of them know about the seamy, exploitative *Mom and Dad*, Babb's only production credit at the time? After all, it had played all over the middle of the country following its Oklahoma City debut, acquiring a certain notoriety.

Perhaps Babb simply played the moral-high-road card, asserting that his *Mom and Dad* was really an indictment of the dangers of premarital sex (exploitation filmmakers in those days often justified their "hygiene"-oriented offerings in that manner). He may have even emphasized his earlier work as the publicist for a theater chain, or his Hollywood connections, through which he could create greater demand for the film by casting (as he ended up doing) real movie actors in his revamped version of the picture.

However he played it, Babb apparently made a suitable impression on Principle's people, since they decided to place their movie in his hands—giving birth to a new picture Babb would initially title *The Lawton Story*. Here's how the 1949 *Tribune* piece described Babb's involvement:

> [The Principle Films officers'] original idea was to distribute a simple movie of the pageant itself to churches and clubs.
>
> Later it was decided to expand the potential audience, and Kroger Babb, president of Hallmark Productions, Inc., Wilmington, Ohio, was invited to assist and become co-producer.
>
> The original production was amended to include scenes from the life of the late Rev. Anthony Wallock, Lawton Congregational minister, who originated the pageant 22 years ago, and who wrote the script and directed the presentation of all pageants since. . . .
>
> The co-producer also added a background story which ties in with the pageant itself and the project was refilmed.
>
> Most of the performers in the picture are native Oklahomans and the portrayal of the pageant provides approximately half of the total film.

Hallmark, with offices at various times in both Wilmington, Ohio, and Hollywood, was the new name of Babb's former Hygienic Productions, distributor of *Mom and Dad*. And for *The Lawton Story*, Babb brought back not only *Mom and Dad*'s director, the B-movie vet William Beaudine, but also that film's scripter and Babb's common-law wife, Mildred Horn, to craft a new story around some of the existing Easter pageant footage.

Horn also wrote *The Prince of Peace*, a souvenir booklet measuring 8½ by 11¾ inches and with front and back covers in vibrant color, offering it for sale at the film's screenings for a dollar. In addition to a lengthy prose retelling of the biblical passion story, illustrated with tinted scenes from the play, the booklet put a highly sentimental spin on the story of Rev. Anthony Mark Wallock—dubbed "The Little Minister"—who, as the story would have it, held onto life from his hospital bed until every bit of the new footage was in the can. Here's the unforgettable way Horn described Wallock's near-death tenacity—and perhaps the assistance of the Almighty—during the final days of shooting:

It was on Nov. 2nd that Rev. Wallock was admitted to St. Anthony hospital in Oklahoma City. A month later—on December 2nd—giant airliners were winging their way toward Lawton from Hollywood carrying more camera crews, directors, producers, writers and actors to the southwest Oklahoma city for final "on location" shooting of the story script. When he was told of the fact by a nurse and also informed that bad weather was threatening to delay the completion of the picture, Rev. Wallock only smiled and in whispered tones, replied: "Don't worry—they'll finish it—the Lord will provide!"

And . . . the Lord did provide! Storms, carrying with them near-zero weather, were pushing down from the Colorado Rockies, riding winds recorded at from 40 to 70 mile an hour velocity. Oklahoma and western Texas were directly in the storms' path. Warnings went out to all ranchers, airlines, highway patrols. Thruout the Southwest, people prepared for the winds, freezing temperatures, snow. The storms swept across both states and far into south Texas, yet at Lawton and within a 30 mile radius the sun shone, the skies were clear, and the final "on location" shooting was completed Saturday, Sunday and Monday, December 4–6.

Back to Hollywood flew *The Lawton Story* company and when on December 16th, producer Kroger Babb wired from Culver City studios that the entire production was finished-shooting, the nurse who read Rev. Wallock the wire reported he smiled knowingly and barely uttered "The Lord 'did' provide!" Ten days later, Rev. A. Mark Wallock died.

Ostensibly a tribute to the life of the Little Minister, as the *Tribune* story indicated, *The Lawton Story* arrived on the screen with reliable character actor Forrest Taylor—who would've been known to audiences of the time for his bad-guy roles in B westerns—essaying the role of Wallock. (In what might be considered a unique demonstration of his acting range, Taylor had also played the no-nonsense obstetrician who gives young unmarried Joan the bad news in *Mom and Dad*.)

Although *The Lawton Story* isn't around to verify this observation, the wraparound footage Babb supervised and Beaudine shot likely took substantial liberties with Wallock's story. That's how David F. Friedman, an exploitation-film giant himself as well as a longtime associate of Babb's, remembered it in a 2007 interview. "Krog came up with the story," recalled Friedman. "It was about two brothers, one of whom was an evil banker, and the other a very good guy, a good Christian, et cetera. I mean, this was strictly out of *Uncle Tom's Cabin*."

And what about *Lawton Story* star Ginger Prince, Babb's six-year-old "find" from Atlanta mentioned in the *Time* article? "Her father was named Hugh Prince, and he was a booker for a little four-house [movie theater] circuit out of Toccoa, Georgia," Friedman explained. "Hugh was a nice little guy, but Ginger's mother was the stage mother of all time. From the time this child was conceived, her mother had ideas of grandeur for her. Every year, from the time she was three until she was six or seven, Ginger Prince was the featured attraction for the banquet of the Georgia-Alabama Theater Owners Association, and she did all of the Shirley Temple routines—'The Good Ship Lollipop,' all that. And she was awful." Friedman added, "Of course, Krog knows all about her, so he signs this little girl to a big Hollywood contract."

While Friedman was less than enthralled with Ginger Prince's talents, others were dazzled. For instance, a former website dedicated to still another famed exploitation-film figure, producer K. Gordon Murray (www.kgordonmurray.com), carried in 2007 a reminiscence from former Lawtonian Charley Crabtree, who was an extra in the Babb-supervised scenes. "She could," he writes, "sing and dance and act—I was in love!!!"

The Lawton Story debuted on April 1, 1949, at three theaters—two in Lawton and one in nearby Fort Sill, very close to the site of the Passion Play. Ginger Prince flew in for the big premiere, along with Hollywood comic actor Hugh "Woo-Woo" Herbert and B-picture star Lynn Bari, though neither of them was actually in the movie. "Krog probably just said, 'How'd you like a free ride?' said Friedman. "He had his own plane." Oklahoma governor and filmmaking booster Roy J. Turner was in on the festivities as well, extending a formal invitation to the premiere to President Harry Truman and his wife, who apparently passed.

With ticket prices that topped out at an incredible $1,000 a seat (probably so Babb could ballyhoo them, as he did in the souvenir book, as "a new all-time world record 'top'"), the benefit premiere of *The Lawton Story* proved a hometown hit, raising an estimated $20,000 to help finance future pageants. But once it got into general release, it didn't do as well. Friedman remembered that *The Lawton Story* stiffed in Atlanta, where

Babb had opened it after its benefit premiere: "'Long about midnight, I'm playing poker at the Variety Club in Atlanta, and Krog comes in [after the screening], the most dejected guy in the world. He says, 'Well, I know what to do,' and with that he ordered a gallon of martinis, checked into his room, stayed there for two days, and came back with the greatest campaign I ever saw—*The Prince of Peace*."

Newly retitled, the film went out and did business, with some of Babb's former Elliot Forbses lecturing and selling, according to Friedman, "a four-color litho of Jesus Christ, suitable for framing, and a miniature bible—those little bibles the midgets used to sell at the circus, about the size of a postage stamp." The *Prince of Peace* booklet, a carryover from the *Lawton Story* days, was made available at the screenings, again at a cost of one dollar.

Those who were *really* taken by the movie could order two different pieces of sheet music—later expanded to three—for songs from the movie, also for a buck each and all featuring Ginger Prince's lovable little mug on their covers. The first two were "Right under My Nose" and "Down in Oklahoma" (the latter penned by performer and B-western sidekick Lee "Lasses" White, who was cast in the ill-fated *Osage* the same year *The Lawton Story* was released). The third one, featuring an artist's rendition of a reverently praying Ginger with the Star of Bethlehem and the wise men in the background, was "Say A Prayer to the Prince of Peace." The song was also recorded by Arthur Lee Simpkins, former vocalist for the big swing band of Earl "Fatha" Hines, on Kaybee Records. It isn't hard to divine whose initials "Kaybee" stood for.

Ultimately, *Prince of Peace* was shown all over the world, with 5 percent of its proceeds pledged to the group presenting the Lawton pageant—an arrangement that later led to a lawsuit filed by the pageant's board of directors.

One of most prestigious places it played, Dave Friedman recalled, was on Broadway, in New York City, quite an achievement for an independent road-show picture. As Friedman remembered it, Joe Solomon—who would go on to found one of the well-remembered exploitation-film outfits of the 1970s, Fanfare Films—was working for Kroger Babb at the time and had been put in charge of the New York screening.

"So Joe's standing out in front of the theater, and he's put up this big blowup that reads, 'The Only Picture about Jesus Christ Approved by Catholics, Protestants, and Jews,'" said Friedman. "And sure enough, along comes a little Jewish lady who stops, reads the poster, and goes over to Joe.

"'Mister,' she asks him, 'who says the Jews approved this picture?'

"He says, 'Well, *I'm* Jewish, and *I* approve of it.'"

Much later, Friedman bought the rights to all of Babb's pictures, but *Prince of Peace* was not among them. It remains to this day a lost movie, although the *Prince of Peace* mentioned earlier, sans Babb's additions and subtractions, was retrieved a few years ago, apparently from Babb's son or one of Babb's associates.

"We had a deal that if the company ever disbanded, went broke, or what have you, the film would come back to us," said Lawton's Richard Matthy, who played Christ for years in the pageant, in a 2007 interview. "We went out to California, and the son wouldn't give us the film. We had to get a lawyer. The son finally sent the film back to us—in little bitty pieces."

A Florida man, the now-deceased Lewis T. Philips, painstakingly pieced the original *Prince of Peace* back together, and a copy of his work is available for purchase from the Holy City in the Wichita Mountains, where the Lawton passion play is still staged each Easter season, once just before Palm Sunday, and once before Easter.

One final series of films from the late 1930s through the early 1950s flew completely below the radar, except in several dozen cities and towns in Middle America, including Oklahoma City, Muskogee, Guthrie, Ada, and Shawnee, Oklahoma. The pictures were made when an itinerant Texas filmmaker named Melton Barker wandered through America, mostly around its heartland, plying his trade. Barker ended up making more than a hundred films—or, more precisely, pretty much the same film more than a hundred times—using casts made up entirely of local kids. Like *The Wrecker*'s Richard E. Norman from a generation earlier, Melton Barker would blow into town with a bunch of impressive filming equipment and a scenario. Then, after forging an agreement with one of the city's movie houses, he would lay out his plans to shoot a professional two-reel comedy short called *The Kidnappers Foil*. Interested youngsters were asked to fill out a form printed in the local paper and then mail it or turn it in at the theater, which would then pass the forms on to Barker for final dispensation.

In those days before home video and DVD, having one's image projected onto the gigantic screen of a theater was something most people could only imagine, and they often did. Hollywood dreams were rampant then, and Barker knew and exploited those longings, offering thousands of middle-American parents and kids an encounter with a real-life moviemaker as well as celluloid immortality. And, though he may never have actually *said* that his little two-reel comedy could lead a talented child onto the soundstages of a Hollywood studio, he probably did nothing to dispel the notion either.

Richard E. Norman reportedly made his money by getting his home-talent creations played in local movie houses or other venues and pocketing the box office take, which often had big-bucks potential. (His 1919 production of *The Wrecker*, for instance, featuring all those Tulsa notables, had played two dozen times over a four-day period at the Majestic, one of the city's showplace theaters.) Unlike Norman, however, Barker didn't share in any of the proceeds his two-reelers (usually shown in tandem with a regular feature or two) generated at local theaters. Instead, he charged a "talent fee" for teaching his young charges how to act for the movies. That's according to Caroline Frick, a professor at the University of Texas at Austin and director of the Texas Archive of the Moving Image, who has made an extensive study of the filmmaker and his work.

"You paid to be in the film, he shot it, and then it was shipped directly back to the theater," she said recently. "I think the usual sum was $10, although in some cases it could've been less. A number of people I've interviewed [who were in Barker's films as children] said their parents saved up so they could do it, so that would indicate it was more than just a dollar or two."

Barker's modus operandi was captured in a Shawnee newspaper, which introduced the filmmaker and his proposed movie to readers.

In an undated clipping of the article, a bold-faced headline, bounded by a star on each side, shouts, "SHAWNEE CHILDREN WILL STAR IN MOVIES." Below it is a photo, presumably of Barker, with a camera operator and an impressive-looking camera in the background. Then comes the pitch:

> Melton Barker, movie producer, will arrive in Shawnee soon to produce a two-reel comedy, according to an announcement by Elmer Adams Jr. of the Bison Theater.
>
> The movie will be made in and around Shawnee and over 100 local kiddies will be used in the cast.
>
> After the cast has been selected there will be 3 or 4 days of rehearsals, teaching them to act before the camera and talk into the movie sound equipment. There will be a small fee for training. However, there will be no charge for registering or try-outs.
>
> Children between the ages of 3 to 14 wishing to try out for parts will have to register at once at the BISON THEATER or clip the coupon below and mail to Box 978, Shawnee, Oklahoma. When the casting director gets in town he will get in touch with those who have registered and arrange for try-outs.

The coupon asked for name, age, phone number, address, and gender of the respondent. The upcoming movie was referred to as "SHAWNEE'S GANG COMEDY"—a rather obvious nod to the wildly popular *Our Gang* series of Hollywood one- and two-reelers, which had run from 1922 to 1944. A few news clippings about Melton Barker Productions alleged that "Barker has the distinction of having discovered Spanky McFarland who is now starring in *Our Gang* comedies"—a claim Caroline Frick deems unlikely.

"I have done exhaustive research on that, and I don't see any record of that anywhere," she said. "I think that particular link between Melton Barker and *Our Gang* was made by a journalist somewhere along the line. I've tracked records of his doing movies in over one hundred cities from Los Angeles to places back East, and I've only seen that connection mentioned one or two times. He may, however, have had some sort of experience in Hollywood."

Still, evidence indicates that Barker did nothing to discourage the appearance of similarity between McFarland's *Our Gang* comedies and his own product. In those far less media-savvy times, the two were sometimes conflated. Former Rose State University professor Jim Lazalier recently recalled a filming of a comedy short at Honor Heights Park in his hometown of Muskogee, just after World War II. Almost certainly the work of Barker, the picture offered "a real deal to the kids—pay some money and get some time in the movie," Lazalier wrote in correspondence with the author, adding that he thought "a few well-off kids got to play alongside Spanky."

The newspaper audition notice was usually only the beginning of Barker's blitz on the town's young would-be movie talent. Frick has turned up a whole series of stories that ran in the *Fremont (Nebraska) Daily Tribune*, heralding the impending arrival of Barker and then describing the "scores of kiddies, each one eager to have an opportunity to appear in motion pictures," who greeted Barker when he blew into town. These articles were apparently taken from Barker-generated press releases and run with minimal editing. A few excerpts from them show not only the relative innocence of the time and place (along with a bit of political incorrectness) but also Barker's masterful way of wringing every dollar he could out of his endeavor, as well as his speedy turnaround time between the end of shooting and the premiere of the finished movie.

> Those children who so far have not had an opportunity to register and those who want to try out for a part in the picture may do so by making an application at the Empress Theater. Every type of child is needed for the picture—tall and short youngsters, "fatties" and "leans," and every other type. There will be some call for singing and dancing types, but neither of these talents is necessary. Mr. Barker wants to get as many applicants as he can to assure himself of having covered the city thoroughly in his search for talent that will later sparkle on the Empress screen.
>
> "The more youngsters I get to look at, the better my chance of selecting a cast that will genuinely represent Fremont's talent," said Mr. Barker.
>
> —November 2, 1939, a day after the initial story ran

> Wm. Mack, manager of the Empress, has contracted with Barker, Hollywood producer, to film a two-reel comedy similar to the *Our Gang* comedies here in Fremont using approximately 75 children as the characters.
>
> The object of making the picture in Fremont is to give local children an opportunity to see and hear themselves on the screen and to compare

themselves with Shirley Temple, Freddie Bartholomew, Spanky McFarland and other celebrities of the screen.

—November 3

Barker is anxious to receive more entries, thus giving him a chance to have a wide range of choice in filling the parts of the story. Children who have not registered may report for the trials during the time scheduled.

—November 9

The first motion picture ever filmed here with an all-Fremont cast will be shown Friday and Saturday, December 8 and 9, at the Empress theater, the management announced.

Last three scenes of the picture, *The Fremont Gang Comedy*, were filmed Sunday afternoon at Barnard park under the direction of Melton Barker, Hollywood producer-director. The picture features a cast of 130 children between the ages of 3 and 12.

The 2,500-foot film will take about 30 minutes for showing, the Empress management announced. It will be co-featured with Loretta Young's current movie hit, *Eternally Yours*.

—November 27

Casting as many kids as he possibly could at each stop, Melton Barker apparently shot the same picture, with slight variations, over and over again for years. He even used the same professionally made credits, touting the film's all-local cast (without going into actual names or any other details that would necessitate the credits being changed from town to town) in multiple versions of *The Kidnappers Foil*.

"The credits were actually changed over time, but it was because the film elements wore out," Frick explained. "Keep in mind that he did this, off and on, all the way through the early '70s. He did *Kidnappers Foil* basically for forty-plus years, and he did other films as well. I've found one called *The Last Straw*, which is a lot like *Kidnappers Foil* but involves bank robbers. Also, he did what was more common at the time for itinerant filmmakers—he went to cities and shot local businesses."

Although well over a hundred versions of the two-reel *Kidnappers Foil* were shot by Barker, mainly in the late '30s, the '40s, and the early '50s, not many of them have turned up. Given that 35 mm theatrical movies were released on unstable nitrate-based film until the early 1950s, a good number of those from the golden age of Barker's movies have either turned to powder or goo or gone up in smoke. One that didn't, however, was the one made in Shawnee, showing at that city's Bison Theater in 1946. Nestled in a forgotten storage cabinet, it was discovered during a renovation of the Hornbeck Theatre, the Bison's successor, a few years ago. After learning of the discovery, the Oklahoma Historical Society, with a grant from the National Film Preservation Foundation, transferred Shawnee's *Kidnappers Foil* to DVD, adding a new introductory interview segment featuring some of the members of the cast, who were at that point mostly septuagenarians.

Remembering the long-ago casting call, Harold Nix said, "It wasn't much of an audition. They took our picture. . . . We had to make our own costumes, or our mothers did . . . big old patches on my britches, and my shirt, and everything."

Some of the same cast members were also interviewed by the *Daily Oklahoman*'s Ann Kelley for a story published on October 8, 2007. A reminiscence from one of them, seventy-two-year-old Ruella Yates, indicated just how much Barker—whose press material sometimes linked him not only to Spanky McFarland and *Our Gang* but to Hollywood in general—played on the innocent movie-star dreams of Middle America. "As a child, I understood that this was a chance to be a movie star like Elizabeth Taylor in *National Velvet*," she told Kelley. "It was a surreal experience, because I was a country girl and had never been around so many children my age."

Indeed, the Shawnee production of *The Kidnappers Foil* is fairly bursting with kids of all ages, undoubtedly because anyone with the "talent fee" was sure of getting cast in some sort of part, if only as a member of a group. Much of the film, in fact—once the actual kidnapping is effected, with Barker himself taking the role of the father of the abducted girl—seems to be composed of large groups of kids sitting outside, all talking about what they'd like to do with the $1,000 reward money offered for the return of young kidnappee Betty Davis. (The similarity in name to one of Hollywood's biggest stars was probably no coincidence.) The lines are mostly distributed one to a customer, with few characters getting any more than a single utterance. Even those with a simple short line sometimes fluff, stare at the camera like a deer caught in high-beam headlights, or give a rushed, high-pitched, or otherwise bizarre line reading. (A Mae West impersonation by a very young lady particularly stands out, as does the youthful "woo woo" that follows.) But after all, these are kids, with no experience at all in moviemaking. And for auteur Melton Barker, retakes were apparently an unneeded drag on his time and expenses.

"I don't think there were any retakes," said Caroline Frick. "It was probably shot in sequence, very minimally edited, processed, and shipped back to the theater where it was going to be shown."

The Daily Oklahoman's Kelley wrote that there were "about 100 children" in the picture, but it seems to be a far larger number than that. When the preteen boys in the group known as "Butch's gang" tromp into the frame, there are so many of them that they resemble nothing so much as a phalanx of Roman soldiers, marching over a hill. And by the time the various aggregations—the very young kids, the older girls, Butch and the boys—all get together, find both of Betty's teenaged kidnappers inexplicably asleep on a hill (with a wide-awake Betty sitting between them), and dogpile the hoodlums into submission, you almost feel sorry for the latter, suddenly buried under huge writhing masses of youthful humanity.

As it turns out, the thousand-buck reward is used to throw a big party for Betty, where a few acts (whose parents may have paid a bit more of a fee) perform on what looks like someone's patio. There's a tap-dancing hula girl, a moppet vocalist, a trio of tappers, and then a performance heavily influenced by Shirley Temple before the whole bunch bring things to a close with a gang vocal on "Hail, Hail, the Gang's All Here." Comedy, music, even a little drama—it was all there. And its creator, Melton Barker was off to the next town, where he'd do it all again.

Most of what we know about Ennis Melton Barker has been unearthed by Caroline Frick. Barker was born in Keller, Texas, in 1903, and his other films include a pair of civic pride–type offerings shot in Missouri called *The Centralia Story* and *The Cape Girardeau Story*. Although Barker ran a movie theater and a drive-in restaurant during parts of his life, he always seemed to return to the old *Kidnappers Foil* idea, resurrecting it again and again until his March 1977 death—"on the road," as Frick noted. Of course, if he hadn't passed away when he did, the impending era of home video, which allowed just about anyone to become a director of talking motion pictures, would have done in his whole *Kidnappers Foil* concept.

Barker shot films all across America, but he actually resided in Oklahoma, at least for a time. A two-paragraph *Daily Oklahoman* piece from October 12, 1945, told of the theft of a car belonging to Barker, who had been staying in Oklahoma City's Skirvin Hotel (and possibly making a *Kidnappers Foil* there at the time). Observing that the thief "didn't realize he also was stealing motion picture equipment valued at more than $2,000," the story gave a Tulsa address for Barker. A person living in today's cynical era might wonder if, in fact, any film equipment had been in the car at all, and whether Barker was simply working some sort of scam. After all, that was what he'd been doing for years with *The Kidnappers Foil*, wasn't it?

Not according to the person who is, essentially, his official biographer. "I don't think he was out to try and convince people that they were going to be stars," said Caroline Frick. "I don't think he was a charlatan. I have not found any evidence that he was this dubious *Music Man* kind of character. I think it was a pretty straightforward endeavor. After all, getting a 35 mm camera and sound equipment in the '30s was a serious investment of capital. I believe he was simply a businessman who found a way to make a living."

Frick has even suggested that, like many of the young people he put in his productions—and some of their starry-eyed parents—Barker may have had his own longings for a career in Hollywood, and when they didn't work out, he decided to do something as close as he could get to his thwarted dream job, even if it wasn't exactly what he wanted.

"After many years of looking for his relatives," Frick added, "I finally met his ex-stepson, and he laughed and said that Melton Barker didn't like children. He liked *dogs*, but he didn't like children very much. I think that's kind of a sad coda to his story."

Whatever else can be said about Melton Barker and his cinematic endeavors, it must be noted that he did what he said he was going to do.

The squeaky-voiced, often jittery youngsters who made their way into one of his two-reelers may never have left their Middle American homes for big careers in Hollywood, but they were at least in a movie with a beginning, a middle, and an end, and they, along with their friends and family and others who lived in their town, got to see their movie in an honest-to-goodness theater on the same bill as a big Hollywood production. Even now, that counts for *something*.

FIVE

State Fair, Stark Fear,
and the World's Greatest Athlete

> In the novel, the farm boy of *State Fair* . . . sought the horseshoe
> pitching championship, but in the current movie this ambition has
> been updated to racing cars. It was the racing scenes for which the
> fairgrounds here were used, because of its grandstand and track being
> just right. . . . One of the stories making the rounds is that Boone one
> day after director Jose Ferrer had left the location, took a car alone
> on several laps around the track at what he thought was a moderate
> speed. But when he came in, his manager was whitefaced. Seems
> Boone's adjusted time for the few laps he drove was just a little more
> than a second over the track record.
>
> > —*Daily Oklahoman* (April 1, 1962)

> It was to have an Oklahoma setting, and it was to be contemporary.
> We knew we wanted the script to have oil, cattle, sex and violence.
>
> > —*Stark Fear* coproducer Joe E. Burke, quoted by
> > Jack Bickham in *Oklahoma's Orbit* (June 21, 1961)

> I'll always know where to come anytime I need actors and
> actresses—straight to Muskogee.
>
> > —Michael Curtiz, director of *Jim Thorpe, All-
> > American*, quoted by Gilbert Asher in the *Tulsa
> > World* (September 8, 1950)

After the flurry of filmmaking activity that marked the end of the 1940s
in Oklahoma, the next decade began with substantial promise—only to
taper off rather dramatically. Perhaps this had something to do with the
end of Governor Roy J. Turner's days in office. Throughout his run as
the state's chief executive, Turner was a relentless booster of moviemaking in his state, especially when the movies made involved cattle and
cowboys from the Hereford Heaven area. In January 1951, Turner was

Burt Lancaster as the titular character in *Jim Thorpe, All-American* (1951). (John Wooley Archives)

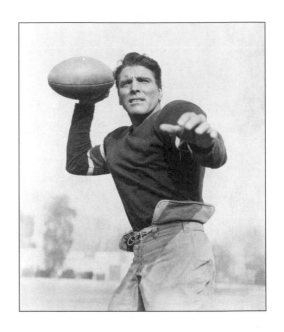

succeeded in the office by Johnston Murray. Like Turner, Murray was a Democrat, but unlike Turner, he apparently wasn't particularly enchanted by Hollywood or especially interested in developing the state as a filmmaking center.

In the early '50s, however, one notable film unit did some significant shooting in the state while Turner was still in office. The crew didn't stay long, only a little over two weeks, and it's not clear how much Governor Turner had to do with the Hollywood unit being in the state in the first place. But it was a very big deal for Muskogee, for that area's Native American population, and for fans and admirers of the greatest American Indian athlete of them all, Jim Thorpe.

In late August 1950 a West Coast contingent of some one hundred actors and technicians flew, drove, or took the train to Muskogee, where they all convened on the campus of what was then known as Bacone Indian College to shoot a number of scenes for a Warner Bros. film, *Jim Thorpe, All-American*. The group included big-name director Michael Curtiz and still-rising star Burt Lancaster, top-drawer talent assembled to create a biopic about a world-class figure: Oklahoma (technically, Indian Territory) native Thorpe, who'd recently been named by the Associated

Press as the outstanding male athlete of the first half of the twentieth century.

Although Thorpe had been born in Prague, about a hundred miles west of Muskogee, and was of Sac and Fox descent (his great-grandfather was the renowned chief Black Hawk), he had never attended Bacone. Instead, the Oklahoma college was doubling for Pennsylvania's Carlisle Indian Industrial School, where Thorpe had achieved national fame as a football player (coached by Glenn "Pop" Warner, who'd go on to be one of the most influential names in youth football). At the end of his Carlisle days, in 1912, Thorpe had become the first athlete ever to win both the pentathlon and the decathlon at the Summer Olympics, held that year in Stockholm, Sweden. A classic story, related by author Bob Bernotas in his book *Jim Thorpe: Sac and Fox Athlete* (1992), involved Sweden's King Gustav V, who presented Thorpe with his gold medals for those two events:

> Before Thorpe could walk away, the king grabbed his hand and uttered the sentence that was to follow him for the rest of his life.
>
> "Sir," he declared, "you are the greatest athlete in the world."
>
> Thorpe, never a man to stand on ceremony, answered simply and honestly, "Thanks, King."

There was a dustup not long after that, however, when Olympic officials yanked away Thorpe's medals because he'd been paid to play semipro baseball. In their eyes, that made him a professional athlete, and at the time pros weren't allowed to compete in the Olympic Games. (It would be exactly sixty years before the International Olympic Committee would restore his medals.)

Thorpe became a professional in earnest the next year, joining the New York Giants as an outfielder. A genuine two-sport athlete (three, if you count a couple of barnstorming stints with an all-Indian basketball squad), he played on three major-league teams and seven pro football teams—including New York's *football* Giants—in a long athletic career. His influence on the latter sport is illustrated by his being named, in 1920, the first president of the American Professional Football Association, which evolved into the National Football League. The NFL's Most Valuable Player award still carries his name.

By the time the *Jim Thorpe, All-American* crew arrived on the Bacone campus, though, the celebrated athlete was sixty-three years old and near the end of an up-and-down life. Never catching on as a coach following his playing days, Thorpe found relatively steady work in movies, especially throughout the 1930s and into the mid-'40s, appearing in such well-remembered Hollywood fare as *King Kong* (1933), *They Died with Their Boots On* (1941), and *White Heat* (1949). Oddly enough, his name and fame were often not taken advantage of, and he appeared many times, including in those three blockbusters, as an uncredited extra.

He did travel the lecture circuit with intermittent success, and—according to the intellectual property rights management website CMG Worldwide (www.cmgww.com)—"even led an all-Indian song and dance troupe entitled 'The Jim Thorpe Show.'" But there were also periods of far less glamorous work in his life. Sometimes the man called by a king "the greatest athlete in the world" found himself working manual-labor jobs to keep the wolf from the door.

Thorpe ended up with both writing and technical adviser credits on *Jim Thorpe, All-American*, although the screenplay itself was penned by Hollywood pros Everett Freeman, whose work included 1947's Danny Kaye starrer *The Secret Life of Walter Mitty*, and Douglas Morrow who, a few months earlier had won an Academy Award for his work on another sports biopic, *The Stratton Story* (1949).

Director Curtiz, meanwhile, had helmed some of the most popular features to light up Hollywood's golden age, including such all-time classics as *The Adventures of Robin Hood* (1938), *Casablanca*, and *Yankee Doodle Dandy* (both 1942). A Hungarian immigrant who'd been in America since the late '20s, he was known for his fractured English and no-nonsense demeanor. It was the latter that caught the attention of *Tulsa Tribune* writer Elizabeth Stubler, when she visited the set for a piece published August 25, 1950—the first day of shooting on the Bacone campus:

> Director Curtiz, with a deep tan and splotches of red on his high cheek-bones, looked as much like an Indian as anyone in the cast. A fast worker, he barked orders impatiently and had little patience with on-lookers who were not immediately involved in the production.
>
> In tan slacks and matching sport shirt with a red monogram, he had a red

scarf knotted at his throat. Moving eagerly from one scene to another, he would mumble briskly to extras, "Don't just be standing around here when you could be off making yourself look better. Comb your hair! It's blown all over."

Helping hold confusion to a minimum was competent Irva Mae Ross, script supervisor who has been with Warners 15 years, and with Curtiz for much of that time.

"It's fun to work with him, because he really knows his job," she said in an aside, "but he really keeps you on your toes."

While Stubler wasn't particularly taken with Curtiz's brusque manner—she was likely one of those "onlookers not immediately involved in the production" who encountered the director's cold shoulder—she was much easier on Lancaster, who told her, "I won't wear any unusual makeup for the part [of Thorpe]. All I'll need is sun tan base for my face, and as you can see they've dyed my hair black." Referring to the star as "easy going and friendly," Stubler observed, "Lancaster spent a good part of the morning sprawled on the grass with Muskogee Indians, helping them run over their lines."

Thorpe himself, meanwhile, was nowhere to be found when shooting commenced. Stubler wrote that crew members were not sure when he would turn up, adding: "A big welcome is waiting for him at Bacone, where members of the state's prominent Indian families are awaiting to show him they're mighty proud of the Prague farm boy who will go down in history as one of the outstanding sports figures of all times."

If Thorpe—who had left Oklahoma as a preteen and was, at the time of the filming, living in California—ever made it to Muskogee during the shoot, his appearance was not reported in Tulsa's two newspapers, which both devoted a significant amount of space to the goings-on at Bacone. Over the course of the twenty-one-day shooting schedule, readers of the *World* and *Tribune* got up-to-the-minute reports on everything from the hundreds of local extras involved to the doings of the Hollywood names who'd gathered on Bacone's campus—including Phyllis Thaxter, who played Thorpe's wife (and sat in on some classes at the school); veteran character actor Charles Bickford (who made a point of complimenting the local cuisine in a visit with the press) as Pop Warner; and Steve Cochran (who stayed in a motor court instead of a hotel so he could have his dog with him) as one of Thorpe's gridiron opponents. By the latter days of the filming, the popular press had warmed up to the gruff Curtiz, and he in turn had become much chummier with the locals. On September 8 the *World's* Gilbert Asher reported that the director had called all his extras together at the end of the day's shooting and pronounced them "splendid." According to Asher, Curtiz was positively enthusiastic about his days on the Bacone campus, saying, "These are wonderful people who are helping us. They listen to instructions and they follow them faultlessly. It's a pleasure to work with them."

The *Tribune's* John H. Booker, on September 15, came up with a filler item that played on the Hungarian director's well-known penchant for mispronunciation. "Director Curtiz—pronounced Cur-teeze—finally overcame his trouble with the name Muskogee," wrote Booker. "For three days he called it 'Muskawgo.'"

Curtiz and most of the rest of the unit headed back to Hollywood from Muskawgo the very next day, to take up the rest of the filming on the Warner Bros. lot. It was almost a year later when female lead Thaxter returned to the city for the big world premiere of *Jim Thorpe, All-American,* an event that mirrored, in a more modest way, all the hoopla that had gone on in Tulsa a little more than two years earlier, when that city's namesake film had received its own world premiere. Four Muskogee theaters showed *Jim Thorpe, All-American* to sold-out crowds, and there was even a parade, with star Phyllis Thaxter in the lead car. In a departure from the Tulsa event, however, the parade emphasized Native Americans and their culture instead of oil field equipment. The *Tulsa World's* J. C. Bradford told all about it in a story that ran on August 21, 1951, the day after the premiere:

> The car which bore Miss Thaxter, an ancient Ford without a top, rattled along at the head of the parade which left from in front of the [Severs] hotel, wound through the main streets of the town and out to the campus of little Bacone Indian college where much of the movie was filmed.
>
> Brightly-costumed Indian dancers and 16 Indian princesses representing eastern Oklahoma towns added color to the blocks-long parade. The cavalcade and a group of Muskogee's leading citizens were served Indian food at a luncheon on the campus.
>
> It was a full day for the stars. After the meal, they visited the Veterans

hospital, gave away autographed pictures downtown and made 30-minute personal appearances at each of the four theaters.

They were also on hand to welcome cross-country runners, representing the Five Civilized Tribes, as they converged on the town from different directions. . . .

By ordinary standards for such events, the celebration was not sensational, but it satisfied those who turned out. It was the day of the Indian and the native Americans took full advantage of it. They came from all over the state, displaying their colorful costumes and feathered headgear. The tinkling of the bells strapped around their legs and arms could be heard through most of the day as they danced through the Indian village which had been set up in the middle of town.

Although Bradford referred to the "stars" in his story, Thaxter was actually the only major *Jim Thorpe, All-American* player who showed up for the premiere. Lancaster sent his regrets from Italy, where he was shooting a picture; an actor named James Brown, in Bradford's words, "represented" the star at the premiere. Texas native Brown, best-known to baby boomers for his role as Lt. Rip Masters in TV's *The Adventures of Rin Tin Tin* (1954–59), may have been there because he was a contract player at Warner Bros. at the time, or perhaps he was there because his wife, Betty Engle, was both a Warners starlet and a Ponca City native. (One of his bigger movie roles had come in 1949, when he'd played Bob Younger in Warners' *The Younger Brothers*, a feature that treated the outlaws with the same sort of sympathy as the 1916 Tulsa-lensed film of the same name.)

Thaxter, Brown, and Engle provided the star power for the event, along with a young woman named Virginia Parlin, who, as "Miss Carlisle," was on hand to represent the Pennsylvania city and former college where Thorpe had first achieved national notice for his athletic prowess. Then there was the local color, both in the parade and the village set up on Muskogee's main street, as well as the cuisine. A luncheon on the Bacone campus, according to an August 18 *World* story, was to include "foods made from centuries-old recipes handed down by Cherokee, Seminole and Creek tribesmen. . . . There'll be fry-bread, crackling bread, sofkee (a kind of corn broth) and blue dumplings (chicken dumplings in berry juices)."

As befits a celebration of a movie about an American Indian athlete, a five-mile marathon race was also held. Five Native American runners from Bacone—each representing one of the Five Tribes—started out five miles from Muskogee on five different highways and raced to the Ritz, the first of the four theaters scheduled to show the film.

But the man about whom all this fuss was about—like the actor who portrayed him in the movie—did not attend. "Thorpe was not present because he had asked for $1,000 to come to Muskogee plus $400 each for five personal appearances," wrote Devlin. "Neither the city nor the studio desired to meet his price. He was paid $50,000 for the rights to film the picture plus other fees which approximated another $50,000, it was learned."

The reporter didn't name his source, although it was probably someone representing the studio. Wherever it came from, its veracity is questionable. Other sources claim that Thorpe—who was far from a wealthy man at the time—got nothing at all for his contributions to the picture, having sold away the movie rights to his life story many years earlier. If the latter is true, perhaps that also explains why he stayed away from Muskogee during the shooting as well as the festivities. (An August 12 *Daily Oklahoman* article, however, reported that Thorpe was scheduled to attend the American Indian Exposition at Anadarko on August 18, "to receive another plaque naming him as the outstanding Indian of the year.")

The day after the premiere, the stars and Parlin traveled to Oklahoma City, where the now ex-governor Roy J. Turner was included in the festivities, along with the current governor, Johnston Murray, who had proclaimed August 17–23 as *Jim Thorpe, All American* Week in Oklahoma. Like Muskogee's event, the Oklahoma City premiere boasted a parade that prominently featured Native Americans, a luncheon for the stars and dignitaries, and a race with American Indian competitors, followed by showings of the film. It began playing at two theaters that day, the Warner and the Midwest.

From there, the actors headed to Carlisle, Pennsylvania, site of the Carlisle Indian Industrial School, for still another premiere. Accompanying Thaxter, Brown, and Engle was La Rue Martin of Anadarko, described in an August 20 *Oklahoman* item as a "Caddo Indian princess who was picked at the American Indian exposition at Anadarko as its 'All-American Indian princess.'" She was to represent the state at the Carlisle premiere.

If Thorpe attended either of those events—or the American Indian Exposition where Martin was crowned—his presence went unreported in the Oklahoma press. The great athlete died about two and a half years later of heart failure in Lomita, California. Patricia, his third wife, asked Oklahoma governor Murray to authorize state money for a monument so that Thorpe could get the burial she felt he deserved, but he denied the request. Then—according to an August 19, 2000, story filed by Associated Press reporter Jonathan Poet from Jim Thorpe, Pennsylvania—his widow went elsewhere:

> Patricia Thorpe announced that she was looking for a place that would honor her husband and ended up here, 70 miles north of Philadelphia in a community nestled in a narrow valley in the Poconos, where civic leaders pledged to give him a monument. They also pledged to merge the boroughs of Mauch Chunk and East Mauch Chunk and incorporate together as Jim Thorpe, which happened in 1954 [the year after his death].
>
> A local newspaper publisher pushed the issue, saying that Thorpe's tomb could help the town become a tourist attraction. Locals even hoped Thorpe's presence would attract the Pro Football Hall of Fame, which ended up being built in Ohio.
>
> Money was raised. The monument was built. And the ground where Thorpe is buried was dedicated in 1957.

The roadside park that's home to Thorpe's remains lies a little over 100 miles northwest of the long-defunct Carlisle Industrial Indian School, where the athlete received his higher education and first sports stardom, and about 1,300 miles east of Prague, Oklahoma, where he was born. Thorpe's children and other family members would prefer to have him much closer to home, where the body could be given a traditional Native American burial, but their requests to move Thorpe's remains have been so far denied by the Pennsylvania town's officials.

So there the long-interred subject of *Jim Thorpe, All-American* remains, marked by a monument with an inscription that echoes the utterance of Sweden's King Gustav V in 1912: "Sir, you are the greatest athlete in the world."

Of all the big-studio productions that visited Oklahoma in the '50s and '60s, *Jim Thorpe, All-American* generated the most press. Part of the reason was readers' interest in one of their own—Sooner State native Thorpe, an Okie kid who'd gone on to international renown. Another factor was the presence of the picture's stars, and the rest of the film crew, in the area for a relatively long time.

A couple of other major motion pictures, however, also benefited from scenes shot in Oklahoma during this period. Both of them, 1956's *Around the World in Eighty Days* and 1962's *State Fair*, had connections, albeit tenuous, to the Sooner State.

Around the World in Eighty Days was the second film ever to be shot in Todd-AO, a widescreen process developed by colorful Hollywood producer Mike Todd. And the first? *Oklahoma!* (1955), which was shot outside the state because the kind of undeveloped land prevalent in turn-of-the-century Oklahoma—the time in which the picture was set—was more plentiful elsewhere. "We had to film *Oklahoma* in Arizona," the garrulous Todd told the *Daily Oklahoman*'s John Dexter for an October 9, 1955, story. "Then we turn around and film these scenes in Oklahoma. They could've been shot in western Nebraska or anywhere else." Todd also noted that *Around the World*'s Shirley MacLaine, whom he called "our feminine lead," had been a member of the chorus in the Broadway version of *Oklahoma!*

State Fair, on the other hand, was the second musical remake of the Oscar-nominated nonmusical movie of the same name from 1933. That version had been a vehicle for Oklahoma's favorite son, Will Rogers, then one of America's top box-office draws. All three of the *State Fair* features were based on the same 1932 novel by Philip Duffield Stong; the latter two (released in 1945 and 1962) benefited from the involvement of musical-theater greats Richard Rodgers and Oscar Hammerstein II, the team behind *Oklahoma!*

Around the World in Eighty Days, whose source was the classic Jules Verne novel, was conceived and executed by Todd as a great big block-buster, full of major stars and exotic locations, designed to explode onto

Four of the stars that studded the cast of *Around the World in Eighty Days* (1956): Shirley MacLaine, David Niven, Cantinflas, and Buster Keaton. (John Wooley Archives)

America's screens via the 70 mm film process that bore the producer's name. David Niven headlined a multinational cast that included his fellow Brits Noel Coward and Robert Morley, Mexican film comedian Cantinflas, and dozens of cameos from American stars ranging from Frank Sinatra and Marlene Dietrich to comic Joe E. Brown and veteran western star Tim McCoy. While Todd and unit director Lew Borzage were busy filming scenes in Oklahoma, wrote Dexter in the *Oklahoman*, "There are film crews shooting today in Spain, England, Suez, Pakistan, in addition to Durango, Colo., and the Wichita mountains area."

Yes, the natural beauty of the Wichita Mountains near Lawton had been called upon once again to serve as a movie setting, as it had in 1920's *Daughter of Dawn* and 1949's *Prince of Peace*. *Around the World in Eighty Days* had more in common with the former than it did with the latter, however, using actors and extras from the area's Native American population as well as the buffalo herd in the Wichita Mountains Wildlife Refuge, just as filmmaker Norbert Myles had done in *Daughter of Dawn*.

The area was apparently chosen by Todd and company because of the efforts of a man named Frank Rush, Jr., who ran the Craterville Park Ranch Resort in the Wichita Mountains. It had been simply Craterville Park in the '20s and '30s, owned by Frank Rush, Sr., and used, among other things, to hold an annual event called the All-Indian Fair. According to Muriel H. Wright's 1946 *Chronicles of Oklahoma* article titled "The American Indian Exposition in Oklahoma," Rush sponsored the first of these events in 1924 and continued until 1932 with fairs that were "widely advertised for [their] special entertainment and agricultural exhibits displayed by the Indians of Southwestern Oklahoma" (vol. 2, p. 159).

In a later *Oklahoman* piece, on September 21, 1955, John Dexter explained how the Wichitas were chosen, adding that "a location crew of 60 film players and technicians" was on the way.

> Movie company personnel, scheduled to arrive here about October 1, will be quartered at Craterville park ranch resort, Frank Rush Jr., resort operator, said. Negotiations for the Oklahoma site have been completed by Rush with Frank Fox, location manager, and James Sullivan, art director of the company. . . .
>
> Originally, Fox and Sullivan planned to film Indian scenes in Black Hills of South Dakota, using the Ute tribe. On a visit here last month, Rush took them to the American Indian Exposition at Anadarko. The movie officials agreed that Oklahoma's redmen were more colorful, and that the picturesque Wichita mountains region was suitable.

Although the term "redmen" is cringe-inducing today, the filming did provide decent, if short-term, employment for hundreds of American Indians from all around the state, with Todd's company signing contracts with officials of the Kiowas, the Comanches, and other tribes. By October 8, the day the filming began, a circa-1870 American Indian village had been put together adjacent to Craterville Park, ready to be inhabited by—as the *Oklahoman's* reliable John Dexter put it in his October 9 report from the scene—"500 colorfully dressed Oklahoma Indians."

Although Lew Borzage was the official director of this unit, Mike Todd apparently took over for at least part of the Oklahoma filming. Wrote Dexter: "Dressed in red shirt and blue jeans, Todd puffed on a long black stogie as he sized up the set and directed rehearsals before the scene was filmed. 'I'm doubling in brass today. I'm supposed to tend to production chores, but I'm a unit director today.'"

Still, Todd found plenty of time to talk to the press, telling Dexter about the placement of the Oklahoma scenes within the movie.

> "You see," he explained, "this trip around the world is made against many obstacles. For example, on location at Durango, Colo., we had the biggest fight you ever saw between the cavalry and some hostile Indians.
>
> "Now, these Indians here are friendly Indians. They have just stopped the train to invite the engineer and fireman to smoke the peace pipe, and these dances are held for them."
>
> But the train of 1870 vintage will have trouble making it to the Indian village, according to the schedule of location shots in the area. It will be stopped this weekend by a herd of buffalo, courtesy of the Wichita Mountain Wildlife refuge. A thousand feet of track, a water tower, a mock engine and the buffalo are waiting for crews to move into the refuge Sunday or Monday.

Since the shooting near Craterville—Dexter gives the location as "Frank Rush's Rocking-R Ranch, north of Craterville Park"—had begun on Saturday, Todd and his crew didn't plan to spend an inordinate amount of time there. But the locals made the most of it. In his October 7 story, Dexter wrote, "Coinciding with the movie company's stay in the Wichita mountains area, a three-day Indian show will be staged at the park over the weekend, beginning Friday night."

So, although they may have had only a brief part, several hundred of Oklahoma's American Indians, as well as the Wichita Mountains, were granted a bit of cinematic immortality in Mike Todd's spectacular widescreen feature, which ended up winning five Oscars, including one for Best Picture. Craterville Park, however, didn't fare as well. The next year, it was closed, due to expansion of the Fort Sill Military Reservation.

Some six years down the road, another major Hollywood company visited the state in search of a suitable location for some specific second-unit footage. A July 20, 1961, unbylined article from the *Daily Oklahoman* told it all in the headline: "Filmland Team Eyes Our Fair."

Tom Ewell and Alice Faye in the 1962 version of *State Fair*. (John Wooley Archives)

The piece told of an upcoming visit to the Oklahoma State Fairgrounds by a cadre from Twentieth Century-Fox that included producer Charles Brackett and director-actor José Ferrer. As Oklahoma State Fair promotion director Earl Schweikhard explained it, the group was planning a second remake of *State Fair*, this time using the Texas State Fair in Dallas, but that fair was missing a racetrack and a grandstand, which were essential to the script. "I don't know yet if they plan to film during our fair or not," Schweikhard said, "but they do like our track and grandstands."

By the next day, it was a done deal. A July 21 *Oklahoman* article quoted Ferrer as saying, "This track is just what we're looking for to film a highly-specialized car-race sequence, which he termed "a mechanized *Ben-Hur*," referring to the memorable chariot race in that 1959 movie. "Ferrer said the company will probably be here two or three days," continued the story, "and may film portions of the sequence during the Oklahoma State

Fair September 23–30. 'If it isn't filmed during the fair, we will probably employ local people as extras to fill the grandstands,' the director said." Indeed, that's how it turned out.

Despite the talk of shooting a car race during the fair, it's likely that the film crew shot only some background scenes then, since it was in town for just a couple of days, and none of the stars came along with it. A larger Hollywood contingent returned October 9, however, including director Ferrer and stars Pat Boone, Ann-Margret (making her first picture), Alice Faye (in her first screen appearance since 1945's *Fallen Angel*), Tom Ewell, Bobby Darin (who brought along his wife, actress Sandra Dee), and Pamela Tiffin (who, coincidentally, had been born in Oklahoma City).

Immediately, two things happened: it began raining, and a call went out for 10,000 extras, all of whom were needed to fill the bleachers for the film's big auto race. Noting that "the would-be thespians must be willing to emote, that is[,] stand up and cheer on cue from a loud speaker," the October 10 *Oklahoman* described the rewards they might reap:

> Since the spectator role is non-paying, the movie makers have come up with several inducements.
>
> For one thing, they're going to give away $100 each hour during the day's filming, for a total of $800. Each spectator will be assigned a number for the hourly drawing.
>
> Also, several of the cast members, including Pat Boone, Bobby Darin, Anne-Margret [*sic*] and Alice Faye, will perform solely for the audience between "takes."
>
> Jose Ferrer, director of the movie, will explain movie-making mechanics to the spectators while cameras and sound equipment are being shifted around for various shots.
>
> In addition, there'll be an honest-to-goodness auto race, the one that will be filmed.
>
> The studio spokesman said the volunteer spectators are to show up on the set—the grandstand—Thursday morning. They should bring their own box lunches, since the filming will likely run into the afternoon.

Considered nearly half a decade later, the incentives don't seem terribly enticing—especially the bring-your-own-meal part. Perhaps they weren't then, either, as the unit personnel ended up getting a little less than half the number of extras they'd hoped for. On Saturday, October 14, a crowd estimated at 4,500 in an *Oklahoman* story from that day —including 200 Civil Air Patrol cadets in uniform—showed up, presumably with lunches in hand, to take seats in the grandstand. The shooting had been delayed by rain for two days, a circumstance that may also have had something to do with the relatively light turnout.

"Far short of the desired 10,000 persons," the article reported, "Hollywood movie-makers were able to take crowd shots for the production Saturday at the fairgrounds." In addition to alluding to a few challenges with the smaller audience—including the observation that "the crowd was more interested in watching the stars of the movie than following Ferrer's instructions"—the article told of another *State Fair* scene shot that same day.

> About 2:30 P.M., Boone, Ewell, Miss Tiffin and Miss Faye, along with Ferrer and a camera and sound crew, journeyed to a county road south of Will Rogers field.
>
> There they filmed a sequence of the Frake family returning home after their stay at the fair.
>
> The stars sang the title song of the movie, "Our State Fair" as they made their way back to their home.
>
> One movie official pointed to the irony of shooting the sequence in Oklahoma since the setting of the picture is Texas—The title song of the movie being shot on a county road in Oklahoma.

The stars left the next day, with some of the crew sticking around for pickup shots and whatever other mop-up work needed to be done. And that was it for Oklahoma City and *State Fair* until April 4, 1962, when the Criterion Theater hosted a premiere screening in conjunction with the movie's debut in several Texas cities. Although none of the major players were on hand, there was a downtown Oklahoma City parade at 7 P.M., preceding the first screening by an hour. Wrote Walt Radmilovich for the next day's *Oklahoman*, "The premiere here Wednesday was devoid of any of the Hollywood stars featured in the film—they were in Texas— but there was accompanying fanfare. A searchlight probed drizzly sky overhead, before show time as a calliope tooted, and a number of sports cars used in the movie were lined up outside the theater."

The Texas premieres acknowledged the film's main setting: the Texas

State Fair in Dallas. The 1945 version had been set in Iowa, and Richard Rodgers (whose songwriting partner Oscar Hammerstein II had died in 1960) wrote a song for the new remake's soundtrack called "The Little Things in Texas," replacing "All I Owe Ioway" in the earlier picture. Other Rodgers and Hammerstein compositions from the previous film were recycled for this second go-round.

The 1962 *State Fair* turned out to be the final production credit for Charles Brackett, the producer-writer who'd won Oscars for *The Lost Weekend* and *Sunset Boulevard*, just two standout movies in an exemplary Hollywood career. He died in 1969. It was also the final theatrical feature directed by Ferrer, who continued to act in films and television until his death in 1992. And, undoubtedly, it was the last—and first—big-screen appearance for a few thousand residents of the Oklahoma City area, many of whom feel that they can still spot themselves in the bleachers whenever *State Fair* plays on television.

Nineteen sixty-two also saw the release of a feature that couldn't have been more different from *State Fair*. It was a small independent effort instead of a major-studio blockbuster. Created by Oklahomans, it was shot almost entirely in the state. And it was as dark as *State Fair* was sunny. "I consider it a film really produced by the people of Oklahoma," said director Ned Hockman in 2005, speaking of his sole feature-film credit, *Stark Fear*. "We raised $150,000, we stayed in budget, and the people sponsored us with their money. You could even buy stock for $10."

Hockman made that comment to interviewer B. J. Wexler in a special presentation of the Wexler-hosted *OETA Movie Club*, a long-running Saturday night film program originating in Oklahoma City and aired statewide by the Oklahoma Educational Television Authority. The occasion was the world TV premiere of Hockman's *Stark Fear* on October 8, 2005, forty-three years after its theatrical debut.

A strange psychological thriller that still packs a wallop today, *Stark Fear* had its origins in the Oklahoma City–Norman area, and specifically at the University of Oklahoma, where a couple of men in the motion picture and journalism departments decided they wanted to get into the feature film business. In his article for the June 25, 1961, issue of *Oklahoma's Orbit* (the Sunday supplement magazine published by the *Oklahoman* newspaper), writer Jack Bickham laid it out for readers:

> Around the University of Oklahoma's motion picture unit, the idea of making a strictly commercial entertainment film—a feature such as you see at your favorite movie house—has been a topic of casual conversation for a long time.
>
> After all, the talk said, why couldn't a prize-winning director like Ned Hockman of OU team up with a seasoned novelist and script writer like Dwight V. Swain, of the Sooner School of Journalism, to make a solidly popular motion picture?
>
> Well, it isn't just talk any more.
>
> They're doing it.
>
> Hockman, Swain and several other key people are taking leaves of absence from the university. Shooting on Oklahoma locations starts July 5.

Hockman and Swain did have some significant experience between them, although Swain's scriptwriting credits lay in the educational and industrial fields. Swain had, however, sold numerous stories to the all-fiction pulp magazines of the 1940s and early '50s and had seen the occasional novel published as well. Both he and Bickham were instructors for OU's acclaimed writing program.

Hockman was a veteran director of industrial and educational movies, as well as television commercials, frequently working in tandem with Swain. Before that, he had shot World War II training films as an enlisted man in the U.S. Army's First Motion Picture Unit, working with Ronald Reagan and Frank Lloyd, the Oscar-winning director of 1935's *Mutiny on the Bounty*.

What was it that made these two men think they could make the jump to a real theatrical feature, a picture that would be able to compete with Hollywood product on the nation's screens? Remember, this was a time when filmmaking was an expensive proposition, well beyond the reach of most people. The overwhelming majority of America's movies were made by major studios with millions of dollars at their disposal, and in order to have any hope of competing, an aspiring filmmaker had to raise a great deal of money, rent the necessary equipment, and hire professional technicians. The time of today's "indie" feature, shot on a wing and a prayer with a skeleton staff using an inexpensive digital camera, was some three decades in the future. The successful independent filmmakers of the early '60s, such as the Chicago-based team of director Herschell Gordon Lewis and producer David F. Friedman, usually turned their profits by blatantly exploiting elements the majors wouldn't touch, including gore and partial nudity. And even then, their movies seldom played in the theaters of Main Street America, depending instead on secondary venues like inner-city grind houses and the up-and-coming drive-in theater circuits.

Still, at that time in U.S. cinema history, things were changing. "Art" films, imported from Europe and often containing rawer elements than stateside product, were gaining in popularity. At the same time, the Production Code Administration, the film industry's self-censoring body, had lightened up significantly from the days when married couples couldn't be shown sleeping in the same bed and Clark Gable's "Frankly, my dear, I don't give a damn," line from *Gone with the Wind* had been denounced from pulpits across the land. The Catholic Church's Legion of Decency, which gave films alphabet-letter ratings based on their moral content, was still a force in the '50s, but increasingly less so as the decade wore on. (Sixty years down the road, it seems almost ludicrous that *Oklahoma!* got a "B"—meaning "morally objectionable in part"—from the Legion of Decency because of the song "I Can't Say No," sung in the film by Gloria Grahame.)

Much of the reason for the Production Code's relaxing standards had to do with the inroads television had made into the motion picture business. Movies simply had to give audiences what they couldn't get on the home screen—whether it was Mike Todd's Todd-AO and similar wide-screen processes, color (most American homes didn't have color television until the early '70s), or the sex-related content, amped-up violence, and/or salty language prohibited on television in those more innocent days.

With the 1960 chiller *Psycho*, director Alfred Hitchcock—whose rotund form and dry hangman's wit had made him a popular television personality—gave his fans something far rougher than anything they could get weekly on his long-running TV program, *Alfred Hitchcock Presents*. Although it came from a major studio and a big-name director, the wildly successful *Psycho* ushered in an era of more "adult" terror on the big screen. With its stark black-and-white photography and use of gritty plot elements that would've been more at home in an independent film, *Psycho* was in many ways the antithesis of the classic Hollywood movie.

Of course, Swain and Hockman were aware of all these factors swirling around them, including the American appetite for abnormal-psychology films awakened by *Psycho*. So was Bickham, who acknowledged the new filmmaking environment in his *Orbit* piece:

> When the film's partners started work toward a shooting script, they agreed that they wanted to have a strongly dramatic psychological story that was definitely in line with the trend toward "adult" entertainment. At the same time, they wanted it to be in good taste. . . .
>
> The story centers around a young woman named Ellen Winslow, whose psychopathic husband deserts her—spurring her into a hectic investigation of his past which includes rape, a symbolic incest theme, violence and the threat of murder, a genuine love story and the stunning scenery of Eureka Springs [Arkansas].

Later in the piece, Bickham noted:

> Small productions such as the one contemplated by BHS, Inc. [Swain and Hockman's company], are a growing trend, according to the Wall Street Journal, which said recently that the "blockbuster trend" is over in films. The influential newspaper noted that more than 40 such low-budget movies were made last year. Firms like BHS have been a resounding financial success in places as different as Harvard and Orlando, Fla.

The "B" in BHS represented Joe E. Burke, a local advertising man and the other producer of *Stark Fear*. Hockman outlined the assembling of the team during his *OETA Movie Club* appearance:

> Dwight and I had worked together on documentary films for years. One day, I was hired by Joe Burke. . . . He had an advertising agency in Norman. We finished looking at the pictures and work I did for him, and I said, "You know, Joe, one of these days we ought to make a film, a major motion picture."
>
> He said, "You think we could do that?"
>
> I said, "I think we could," and I left. Within about three days, he came into my office and he said, "You know, Ned, I've checked your idea out, and I'm going to put together a group and let's do it." So he went to work, and we established Burke-Hockman-Swain Productions.

At first, the three wanted to do a feature about the life and death of nineteenth-century Native American leader Elias Boudinot, a Cherokee who started the tribe's first newspaper, lived a colorful life, and was ultimately killed by members of his own tribe. Although it was "a great story," Hockman told B. J. Wexler, "we figured it out and it was going to cost $500,000."

With a budget that ended up being less than a third of that amount, the three jettisoned the idea of doing a period piece. Instead, Swain came up with that "strongly dramatic psychological story" referred to in the *Oklahoma's Orbit* story, which he initially called *Black Lace*, after a frilly undergarment that the protagonist buys early in the story to try and rekindle the interest of her increasingly disturbed husband.

That married couple, Ellen and Jerry Winslow, were played by two of the three bona fide Hollywood actors recruited for the film, Beverly Garland and Skip Homeier. Swain, Hockman said, was especially sold on Garland after seeing her in her syndicated TV series *Decoy* (1957–58), one of the first action-adventure television shows to feature a woman as the main character. A busy and versatile actress for decades, Garland was probably best known for her work as a heroine in classic '50s science fiction and horror films like *It Conquered the World* (1956), *Not of This Earth* (1957), and *The Alligator People* (1959). Homeier was a former child star who was, as an adult, especially good in villainous parts. During TV's crime-show craze of the late '50s and early '60s, he'd starred as a Hollywood-based police detective in the NBC series *Dan Raven* (1960–61).

Rounding out the cast, as oilman Cliff Kane, was Kenneth Tobey. Like his two costars, he had toplined his own TV show—the syndicated *Whirlybirds*, which originally ran at roughly the same time as Garland's *Decoy*. He had also scored with audiences as the lead in 1951's *The Thing from Another World*, one of his many roles in both big- and low-budget movies.

All three principals in BHS Productions traveled to Southern California to pick the actors for the three top roles, and in his *OETA Movie Club* appearance, Hockman recalled visiting Garland at her home and telling her about his time working in the First Motion Picture Unit during the war. As he remembered it, "On her own, after we left, she picked up the phone and called Frank Lloyd and asked about Charles Nedwin Hockman. And he says, 'Oh, *Charlie*. Yeah, he's all right. Go ahead. He'll take good care of you.'"

The cast was augmented by local actors, notably Hannah Stone as Ruth, Ellen Winslow's friend, adviser, and sometime roommate, and George Clow, chillingly effective as a brutal, concupiscent redneck named Harvey Suggett. Both Stone and Clow had spent years performing on Oklahoma City stages before being cast in *Stark Fear*. And the original music for the film was composed, orchestrated, and conducted by Lawrence Fisher, assistant director of the Oklahoma City Symphony.

Oklahoma City stands out in the setting of the picture, with Garland emerging from the downtown Liberty Bank building in the film's opening. Other Oklahoma locations include the towns of Norman—where OU's Delta Delta Delta sorority house was rented for use as a studio (the film was shot in July and August, when the house was vacant)—and Lexington, which was given the name "Quehada" for the film. An odd little jukebox museum in Lexington figures prominently in the movie.

"We tried to do all that we could in Oklahoma," Hockman said in his OETA interview. "We did go to Eureka Springs, Arkansas, for the section where there was to be a big oil meeting and so forth. . . . We went up there and worked three days."

In *Stark Fear*, the Eureka Springs scenes, with Ellen and her employer sharing a tender moment, contrast wildly with the ones in "Quehada." That backwater Oklahoma burg, as it develops, is the hometown of Jerry Winslow, and when his wife visits it to try to ferret out some clue to his bizarre behavior, she is ogled, manhandled, shouted at, and ultimately assaulted in a cemetery—a scene that, viewed decades later, remains disturbing. The town itself seems to exude sinister vibes, as do the Native Americans whom Ellen runs into—literally—during a stomp dance beside the graveyard. Indeed, there seems to be a particular menace connected with the American Indians in *Stark Fear*, summed up by a line Jerry spits at his wife: "The Comanches know how to deal with your kind. Did you ever see a woman with her nose cut off?"

As might be inferred from that statement, Jerry has some issues, especially when it comes to the opposite sex. As Swain's script has it, they all date back to his relationship with his mother (echoing *Psycho*), and they clawed their way to the forefront of his psyche when Ellen—forced to become the breadwinner after Jerry's income dried up—went to work as secretary for Kane, Jerry's oil business rival.

Stark Fear is an oddly compelling, off-trail piece of work, made all the stranger by its protagonist's dogged determination to stick by her husband no matter what, when everyone else around her (and in the audience) knows that he's seriously disturbed. It's part female point-of-view love story, part exploitation film, and part psychological thriller—a combination that was better reflected by either of its two working titles, *Black Lace* and, later, *Brink of Love*. A third title was ultimately chosen for its release, but BHS Productions ran into outside problems with that one, as reported by Aline Jean Treanor in the December 12, 1962, *Daily Oklahoman*:

> *Dark Brink of Love* was the original title chosen by writer Dwight Swain. But when camera work started, it was diminished to *Brink of Love* by common consent, the way a Richard gets called Rick. . . .
>
> Then it was discovered that violent Norseman, Ingmar Bergman, had already made a *Brink of Love* [actually, *Brink of Life*]. And namesakes are no good in the movie business. Not only are namesakes out, but so are names similar enough to be considered a damaging infringement.
>
> This was when the parental B-H-S got themselves a title list of all the movies so protected—current, recent, and future. Then they started trying to compose an entirely original title that would be appropriate for their child.
>
> Out of 200 they were able to put together, they deemed *The Hate Within* most likely, and registered it (for $85) with the American [*sic*] Motion Picture Association of America, more familiarly known as the Spurlock Committee, for Geoffrey Spurlock, production code administrator.
>
> *The Hate Within* was posted and circulated among moviemakers for the required two-week period in which it could be protested. And it was protested.
>
> Twentieth Century Fox had bought Robert Kennedy's book *The Enemy Within*, with intention of using the book title for the movie. B-H-S challenge [*sic*] the protest, and the matter in controversy went to production code adjudicators. Verdict—for Twentieth Century Fox.

"They said we were trying to ride off their title with *The Hate Within*, and we didn't know anything about that book at all," Hockman told B. J. Wexler during the *OETA Movie Club* appearance. "So we had to go up to New York City . . . to mediate, and finally we told 'em, 'We understand,' and we told Mr. Ellis, who was our distributor, 'Well, name it anything you want.'

"And immediately, he says, 'I've been thinking about it, and I want to call it *Stark Fear*! It'll be great up on the marquee—*Stark Fear*!'

"Well . . . there *is* that element of fear in it. But one time [after the film's release under that title] I took a print, on my military duty, down to Orlando, Florida, and I changed the name to *Cry Deep, My Love*—'It's a Woman's Story!' And we had people lined up around the block to see it."

The New York–based distributor had been secured several months earlier, as the *Oklahoman*'s Treanor reported on August 15, 1962:

> First, Burke-Hockman-Swain had to put their product in the hands of a 42nd Street agent, Donald T. Gillen, Inc., who in turn contracted it to a Broadway distributing firm, Ellis Films, Inc.
>
> Next, it goes to a booking firm, after which the 30 release prints that are to be made of the film will be ready to start their rounds. . . .
>
> Ellis Films specializes in handling low budget films, i.e. made for $250,000 or less, and will let *The Hate Within* be booked freely, as a main feature, a second feature, or to an art theater or drive-in.

Ellis Films had been around since the late 1940s, distributing mostly foreign pictures (including several from England). A couple of years before the *Stark Fear* deal, it had gained a measure of notoriety by securing the American rights to a 1952 French comedy called *Le trou normand* and releasing it stateside as *Crazy for Love*. The selling point for the picture was Brigitte Bardot, by 1960 the sex-kitten queen of American art houses, who was, in 1952, just beginning her movie career.

Stark Fear didn't do as well as *Crazy for Love*, although—as Hockman noted on OETA—it's hard to discern exactly how well it *did* do, since BHS Productions never saw a dime from its release.

"We should've raised enough money for two films at least, maybe three, and then we could've kept going, see," he told Wexler. "All the money in distribution was stolen from us. By 'stolen'—they just said it was being used."

　　　　　　　　　　　　　　　　　　SHOT IN OKLAHOMA

But whatever the verb, the fact is that *Stark Fear*'s distributor never returned any proceeds to BHS, and that was it for the company. Each member of the trio went back to what he'd been doing before the film, with Burke continuing his ad agency, Hockman heading the film program at OU, and Swain continuing to write books and teach at the university.

Over the years, *Stark Fear* has sometimes been referred to as Garland's least favorite film in her entire oeuvre. Sources, including IMDb.com, even indicate that Hockman stormed off the set and was replaced in the director's chair by Homeier. If any of that is true, it certainly wasn't evident in Garland's gracious appearance in Norman on October 24, 2003, when OU Filmmaker-in-Residence Shawnee Britton presented a fortieth-anniversary screening of the picture. (It was intended as a reunion of Garland and her director, but Hockman was unable to attend because of a bout with pneumonia.)

"It wasn't bad, was it?" said a smiling Garland after the big-screen presentation, in a speech preserved on video by Britton and his students. "I hadn't seen it in 40 years . . . and I just remembered what fun we really had. What fun we really had, you know? Ned and Tobey and Skip . . . we really worked hard, but I look back on it now and I remember all these things, and I think it was fun. Acting can be just so joyful when you have fun with it."

Two years later, on OETA, Hockman had similarly positive memories of his star. "It took us thirty days to shoot this movie," he said, "and Beverly stayed over an extra two weeks so that we could do some advertising, going to the various television stations and doing some interviews and so forth. She was really a great professional actress, an actor of A-1 quality, and a wonderful personality. We didn't experience a negative thought from that woman."

Beyond that oddball indie effort and the three major-studio stopovers, Oklahoma didn't have a lot of other filmmaking going on during the '50s and '60s. The rest of what came out of the '50s consisted of a couple of travelogues, a brief flurry of cattle-ranch activity that called to mind the

Hereford Heaven–set features of the previous decade, and some short films from a semipro outfit that at least seemed to be having a good time.

In 1952 the husband-and-wife team of Hal and Ruth Ayers arrived in Oklahoma from Dallas, Texas, to do some location scouting for a documentary to be called *The Oklahoma Story*. He was a producer, she was his scripter, and among the places they visited was the Fort Gibson Reservoir area, described in a June 20, 1952, *Tulsa World* story as "Oklahoma's newest playground."

"They were searching for 'locations'—sites from which camera crews can best record for theater and television viewers the beauties of northeastern Oklahoma," wrote the unnamed reporter, who also said that the filming had the "blessing of the state planning and resources board." The term "blessing" likely had financial implications; it's probable that the state footed the bill not only for the filming but the prints of the final movie as well, in addition to providing support personnel to Ayers and his company, the grandly named Continental Nationwide Films, Inc. *The Oklahoma Story*, was, after all, designed to make people want to travel to the state, as indicated by the chamber-of-commerce sentiments in the final paragraphs of the article:

> Hal Ayers, whose professional interest in the area was in connection with locating prime spots for his camera crews which will enter the region within the next 2 or 3 weeks, came away from his trip with this to say:
>
> "The richness of northeastern Oklahoma can only be realized if everyone in the state will back up the efforts of those interested in making these places known to everyone in America. The tourist spending potential here is simply limitless."
>
> Ayer's movie—*The Oklahoma Story*—when completed will be released to 83 television stations throughout the nation and will be shown in more than 1,800 theaters. As a documentary on the resources of Oklahoma it will be, in the words of Gov. Johnston Murray, "the most valuable advertisement of Oklahoma ever produced."

Although one can rightfully wonder where those specific numbers came from, both television and movie theaters were far less rigid in their programming than they are today, and if station managers or theater owners could get a print of something with a decent amount of entertainment value for free—which was likely the plan for *The Oklahoma Story*—many would have been glad to sign on and make it a part of their programming schedules.

Mr. and Mrs. Ayers and the rest of the company did more travelogues under similar circumstances. The very next month, a crew from Continental Nationwide began shooting in neighboring Arkansas and Missouri for another picture called *The Ozark Playgrounds Story*. Among the many other productions lensed by Ayers and his enterprising company was the 1954 featurette *The Tulsa Story*. By that time, television viewings were being increasingly emphasized. For the twelve-and-a-half-minute *Tulsa Story*, noted the *Tulsa World* on October 27, 1955, Continental had gotten a distribution contract from Sterling Television Company of New York that called for "a minimum of 300 showings in not less than 100 of the principal cities" in America. Reported the *World*, "In the 6-week period of Aug. 10 to Sept. 30, the film was shown in 53 telecasts in 44 cities with an estimated viewer audience of 1,739, 398."

In those days of looser television and movie theater programming, Hal Ayers had found a workable formula for filmmaking. And, for at least a while, it was apparently a profitable one.

A few years later, in November 1956, the *Daily Oklahoman* column "The Smoking Room" brought another documentary, *Oklahoma Holiday*, to the public's attention. This project, too, was tied in with Oklahoma's Planning and Resources Board, which had thirteen prints of the twenty-eight-minute picture available for rental "free to schools, clubs and conventions." Wrote the columnist:

> There have been other color movies emphasizing the state parks, industries, forests, agriculture, etc., and they were plenty good, but this new one perhaps is the best one yet. . . .
>
> The pictures were made by a topflight color movie artist who spent many months getting them. . . . The film will give you a new appreciation of scenic outdoor Oklahoma. It will be shown somewhere every day or night this week, which is Pride in Oklahoma week, but it will be just as interesting and eye-opening next spring or next autumn as it is now. It will really cause you to resolve to do more traveling within the state to see for yourself the scenic spots which your Oklahoma possesses the year round.

During that same month and year, on a ranch just outside of the northeastern Oklahoma town of Vinita, a local actor, recently returned from location shooting, was making some noise in the press. And while "King Tut" probably wouldn't qualify as one of the "scenic spots" mentioned in the *Daily Oklahoman* column, he was just about big enough to be a scenic area all on his own.

Clear View King Tut was a world champion Brangus bull, two-fifths Brahma and three-fifths Angus—the product of a couple of decades of breeding and development at Raymond Pope's Clear View Ranch. And in late 1956 he was just getting back to his Vinita stomping grounds after being borrowed for a few weeks by a Hollywood film unit helmed by A-list director George Stevens.

Writer Mark Sarchet told readers all about it in a November 18, 1956, spread in the *Sunday Oklahoman*, after first explaining how fitting it was, as Oklahoma neared its fiftieth anniversary, "that both Texas and California get their come-uppance and have to call on us Sooners for help before they can film a story about our neighbor across the Red river on Lone Star ground." The story—part tongue-in-cheek, part chip-on-shoulder, continued:

> When Hollywood needed a bull to take the animal star role in the movie, *Giant*, there wasn't a gentleman cow in all of the Longhorn domain who could qualify. No, sir! When Hollywood needed a bull for Rock Hudson to brag about, they wanted no part of those Texas runts. The film version of Edna Ferber's novel also stars Elizabeth Taylor and the late James Dean.
>
> And so Clear View King Tut, the 1955 champion Brangus bull of Ray Pope's Clear View ranch just north of Vinita, was cast in the role. All 2,500 pounds of the jet-black stupendous, colossal, mightiest of them all, native born Oklahoman, King Tut, is a star.
>
> King Tut, Pope and Billy Coppedge—the Clear View herdsman—spent three weeks on location in Texas with Hudson and the rest of the Hollywood minor human stars of the picture.
>
> King Tut, when asked about the life of a movie star, pawed the ground with his left front hoof and snorted three short but powerful dust-swirling blasts.
>
> "Nuts," Pope translated for the king. "Those Texas cows didn't show

me a thing. And as for Hollywood, I would be ashamed to take as long getting ready for the show ring as they take to stand in front of a camera for a few minutes."

The epic tale of a Texas cattle-ranch operation, *Giant* was adapted from the novel by Edna Ferber (whose best-selling book *Cimarron* formed the basis for two similarly sprawling movies about early Oklahoma) and released with much ballyhoo by Warner Bros. in 1956. Audiences responded by making it a box office hit, and the industry gave Stevens an Academy Award for Best Director. The film's nine other Oscar nominations included Best Picture, Best Leading Actor (for both Hudson and Dean), and Best Supporting Actor (Mercedes McCambridge). King Tut, however, was passed over in the balloting.

Perhaps his owners took some consolation in a proposed television pilot that was partially shot at their ranch around the same time, after Tut's *Giant* appearance apparently piqued the interest of the Southern California–based producer-director Harry Donahue. The name of the projected series has been lost to history, but there was a working title for the pilot episode. It was revealed by scriptwriter Ed Erwin, who also had a minor career going as an actor at the time, in a rather breathless interview with journalist Jim Downing, published in the November 5, 1956, issue of the *Tulsa Tribune*:

> "This is going to be a modern story, a sort of a western, but no shooting and—so far—only one horse," explained Erwin.
> "It's been called 'The Blue Ribbon Hijack,' and it's about a prize bull—one of Pope's—being taken to the Fort Worth livestock show and it is hijacked by a Mexican or a South American or a—well, you'd better say a Latin American—who has been trying to buy it so he can start a herd of Branguses himself but they don't want to sell the bull, so he enlists a girl—that's Jan Young—to pretend her car is wrecked on the highway—we got the Highway Patrol's permission to do that—and Jim Davis, he's the foreman who's taking the bull to Fort Worth—he stops and offers to help her and she sticks a gun in his ribs and she and the, well, the Latin American—that's Bob Tafur—and Bill Hale—he's a heavy—they go off with the bull. . . .
> ". . . [T]hey leave Jim stranded by the side of the road and afoot and

along comes a ranch kid on a horse and Jim talks him out of the horse and he rides off after the bull and catches them and overcomes them and saves the bull and that's the story."

The actors mentioned by Erwin were all bona fide working pros, beginning with hero Davis, a veteran movie actor known best for his cowboy roles. In the 1954–55 television show *Stories of the Century*, he'd starred as Matt Clark, a railroad detective in the Old West. But his most lasting fame would come in a much later TV series, the long-lived *Dallas* (1978–91), in which he played patriarch Jock Ewing. Davis died in 1981, when the series was well on its way to becoming a national phenomenon. Although ingénue Jan Young doesn't seem to have had much of a career, Bill Hale (brother of cowboy-movie star Monte Hale) and Bob Tafur were both busy character actors, mostly on television, with the latter usually playing Hispanic roles, as he did in "The Blue Ribbon Hijack." Billy Coppedge and Ray Pope's son Walter "Buckshot" Pope also had small parts in the pilot, as did several other Vinitans.

The plan, according to an October 8 *Tulsa World* article that quoted producer Harry Donahue, was to shoot exteriors for the thirty-nine episodes in and around the Pope ranch and do everything else back in Hollywood. Given Erwin's synopsis of the pilot, it's hard to imagine thirty-eight more half-hour episodes coming out of that premise. Life on a modern-day Oklahoma cattle ranch could indeed be the source of compelling stories, but that in itself wouldn't be enough to hang a whole series on. There had to be something more—a hook, created by a strong lead character or something unusual about the ranch itself. For a series to succeed, it had to be special in some way. Maybe this one would have been, but it's not apparent from the existing evidence.

Perhaps the hook wasn't apparent to potential sponsors either. While Sarchet's *Sunday Oklahoman* piece stated that the shows were "being produced for a feed company" and the October 8 *World* article relayed producer Donahue's prediction that "the TV series should be completed and ready for showing on a national network by early in 1957," Vinita's time in the Hollywood sun began and ended with a forgotten pilot that was, if nothing else, full of bull.

"They went broke and didn't finish the movie," said former Clear View

Ranch herdsman Billy Coppedge in a recent telephone conversation from his Las Vegas home. "They shot one or two scenes at the ranch, and then it went kaput.

"We had a little old shack up there, and they shot a scene with a woman in a long skirt outside that shack, washing clothes in a washtub," he added. "I remember Jim Davis came up and talked to her. That's the only scene I got to see. They went back to Hollywood, and then they called and said they were out of money. And that was it."

Now and again during the '50s and '60s, local semipro aggregations, like Oklahoma City's Slipshod Productions, Inc., would attract some press attention. A June 8, 1958, *Sunday Oklahoman* piece by Joe Looney chronicled the story of Slipshod, which appeared to have been a way for a bunch of local television personnel and their pals to shoot off guns and otherwise have some fun away from work. The group, including a TV copywriter named Barbara Powell and local-station cameraman Ernie Crisp, shot several comedic westerns that included *11:59 A.M.* (a parody of *High Noon*) and *A Close Shave*, which spoofed the then hugely popular TV series *Gunsmoke*. It was filmed at Oklahoma City's Frontier City amusement park.

"Slipshod is a non-profit corporation," noted Looney. "Crisp said films are available to church or civic groups strictly for entertainment. There's a small fee, 'to pay for the film for the next movie.'"

Slipshod lasted at least four years before it, like the western-movie characters it parodied, rode off into the sunset.

Following the filming with Jim Davis at Vinita's Clear View Ranch in '56, no other name actors took the trip from Hollywood to the Sooner State for moviemaking purposes for several years. About as close as Oklahoma got was on November 30 and December 1 of 1960, when film luminaries Glenn Ford, Anne Baxter, and Maria Schell made a two-day visit to Oklahoma City to lend star power to the festivities surrounding the world premiere of the second film version of *Cimarron*. (Like the movie *Oklahoma!* however, *Cimarron* had been shot in Arizona.)

Several months earlier, a July 26 *Tulsa Tribune* story had announced that actor Michael Ansara was on his way to the state to star in another picture, albeit a smaller one than *Cimarron*, that was also based on a novel. The proposed picture, *Indian Paint*, had as its source Glenn Balch's 1942 juvenile-adventure book of the same name. Ansara, then most famous for playing the Apache chief Cochise in the TV series *Broken Arrow* (1956–58), told the unnamed reporter that he was eager to get to Oklahoma—where shooting was to take place at Altus, Lawton, and various Osage County locations beginning in early August. Said Ansara, "I'm really getting excited about it. I love Oklahoma—been there many times. I was at a rodeo in Lawton and made a personal appearance at Okmulgee and I was at some park in Oklahoma City once. Went through Tulsa on the way to Fort Smith one time."

For all his eagerness, Ansara apparently never appeared in any footage for *Indian Paint*—in Oklahoma or anywhere else. Despite the plans of producers Oscar Nichols and Bob Callahan and their Oklahoma Films Corporation, whose stock was publicly offered, *Indian Paint* didn't get made for several years, and when it did, it wasn't filmed in the Sooner State. In 1965, when the picture finally hit the nation's screens, its production company had been changed to Eagle American, its location to Texas, and its lead to Jay Silverheels, well known as Tonto in TV's *The Lone Ranger*. Another familiar television presence, young Johnny Crawford (Mark McCain on *The Rifleman*, which aired from 1958 to 1963), costarred as the Native American lad who owned the titular horse. The only major holdover from the previously announced Oklahoma version was the coproducer, then going by the name Robert L. Callahan.

Although the movie horse that portrayed Indian Paint never ran on Oklahoma soil, a dog named London did. In winter of 1960 the photogenic German shepherd came to Tulsa after starring in two films: 1958's *The Littlest Hobo*, released by Allied Artists, and 1960's *My Dog, Buddy*, brought to the screen by McLendon Radio Pictures, the short-lived company headed by Dallas-based radio mogul Gordon McLendon. A few months after the latter movie's summer release, London was in Tulsa with

London (or a stand-in) and Marcia Becton in 1961's *Just between Us*.
(Courtesy Marcia Becton Wright and *Oklahoma Magazine*)

his owner, Chuck Eisenmann, to shoot a third picture, *Just between Us*. A former minor-league pitcher of some standing (he'd played for the Tulsa Oilers in '46 and '51), Eisenmann had gained even more fame as a dog trainer. His unorthodox methods produced some startling results, as musician and writer Jim Downing recalled recently. Downing's father, who went by the same name (Downing refers to him as "Dauntless"), was a popular columnist for the *Tulsa Tribune*.

"Dauntless brought [Eisenmann] home, and his dogs understood conventional English," remembered Downing. "It was astounding. London had two stand-ins named Toro and Thorn. Toro responded to English and German commands, Thorn only German. These dogs understood very abstract commands: 'London, get me something to cover a typewriter.' London went to Dad's bookcase [at the *Trib*] and pulled out the typewriter cover. 'Now put it where it belongs.' London laid it on the typewriter!"

In a separate interview, Bill Pitcock IV, whose orchestra-leader father played one of the dogcatchers, added, "Chuck Eisenmann had a thing about training his dogs to be intellectuals. He would come into a room, introduce the dogs to everyone, wait about fifteen minutes, and then say, 'Toro, take the phone and bring it to Billy.' And he would."

For *Just between Us*, producer-writer Eisenmann devised a screenplay in which a young girl (played by Marcia Becton) rescues London from a couple of dogcatchers (Billy Pitcock and David Sipes) and, in order to raise the three dollars necessary to buy him a license and thus make him street legal, starts a dog-sitting business. She and London end up with six charges of varying breeds, and while she's off rounding up a lunch, all the dogs but London split. The rest of the film deals with the girl and her dog, as they hunt down the runaways through the likes of the Tulsa Zoo, the Tulsa Christmas parade, and even the grounds of Oklahoma Military Academy in nearby Claremore—where, according to the senior Downing's column of June 5, 1961, "there's one thigh-slapping scene where he [London] actually goes through the calisthenics with cadets."

The film was cast with local actors and was apparently made with Tulsa money as well. In the above-mentioned *Tribune* column, Downing wrote that the film was "financed by a Tulsa combine, headed by Robert J. Farris, attorney, who is listed in the credits as executive producer."

"He was the financial guy," affirmed star Marcia Becton Wright in a recent interview. "He would come and watch the filming."

Becton was eight years old when Eisenmann came to town and began contacting local dance studios to find a suitable young lead. "I did a lot of dancing, and I was always in a lot of numbers in the recitals and that kind of stuff," she recalled. "I'd been the University of Tulsa's mascot for two years, twirling the baton at halftime with the TU band, and the girl who'd been mascot before me danced at the same studio. So our teacher sent us both from her studio, along with maybe a couple of other girls, and there were about one hundred fifty to two hundred girls [at the audition]."

The local players included one who'd go on to considerable show-biz fame—future TV and Broadway star Rue McClanahan, a Healdton native who'd grown up in Ardmore and graduated cum laude from the University of Tulsa with a double major of German and drama. At the time of the Tulsa shoot, she'd done some theater work back East, but she hadn't performed in many films. *Just between Us* may have been her first picture.

For the audition, Wright recalled, she had to do a scene at the breakfast table with McClanahan, who was cast as the little girl's mother. According to both Wright and Pitcock, the future *Golden Girls* star doubled as the film's makeup artist as well. She may also have been instrumental in getting the director, John Patrick Hayes, onto the set. An IMDb.com entry claims that he "proposed marriage to a 20-something Rue McClanahan after they were together for 4 years, but she turned him down"; he would direct three other early '60s pictures featuring McClanahan, on his way to a long career in independent and exploitation films.

Just between Us was scored by Ronald Stein. Like Hayes, Stein would make his mark in low-budget pictures, including London's earlier starring effort, *The Littlest Hobo*. Stein's other work includes such well-remembered B and Z pictures as *Zontar—the Thing from Venus*, *Spider Baby*, *The Terror*, and *Psych-Out*.

The budget couldn't have been much on *Just between Us*, either—or, if it was, the lead human in the film didn't see much of it. "They were all real sweet dogs," said Wright, recalling London and his two stand-ins, "but I wore my own clothes for the movie, and they tore holes in the sleeve of my coat. Then, in one scene, I'd taken off my belt to use as a collar for the dog, and it had gotten cracked. And I had also used my shoe, one time, to give all the dogs some milk, which had kind of ruined it.

"So they gave me a check for a hundred dollars after it was all over, to go buy a new coat, belt, and shoes. And that was *it*," she added. "That's all I got paid."

The film debuted at Tulsa's Premiere Theatre and Airview Drive-In on July 26, 1961. The elder Downing, who'd seen the movie via an invitation-only screening some six weeks earlier, wrote:

Friends, this is one of the funniest, cleanest family pictures since *The Shaggy Dog* and I am not kidding. Also, I am not prejudiced. There are glaring deficiencies in the filming and in the acting in spots—murky photography and self-conscious amateur actors don't help it along—but overall it is a winner.

The title is poor because it just doesn't suggest the hilarity of the picture. I'd call it *And the Dogs Ran off in Every Direction* or some such. Because that's exactly what happens.

Despite the columnist's endorsement—or, perhaps, because of the flaws he cited—*Just between Us* did not pick up a major distributor, so it's unclear how many more bookings the film received. No matter how many there were, however, it would've been hard to beat the first one, which featured not only a special live performance by London prior to the screening but also, a day earlier, an incredible stunt from one of Eisenmann's canines. The July 24 *Tribune* described it all in a three-paragraph announcement:

> What is believed to be the first civilian dog parachute jump in history will come off at 7:15 A.M. Tuesday at Harvey Young Airport, 1500 S. 135th E. Ave.
>
> London, dog star of the Tulsa-made movie *Just Between Us*, which will have its world premiere here Wednesday, will attempt to jump from a small plane at about 2,000 feet.
>
> Chuck Eisenmann, the dog's trainer, said that if wind conditions are wrong for London's weight, the star's son, Lance, who was flown in from Hollywood Monday, will make the jump.

The *Tribune*'s Downing was there for the stunt, reporting in a July 26 column that it was indeed "Lance, the Parapup" who parachuted from the plane. Downing's son saw it all as well and still remembered it nearly fifty years later.

"Sadly," said Downing, "the dog could not control the parachute and he landed in a frog pond just west of the airstrip. This was a commercial frog operation and said pond was surrounded by a fence, actually a wall, of vertical corrugated sheet metal, which I recall was eight feet high. When we saw that [the dog] was landing on the other side of the wall, Chuck made a flying run at it and leapt. He actually got hold of the top of the wall and pulled himself up and over. Dauntless was very impressed [and said]: 'He loves that dog. That's his bread and butter. I never would've thought anyone could climb over that!'"

Lance's jump was, of course, not part of the on-screen action in *Just between Us*, which had wrapped months earlier. But it may have been filmed, and if so, some of the sequence may have shown up later in the Canadian television series *The Littlest Hobo,* which also starred London (although, like Lassie, there was more than one dog actor with that name). Based on the 1958 feature, a black-and-white TV series (which recycled the *Just between Us* plot into a two-part episode called "The Five Labors of Hercules") ran from 1963 to 1965, and a color series from 1979 to 1985. The background footage running under the credits for the first series featured shots of a parachuting dog.

Apparently, however, the encounter with the frog pond soured Eisenmann on any further four-legged paratroopers. "In the series shot in colour in Toronto, there was an episode titled 'Smoke' starring Monte Markham, in which the Hobo dog allegedly parachuted from an airplane to deliver some life-saving medicine," recalled Simon Christopher Dew, supervising producer of the second *Littlest Hobo* series, in recent e-mail correspondence. "I say 'allegedly' because Chuck insisted on using a dummy dog for the airborne stunt. And a good thing too because not unlike the incident you relate, the 'dog' was carried far off-course and landed in the middle of a cornfield. Needless to say the farmer was less than amused when 4 large prop guys raced onto his property to 'rescue' their dummy dog which had carved quite a swath through his ripe and ready corn."

As the '60s drew to a close, with the old studio system disintegrating and Hollywood decentralizing, lots of theatrical films were being shot in places other than Southern California. They were not, however, being shot in Oklahoma. Since the video technology that put moviemaking capabilities in the hands of just about anyone was still a couple of decades away, there weren't many student or experimental films launched in the state either.

But there were a few. Tulsa entertainment historian Mike Ransom, the man behind the impressive TulsaTVMemories.com website, has run down a few Tulsa-lensed narrative movies from that period, including one called *Violin Man* (circa 1970). It featured Armin Sebran as a wild-looking street violinist traveling among Tulsa's disenfranchised. (The character was the prototype for Sebran's Yahootie Menu, a regular on the fondly remembered late-night Tulsa TV show, *The Uncanny Film Festival and Camp Meeting*, featuring future Hollywood character player Gailard Sartain and writer-performer Jim Millaway, with another future movie star, Gary Busey, coming along later in the show's two-year run.)

Director-photographer Paul Stevenson recently recalled the shooting of *Violin Man*:

> Armin and I spent many days wandering around "skid row," he in full beard and wild hair with a tailcoat and violin, me with a sixteen-millimeter camera. I suspect that since we looked so odd, the "ragged people"—Paul Simon called them—accepted us. We had many long conversations with alcoholics, prostitutes, and the other invisible people who inhabit our cities. We heard many life stories—the Native American veteran, "My grandfather hunted buffalo here!"—that echoed in our dreams and somehow ended up forming the tone of the movie.
>
> It is a series of scenes of the violin man wandering the streets of the inner city, playing his violin, and, to me, [it]echoed the sadness but also the persistence of the lives we experienced. The violin man as he evolved is an odd mix of Marc Chagall, Charlie Chaplin, *Waiting for Godot* (which I was trying to read in French), the people we met, and many other influences.

A couple of years earlier, University of Tulsa graduate Dale Pelton, a philosophy major who'd spent some time around the City Lights bookstore's beatnik scene in San Francisco and had run his own Tulsa-based coffeehouse, debuted a forty-five-minute feature called *A Season of Visions, A Dwelling of Mine*. Written, directed, and coproduced by Pelton, it had its only public showing at the Tulsa Public Library's Aaronson Auditorium on August 28, 1968. Like the later *Violin Man*, it was shot without sound, and a music track was added later.

"I found this guitarist [Steve Trosberg] who'd come into town from God knows where, and we recorded him at All Souls Unitarian Church," remembered Pelton recently. "That was our music track. It was almost like a music video, with no dialogue."

A press release announcing the premiere explained that *Season* told of "twelve hours in the life of a forty year old man who finds aimlessness and small pleasures, beauty and agony as he wanders the corridors and haunts of a small Midwestern town." Coproduced by Pelton and his then roommate David Ward, *A Seasons of Visions, A Dwelling of Mine* featured an all-Tulsa cast that included Norman Hawk as the man and Kelsey Bartholic as a girl "of enchanting vigor and beauty, a face and body which teases, entrances and plagues him as the night continues," according to the press material.

"I made it because, first of all, I wanted to make a film, and second, I wanted to get into film school at UCLA or USC, and I needed some credentials," Pelton said. "I hadn't had any actual film classes or anything, and there was a huge amount of people trying to get into those film schools."

The screening of the finished product was sponsored by the University of Tulsa's English department, even though Pelton had long since graduated. "My roommate was a teaching assistant in the English department, and he let me use his Bolex [camera]," Pelton said. "I also got some help from the guy who was the head of the media department, Bill Hayes. But the film had no official connection with TU.

"After that, I showed it to one of my teachers at UCLA, but I never had a formal screening," he added. "It didn't have dialogue; it was overly long. It did have beautiful images and evocative, poetic music. But I didn't show it to anybody else. I haven't seen it myself since 1968."

If nothing else, *Visions* served its purpose by helping Pelton get into UCLA's film school, where, for his master's thesis, he created the groundbreaking *Death of the Red Planet*, which he described as "the first laser-generated film."

"It was in thirty-five-millimeter Cinemascope, with quadraphonic sound, sixteen minutes long, an all-abstract film with laser images and a beautiful avant-garde sound track, with music from the group Yes and organist Rick Wakeman," he said. "It was released in 1973 to over six hundred theaters—it played with features like *Phantom of the Paradise* [1974] and an incredible Czech animated film called *Fantastic Planet* [1973]."

Visions also brought its creator into contact with another beginning Tulsa moviemaker, one who would earn both praise and criticism for his studies of seriously wayward youth, notably 1995's *Kids*. "Back then, the cameras were very heavy, and there was a rig to help you carry the equipment while you were filming," recalled Pelton. "Larry Clark was making a film in Tulsa about gangs, and while he was doing an interview with a criminal, the police came in and busted the guy. I saw a story in the *Tribune* about it, and I thought, 'Here's a fellow filmmaker.' So I called him up, and he lent me the rig to carry the camera for *my* film."

Although Pelton ultimately became a successful production designer and art director—helping design the spaceship for the original *Battlestar Galactica* TV series and working on such films as 1985's *The Goonies* and 1991's *Doc Hollywood*—he had to go to Hollywood to do it. In the late '60s, when he made *Season*, Hollywood was showing little interest in heading toward Oklahoma, regardless of what talent might exist in the state.

Then, along came a man whose efforts went a long way toward changing all that. He too went to Tinseltown, but he never intended to stay. Instead, his idea was to bring as much of it as he could back to his home state.

George Nigh was a lieutenant governor, not a filmmaker. But he was someone who loved movies and the movie business. And because he was in a position to act on that love, he became the man who threw open the doors to a golden age of Oklahoma filmmaking.

SIX

Hollywood Hippies and Hound Dogs

I know it's a longhair type show, but that's what the kids are going to see nowadays. All our children are looking forward to seeing the movie.

> —Boswell resident Mozell Hampton talking about *Two-Lane Blacktop,* quoted by Doug Hicks in the *Tulsa World* (September 20, 1970)

Where the Red Fern Grows is the movie that put Oklahoma on the map, and the person who drew the map was George Nigh. He was the state official who saw the potential for major filmmaking in Oklahoma.

> —Vern Stefanic, former movie critic for the *Tulsa World*

Filming is a solid, clean industry that boosts the economy of the state without diminishing its natural resources. It leaves the sky clean and the water clear while forty percent of its budget remains in the community.

> —Oklahoma lieutenant governor George Nigh, quoted in the *Tulsa World* (May 9, 1973)

A lot of Hollywood people are laughing and scoffing at what we're trying to do. But it'll just take one hit to make them stop laughing.

> —G. D. Spradlin, quoted in the *Tulsa World* (June 13, 1972)

"A short time back," wrote Jon Denton in the Sunday Oklahoman magazine Showcase from May 21, 1972, "a joke drew chuckles in the Capitol corridors. It went something like: 'George isn't satisfied going to Hollywood. He wants to bring it home.'"

Continued Denton: "George Nigh is laughing now. It is true. Hollywood is coming to Oklahoma. After two years and four movie-seeking jaunts to California, the lieutenant governor is cashing in the door prize."

Perhaps George Nigh's deep interest in bringing show biz to Oklahoma was foreshadowed early in his political career. In 1953, during his tenure as a state representative, the McAlester native introduced the legislation that officially designated Rodgers and Hammerstein's "Oklahoma!" as the theme song for the Sooner State. Five years later, at the age of thirty-one, he became Oklahoma's youngest lieutenant governor.

Nigh, a Democrat, left politics in the early '60s and started a public relations firm. But he didn't stay away from politics for long; in 1966 he was elected to another go-round as the second-highest elected official in the state. He remained lieutenant governor for three consecutive terms, from 1966 to 1978, and then stepped up to governor, becoming the first person to serve two consecutive terms as Oklahoma's chief executive.

It was his second tenure as lieutenant governor, however, that is most germane to the history of moviemaking in Oklahoma. In that office, Nigh's duties included heading up the Oklahoma Industrial Development and Park Commission (the predecessor of the current Oklahoma Tourism and Recreation Commission), and one of the major industries he decided to try to develop in his state was the one based in Hollywood. So, in early 1969, Nigh began traveling westward to confab with studio representatives, especially those who were eyeing potential filming sites outside of Southern California. By the time the year was over, he'd made repeat trips—once, in June, with what was reported in the *Daily Oklahoman* as "a group of 123 state residents" (one wonders if they all traveled together)—and received several promises from film executives to shoot in the state. In a luncheon speech to the Edmond Kiwanis Club in early November of 1969, he even named three movies and the Oklahoma locations their producers planned on using.

But, as movie mogul Samuel Goldwyn once said, "a verbal contract isn't worth the paper it's written on," and nowhere has that been truer than in the movie business. Despite stated commitments from movie people and Nigh's confident announcements, films such as *The Longest Yard*, *Confederate Indians*, and *The Texans*—all of which Nigh had named as upcoming Oklahoma productions in 1969—were either made elsewhere (the 1974 Burt Reynolds starrer *The Longest Yard* in Georgia, South Carolina, Florida, and Hollywood) or not made at all. The never-lensed *Confederate Indians* got the most buzz, not only because it was to involve a couple of top-drawer western moviemakers, producer Richard E. Lyons (*Ride the High Country; Coogan's Bluff*) and director Burt Kennedy (*The War Wagon; Support Your Local Sheriff*), but also because it planned to focus on a famous figure from Oklahoma's history, the Confederate brigadier general Stand Watie, a Cherokee. Kennedy's wife, Sue, was from Jay, further cementing the Oklahoma connection. According to a June 24, 1969, "On with the Show" column by the *Tulsa World*'s Pericles Alexander, both producer and director "swore on a copy of the book, *Confederate Indians*, that the biographical motion picture about Cherokee General Stand Watie would be filmed in northeastern Oklahoma before too many full moons have passed."

But *Confederate Indians*, along with several other proposed features, simply didn't happen for Nigh and his state, and that initial round of fizzled projects must've been disappointing—and probably a little embarrassing—for the lieutenant governor. To his credit, however, he persevered, not only continuing to visit the film capital and cultivate his connections there but ultimately going on location for a day to see for himself how movies were constructed outside of Hollywood soundstages. A *Tulsa World* story from April 26, 1970, by Mike Flanagan told of his accompanying Nigh to a Louisiana plantation where *The Beguiled*, starring Clint Eastwood, was being filmed. The lieutenant governor and Flanagan, along with a second newspaper reporter and a photographer, had flown there in an Oklahoma Highway Patrol plane following an invitation from Claude Traverse, the movie's associate producer and a native of Driftwood, Oklahoma. (Later, Traverse was also attached as associate producer for another scuttled Sooner State project, a film adaptation of Larry McMurtry's novel *Leaving Cheyenne*.)

"Although he denies any ambition even for a bit part," wrote Flanagan of the lieutenant governor, "Nigh admits he will point out 'his' tree to friends who see *Beguiled*. 'See that tree on the right of the gate?' he'll ask. 'I spent all afternoon behind it.'"

Just about five months later, Nigh visited another set and watched another theatrical motion picture being filmed. But this time the experience was sweeter, because it was in his home state. Finally, after all the promises, promotion, and canceled projects, a Hollywood film unit had made it to Oklahoma for real. All his effort had begun to pay off.

On September 4, under the headline "Crew to Shoot Movie in State," an announcement appeared in the *Daily Oklahoman*. It was a small story, but it portended great things:

> The campaign to bring movie making to Oklahoma has achieved its first success, Lt. Gov. George Nigh said Thursday.
>
> He said that Boswell in Bryan County will be the on-location site for a new movie, *Two-Lane Blacktop*, to be released by Universal Pictures.
>
> Nigh said a crew of 45 will arrive in Durant from Hollywood Sept. 14 for 10 days of shooting. Stars of the film will be James Taylor, Lori Bird and Warren Oates. Director will be Monte Hellman.

A day earlier, an unbylined *Tulsa Tribune* piece had noted that it had all started during one of Nigh's visits to California in the summer of '69. The lieutenant governor was quoted as saying, "Hundreds of small towns are suitable for making this film. Oklahoma was chosen because we went after it and then responded in the right way when they came to look us over." And so the new era of Oklahoma filmmaking began, thanks in great part to a lieutenant governor who wouldn't give up.

In fact, it wasn't just a new era in *Oklahoma* filmmaking. It was a new era in filmmaking itself. Hollywood's old self-censorship barriers, guarded zealously by the Production Code Administration, had begun weakening many years earlier, and the changing social mores reflected in America's movies had made the old taboos not only quaint but also unenforceable. (The Catholic Church–affiliated Legion of Decency also continued losing influence with filmgoers, although it didn't officially expire until 1980.) In 1968 the Production Code was scrapped by the Motion Picture Association of America, replaced with a four-level rating system of G (general audiences), M (mature audiences), R (restricted, with those under seventeen admitted only with a parent or adult guardian), and X (no one under seventeen admitted).

The year after the MPAA ratings system came into being, a low-budget little movie called *Easy Rider* reshaped the cinematic landscape, as Hollywood suddenly discovered the baby-boomer appetite for films about disaffected young people coming of age in modern America, surrounded by sex and drugs. *Easy Rider*'s hippified existentialism had coined box office gold for the film's counterculture-savvy creators Dennis Hopper and Peter Fonda. Hoping to duplicate their success, studio heads green-lighted project after project brought in by intense-looking longhairs hoping to paint their own visions of reality on the canvas of the big screen.

Out of that environment came Universal Pictures' *Two-Lane Blacktop*, whose cast and crew began filming in the southern Oklahoma town of Boswell (with a population of just over 750 at the time) on September 16, 1970. In an article for the *Oklahoma Journal* newspaper published six days later, Skip Largent wrote about the film and its youth-culture predecessors:

> *Two Lane Blacktop* is a child of the recent germination of small-budget quality movies. Its parenthood can be traced to such low cost successes as *David and Lisa* and *Easy Rider*.
>
> A glance at the synopsis of the film suggests similarities to the recent Dennis Hopper shocker, but [director Monte] Hellman denies any resemblances the script may have to *Easy Rider*.
>
> "The film is like *Easy Rider*, only in the sense that it deals with young people in the movie. It is really a traditional love story told in today's terms."

Two-Lane Blacktop saw two figures from the world of pop music make their dramatic-feature debuts as a pair of detached hot-rodders from L.A., driving their souped-up '55 Chevy across America. Balladeer James Taylor played a character known simply as the Driver, while Beach Boys drummer and vocalist Dennis Wilson was the Mechanic. Along the way, they pick up the Girl (Lori Bird, another movie newcomer, then only seventeen years old) and get into a cross-country race with the driver of an orange Pontiac GTO (Warren Oates).

It was definitely, as Boswell's Mozell Hampton put it in the epigraph at the beginning of this chapter, a "longhair type show," and in 1970 long-haired hippie boys were still looked upon with disfavor in many rural areas of the country, including much of small-town Oklahoma. Still, reports at the time indicate that the citizens of Bryan County and the "amiable, hippie-appearing longhairs"—as the film crew was described by reporter Doug Hicks in a September 20 on-the-scene *Tulsa World* story headlined "Longhair Hollywood Group Putting Oklahoma in Movie"—got along swimmingly. Hicks described a couple of old guys warbling the line "They're gonna put me in the movies" from Buck Owens's hit country tune "Act Naturally" while they watched the crew. Hicks further noted: "Highway Patrol troopers J. R. Jones and Don Langley have remained on location through the week, assisting in roadblocks and leading the 'parade' when high speed runs are made on the two-lane highways exiting the town." About the only jarring scene in Hicks's piece occurred when Bird "failed to properly use the clutch in the Chevy parked just outside town." Reported Hicks: "'Oh . . . it,' she yelled, pounding on the steering wheel. 'I . . . can't do it.'"

After its week-plus in Boswell, the outfit pulled up stakes and headed for other locations, reflecting the cross-country nature of the story. A UPI report dated September 16 quoted location manager Steve Henschel, then in Boswell: "We started in Los Angeles, went to Needles, Calif., Flagstaff, Ariz., Santa Fe [and] Tucumcari, N.M., and now here." Additional filming was to take place in Arkansas, Tennessee, and North Carolina.

Unlike many youth-oriented films of its time, *Two-Lane Blacktop* has aged well. Although *Esquire* magazine had proclaimed it the movie of the year, reprinting the minimalist script (by Rudolph Wurlitzer and Will Corry) in its April 1971 issue, and the picture got some decent if not overwhelmingly positive notices elsewhere, any hopes Universal had for approaching the box office take of *Easy Rider* were quickly scotched. *Two-Lane Blacktop* lived on, however, accruing an increasingly more stellar reputation. In a piece done for a July 2008 screening of the film in Austin, Texas (reproduced on the Alamo Drafthouse Cinema site at blog. originalalamo.com), noted director Richard Linklater called it, simply, "the purest American road movie ever."

Two-Lane Blacktop was not the only picture shot in Oklahoma that year—or even that month. Almost surreptitiously—especially when compared with the interest stirred up by the film crew's activities in Boswell—another movie was being shot 125 miles due north, in the hills southeast of Checotah, beginning at roughly the same time. And strangely enough, George Nigh wasn't involved.

"I don't think we had anything to do at all with any state lawmakers of any sort," said Herschell Gordon Lewis recently, reminiscing about his Oklahoma-lensed picture, *This Stuff'll Kill Ya!* (1971). "Our relationships were purely local. In most cases, we just went out and shot. Nobody gave us any trouble."

It wasn't that George Nigh, given the chance, wouldn't have welcomed Lewis's bunch to the state. In fact, after the picture was done, he would cite it as one of the examples of early '70s Oklahoma moviemaking. It's just that Lewis and his Chicago-based Ultima Productions, Inc., flew well under Hollywood's radar, and Hollywood was where George Nigh was looking.

Today Herschell Gordon Lewis has a wide following among fans of horror and exploitation cinema. Aficionados affectionately know him as the Godfather of Gore, thanks in part to the taboo-breaking, over-the-top horror films *Blood Feast* (1963) and *Two Thousand Maniacs!* (1964) he created with his then-partner, producer David F. Friedman. An erudite former English professor and current marketing and advertising specialist, Lewis continued for years to specialize in films featuring extreme gore effects, which—prior to the advent of home video—were viewed mainly by audiences in inner-city grind houses and less discriminating drive-ins. A clue to Lewis's thoughts about his oeuvre can be found in a quote he gave interviewers Todd McCarthy and Charles Flynn for their book *Kings of the Bs* (1975): "*Blood Feast* I've often referred to as a Walt Whitman poem—it's no good, but it's the first of its type and therefore deserves a certain position."

While *This Stuff'll Kill Ya!* isn't exactly a gore film, it does feature some of the money-shot scenes Lewis fans have come to expect. A *Tulsa World* story from October 1, 1970, hinted at one of them, noting, "The company spent most of the morning Wednesday trying to perfect a scene in

Newspaper ad from 1971. (John Wooley Archives)

which a dummy's head is blown off, simulating the death of a character in the film."

The film also depicts a graphic stoning, a double crucifixion, and a charred corpse. There's also a rather squirm-inducing, albeit implied, scene involving several men and a young bride in a church, whose preacher (Lewis regular Jeffrey Allen) and congregation are all fueled by illegal moonshine, and plenty of it. The film was classified GP, which had

Larry Drake (second from right) and Jeffrey Allen (far right) enjoy some down-home honeymoonin' in *This Stuff'll Kill Ya!* (Courtesy of the James Edwards Collection)

taken the place of the MPAA's M rating in 1970 (and would become PG in 1972).

Lewis had worked the same kind of cinematic turf before with 1964's *Moonshine Mountain*, which had turned out to be a highly successful picture for him and his company. (Noted Lewis: "*This Stuff'll Kill Ya!* might be considered the illegitimate child of *Moonshine Mountain*.") But that picture had been shot in South Carolina; the Chicago-based Lewis had never made a movie in Oklahoma until *This Stuff*. He did, however, have some experience in Oklahoma's entertainment industry. And that's what ultimately led him back to the state.

"Some years before, I had been a producer-director at WKY [television station] in Oklahoma City," explained Lewis, "and one of the shows I'd handled there was called *The Chuck Wagon Boys*. The Chuck Wagon Boys were three musicians, just nice guys. One was named Julian Aiken, one was Willie Wells, and the third was Jack Beasley. They'd had a fairly successful daytime TV show in which they played guitars and string bass and sang country and western songs.

"I had stayed loosely in touch with Jack Beasley, who'd started a radio station in Oklahoma City called KJAK. And he invited me to come down there and shoot this movie. I accepted with alacrity because, first of all, I had some familiarity with Oklahoma City, having been in the control room there; and second, he said that his radio station had a fairly big studio, and we could shoot a lot of scenes inside it. Also, he would help cast the thing. So for me it was a no-brainer, and off we went."

Although some of the picture was shot in Beasley's studio, most of the film was done in and around Checotah, about 120 miles east of Oklahoma City. The former Chuck Wagon Boy also assisted Lewis by recruiting several cast members from the University of Oklahoma drama department. Those student actors included Tulsa native Larry Drake, whose portrayal of a dull-witted hillbilly named Bubba launched a long career that would bring him, among other things, a couple of Emmys for his work on the TV series *L.A. Law*.

While Drake was at the very beginning of his film career, another one of the film's stars was on his final go-round. *This Stuff'll Kill Ya!* was the last of several dozen movie credits for Tim Holt, a bona fide star of B westerns who occasionally acquitted himself well in major pictures, notably the 1948 classic *The Treasure of Sierra Madre*. Following the demise of his series of western movies (the last was made in 1952), Holt had been able to amass only a handful of credits, and he was working an advertising job in Oklahoma City when Lewis and his Ultima cohorts hit town.

"I had an assistant named Alex Ameripoor, whose real first name was Eskandar, and he was convinced that the best movie anybody had ever made was *Treasure of Sierra Madre*, with Humphrey Bogart, Walter Huston, and a rising young star of the time named Tim Holt," remembered Lewis. "Alex, in fact, was such a fanatic about *Treasure of Sierra Madre* that he carried a sixteen-millimeter print of the movie with him. So here we come into Oklahoma City, and who was selling radio time for KJAK? Tim Holt. And Tim Holt, of course, by that time had aged considerably and was somewhat long in the tooth, but nothing would do but that we put him in this movie—which, of course, I was delighted to do."

Working with the Iranian-born Ameripoor as the film's director of photography (under the *nom de cinéma* of Eskandar Ameri), Holt got special billing as a Secret Service agent named Clark, who matches wits with the preacher and his moonshine-loving cohorts. "It was quite obvious, in the handful of scenes in which Tim Holt was present, the guy was still a *total* professional," noted Lewis. "He still had the voice, he knew his lines, and he really set a pace for the other people on the set. So that was truly a pleasure."

Produced, directed, and written by Lewis under the working title of *The Devil Wears Clodhoppers, This Stuff'll Kill Ya!*—according to the *World* article—used a lake cabin owned by Checotah's Newell Smith for a major set and cast the town's chief of police, Jess Frazier, in the picture, along with patrolman Ron Beaver and McIntosh County deputy sheriff Dalton Turner. "We had one scene where we had to burn a car, and the police knew what we were going to do, and there was no objection whatsoever," said Lewis. "They helped put out the fire, and then they towed that car away someplace. I said, 'Get rid of it,' and they said, 'Delighted.' So we had total cooperation."

Those who see the picture today may notice a scene-transition technique used extensively in the popular TV series *The Dukes of Hazzard* (1979–85). In that series, viewers saw only the hands, and never the face, of country artist Waylon Jennings as he strummed his guitar. It was a shot used again and again, with variations, as a bridge between scenes—the same kind of shot on display in *This Stuff'll Kill Ya!*, with the hands on the guitar belonging to Lewis's son Bob. The filmmaker believes he was the first to use it and doesn't think it impossible that it was seen and copied by someone with *The Dukes of Hazzard*.

"It became a popular technique, and I'd like to take credit for that, although people will say, 'Well, your picture was too offbeat for anyone to have even seen it.'—which is possible too."

Speaking of guitars and music . . . Throughout most of the '60s, Oklahoma native Leon Russell had been busy building up a stellar reputation in the West Coast music industry as a session player, arranger, and songwriter. By 1970 he'd started making some noise as a solo artist as well. Moving back to Tulsa, where he'd grown up, he established Shelter Records with his partner, British producer Denny Cordell, and made his Oklahoma hometown—at least for a few golden moments—one of the world's crossroads of rock.

Among Russell's notable accomplishments in the early '70s was assembling and leading the band that backed vocalist Joe Cocker on his hugely successful Mad Dogs and Englishmen tour (with the name, taken from a 1930s Noel Coward song, intended to reflect the composition of the band.) The group itself was huge, sporting, among other musicians, three drummers and a chorus of ten vocalists; its full-throttle performances in such cities as Detroit, Dallas, San Francisco, and New York were chronicled in the MGM documentary *Mad Dogs and Englishmen*, released in 1971.

The film is an engaging and sometimes dizzying rock 'n' roll spectacle, with Russell's charisma at its absolute peak. Although the whiskey-throated, twitchy Cocker is the star attraction, Russell and his handpicked group—including several top Tulsa rockers as well as a pre-star Rita Coolidge—command the viewer's attention on at least an equal basis.

Several offstage scenes for *Mad Dogs and Englishmen* were shot in Tulsa by director Pierre Adidge (who did another highly regarded music documentary, *Elvis on Tour*, soon afterwards). They do much to reinforce the notion that, thanks to Russell and his influence in the industry, Tulsa was a very cool place to be in the early '70s.

Universal reissued *Mad Dogs and Englishmen* on DVD in 2005, and it remains readily available. Not so a second Russell-based documentary, *A Poem Is a Naked Person* (1974), shot between 1972 and 1974 by noted documentarian Les Blank, perhaps best known for his 1982 treatment of filmmaker Werner Herzog, *Burden of Dreams*.

Sources indicate that Blank lived at Russell's recording-studio complex on Grand Lake O' The Cherokees, about ninety miles northeast of Tulsa, while making the feature-length picture. Sometime after the filming, however, there was apparently a dispute between Russell and Blank that led to legal action. Blank's website (www.lesblank.com) explains it this way: "According to Les's contract, he is legally able to show his own

16 mm print if personally presenting it and a non-profit organization is sponsoring the showing."

Although *A Poem Is a Naked Person* allegedly received theatrical distribution through the Blank-affiliated Flower Films, it's unclear if there was ever a for-profit showing. The few who *have* been able to see it tell of some fascinating footage featuring Russell and country star George Jones in a laid-back mood, as well as bizarre scenes involving animals—for instance, a sequence in which a young man traps scorpions on the walls of Russell's empty swimming pool, and another in which a baby chick is fed to a snake.

At this writing, *A Poem Is a Naked Person* remains available only through showings by the filmmaker, under the conditions listed above. Rumors continue to surface about other prints being available, but the documentary remains one of the most notable unreleased rock movies of its era.

By mid-1972, Oklahoma's share of the film business was expanding nicely, as Jon Denton affirmed in the *Showcase* magazine article quoted at the beginning of this chapter. Under the title "Nigh's Movie Industry Wooing Pays Off," Denton summed up the lieutenant governor's "batting average" by noting he had "six hits, one of them a homerun." That half dozen included *Two-Lane Blacktop* ("Some reviewers gave it excellent billing as a protest product") and *This Stuff'll Kill Ya!* ("It's strictly drive-in theater fare"), along with an ABC-TV documentary "about land settlement and frontier pioneers" shot under the title *Getting There First*. (Intended as a U.S. centennial offering, it never aired under that title, and it's not certain that it was broadcast at all.)

The remaining three were all theatrical pictures, including the one Denton must have considered the home run, Cliff Robertson's *J. W. Coop*. Robertson was making the climb from TV to movie stardom at the time, boosted by his Academy Award–winning turn as the mentally challenged subject of an IQ-increasing experiment in 1968's *Charly*, based on Daniel Keyes novel *Flowers for Algernon*. *J. W. Coop*—known simply as *J. W.* during its filming—was Robertson's baby all the way, his first stab at producing and directing (as well as starring in and cowriting) a theatrical feature.

Sad and downbeat, it told the story of an imprisoned cowboy who keeps his chops up by riding in prison rodeos, where he earns something of a reputation. Upon his release, however, he finds that the society around him has changed, and his attempts to cope with those changes and reestablish himself on the outside forms the crux of the film—which, with its alienated, wandering protagonist and a laid-back, near-documentary style, had something in common with *Two-Lane Blacktop* and other films in the then popular youth-culture mode.

J. W. Coop was released by Columbia Pictures on January 1, 1972, with an official world premiere held twenty days earlier at the Westwood Theater in Oklahoma City. Lieutenant Governor Nigh and Governor David Hall hosted the premiere, with participants in the National Finals Rodeo (then held annually in Oklahoma City) on hand for the festivities as well.

In the summer of 1971, Robertson and his film outfit had visited the Oklahoma State Penitentiary in McAlester for several days of shooting— a December 2, 1971, *Tulsa World* story told readers that "the prison scenes and some rodeo footage" were shot there. An L.A. native, Robertson owned a horse ranch in Yukon, which may have played a part in his decision to film in the state.

At the premiere, wrote Denton, Robertson said "he felt Oklahoma had plenty of 'elbow room.'" Robertson added, "This is very conducive to movie making. There is a great range of topography in the state, too. . . . We also found excellent cooperation here."

An Associated Press story, datelined McAlester and dated July 12, 1971, just after Robertson had finished his work at the penitentiary, reinforced that positive assessment:

> A Hollywood movie producer and director had nice things to say about Oklahoma as he left the state prison here after filming a motion picture.
> Cliff Robertson, who wrote, produced, directed and starred in the movie *J. W.* said if the rest of Oklahoma was like McAlester, not only would he return, but he would encourage other film companies to do location shooting here.

Interestingly enough, that endorsement followed a UPI article from three months earlier that did nothing at all to encourage filmmakers to visit the state. That article, published on April 16, quoted Twentieth

Century-Fox art director Joel Schiller as saying that Oklahoma was "dirty and down and depressing and full of junk cars everywhere." Schiller was, according to the story, "looking for a 'relatively untouched town of the 1926 period that has charm'" and had in fact found three in Kansas—after spending "several weeks" unfruitfully searching for that kind of a place in Oklahoma. "'In comparison [with Oklahoma],' he said, 'Kansas is gorgeous. It was a shock to me. Like 10 miles away across the state border it's completely different. There must be a wholly different kind of temperament in the two states.'"

The art director had been scouting locations for a period picture about a stunt pilot and his son that ended up being called *Ace Eli and Rodger of the Skies*. Released in 1973, it did not do well at the box office and is largely forgotten today. It deserves mention in these pages, however, not because its script was written by a young up-and-comer named Steven Spielberg or because it featured Bernadette Peters in her big-screen debut, but because it starred that booster of Oklahoma location shooting, Cliff Robertson.

In addition to the protagonists of *Two-Lane Blacktop* and *J. W. Coop*, a third batch of alienated and ultimately doomed young characters played out part of their fates in an Oklahoma setting. A quartet of Vietnam vets known as Danny, Shooter, Fatback, and Kid, they were portrayed by four actors early in their careers: Joe Don Baker, Paul Koslo, Elliott Street, and Alan Vint (a Tulsa native who, like his brother Jesse, found steady employment in Hollywood beginning in the late '60s). The characters were the focal points of a film titled *Welcome Home, Soldier Boys* (although it was shot under the title *Five Days Home*) and released by Twentieth Century-Fox in 1972. It would be one of several '70s movies featuring disaffected young veterans unable to understand or readjust to the America they'd left for the killing fields of Vietnam.

The first U.S. war broadcast into the nation's living rooms, the Southeast Asian conflict had split the country into two angry camps, with the antiwar faction drawing deeply from the baby-boomer pool of high school and college-age (and, in the case of the males, draft-age) young people. That huge demographic, chock-full of war protesters, was also the major audience for the wandering-youth film craze begun by *Easy Rider*.

As in *Easy Rider*, the protagonists in *Welcome Home, Soldier Boys* are traveling across America, in search of its soul or, perhaps, their own souls. The disillusioned characters in *Welcome Home* are all fresh from combat in Vietnam, and upon their discharge from the service they pile into a big black Cadillac and head down the highway to try to reconnect with the country and their people. But they've changed, and so has everything around them. The accidental murder, early in the film, of a young woman they've picked up foreshadows a violent finale, when the apathy and hostility they encounter lead them to attack a small New Mexico town as though it were an enemy stronghold—which, in a sense, it is. At least, that seems to be the premise advanced by scripter Guerdon Trueblood and director Richard Compton, both of whom would go on to pretty good careers in television and low-budget theatrical features.

Given the antiwar nature of the film, it is perhaps surprising that the crew got so much help from the residents of a small western Oklahoma town. Folks in the map-dot communities of America's heartland leaned heavily toward the patriotic, my-country-right-or-wrong philosophy, even during the darkest days of the Vietnam War. But when Compton and his outfit blew into Cordell for a few days in early March 1971 to shoot several scenes for the picture—including one in which Joe Don Baker's character has an unsatisfactory reunion with his mother, played by television actress Florence MacMichael—he apparently got nothing but cooperation from all the town's residents.

There was, for instance, Mrs. Jess Wesler, who opened her big two-story home at the corner of Grant and Fourth Streets to the cast and crew and seems to have remained nonplussed when the company piled in and took over. A March 7 article in the *Oklahoma Journal Fun Guide* reported that filming in the Wesler house "was like trying to stage World War II in Times Square."

"A great beam of wood had to be placed square in the middle of her living room so the ceiling would not collapse under the tons of equipment and people up on the second floor," wrote the author of the piece, Howard Davis. "Efforts to keep the house quiet during filming virtually

Disaffected Vietnam veterans and their distaff passenger in *Welcome Home, Soldier Boys* (1972). Clockwise from left are Alan Vint, Paul Koslo, Cherie Foster, Joe Don Baker, and Elliott Street. (John Wooley Archives)

floundered in a sea of floor-squeaks, which Mrs. Wesler, who had donated her house free of charge, was powerless to stop."

Meanwhile, others in the town, including members of the local constabulary, were providing their own services to the company. Wrote Davis:

> Cordell chief of Police Eby Don Walters has promised his full cooperation in assisting with downtown location shooting.
>
> He has agreed to block traffic off from the Main Street square for as many five-minute periods as the director finds necessary, and has even agreed to attempt the unusual task of keeping the entire square perfectly noiseless when necessary. . . .
>
> More than a dozen bit parts have been assigned to local persons, and there have been still more hired as stand-ins.
>
> None of them are doing it for the money. Just for fun, or the glamour.
>
> Ron Cochran, a 27-year-old unemployed oilfield worker, says he agreed to take his bit part, "just for the hell of it."
>
> Therese Jarvis, sophomore at Southeastern State College [in Durant], took her part "because it's one of those things you always dream about, and then it suddenly happens."
>
> And four-year-old Glen Wilhite is taking his part because he likes to "shoot Indians."

Davis saw in director Compton an "ability to turn quirks of circumstance into esthetic effects":

> For example, the Christmas lights still strung from the Cordell courthouse Compton decided to let stand, even though the city officials would have been more than happy to take them down.
>
> "It's typical," was his reasoning.
>
> Also, Compton decided to let stand the name "Cordell Lounge" of the beer tavern where the four soldiers get hustled in a game of pool.

The thirty-five-member cast and crew left a few days later for Carlsbad and Hope, New Mexico, where they wrapped up the film. (IMDb.com gives Little Rock, Arkansas, as the primary shooting location.) "Budgeted low, under a million dollars," according to Davis, the movie probably earned money, even though it was not a huge hit. A few years later, however, Compton would reteam with Alan Vint (along with his brother Jesse) to make the classic southern-redneck exploitation film *Macon County Line* (1974). Although it was also brought in on a low budget, it ended up making multimillions for its distributor, American International Pictures, a specialist in movies aimed squarely at the youth and young adult market.

The final feature of the half dozen on Jon Denton's *Showcase* rundown is a little different. In fact, it could've been the beginning of something really big in the state, the harbinger of Oklahoma as a filmmaking center all on its own. That didn't exactly happen, but that's not because G. D. Spradlin didn't give it a very good try.

The other early '70s movies had been made in the state by filmmakers from Hollywood (or Chicago, in the case of *This Stuff'll Kill Ya!*), all outsiders persuaded to come to Oklahoma for a short time, shoot a little and spread a little money around, and then return home when their work was done. Spradlin was just the opposite—a man born in Garvin County, Oklahoma, who'd had careers in both law and the oil business before making his way to the West Coast, where he'd broken into television and then movies. By the late '60s, he'd guested in several TV series, including *I Spy*, *The Big Valley*, and *The Iron Horse*, the latter a western program starring fellow Oklahoman Dale Robertson. In 1968, Spradlin had gotten his first big film break (appearing with another Sooner State actor, Ben Johnson) in the Charlton Heston western feature *Will Penny*.

Spradlin's career as a character player was clearly on the rise in the early '70s, which is when he got the idea that he might be able to continue his film career and work out of his native state at the same time. He also had aspirations of producing and directing his own films and saw no reason why he couldn't do it in Oklahoma as easily as—or easier than—he could in Hollywood.

So, on July 2, 1971, a *Tulsa Tribune* story by Lillian Newby announced that Spradlin was returning to the state to make a new movie called *The Only Way Home*, adding that the actor had said the main reason he'd come home to film the movie was that "he wanted to." Wrote Newby:

> "I love this business . . . and I would rather live at home. That's been Hollywood in the past," he said. Technical changes and financial changes have made it possible to move around the country to film today.

Beth Brickell and producer-director-actor G. D. Spradlin in *The Only Way Home* (1972). (John Wooley Archives)

Spradlin said Oklahoma has the actors and the scenery for a film industry, although at present it lacks some of the technicians such as cameramen, soundmen, script supervisors and management personnel. . . .

"It's my hope that all of us working together can develop a film-making capacity in Oklahoma," Spradlin said.

Newby also noted the lieutenant governor's part in getting Spradlin and his production to the state, writing that the filmmaker "praised Nigh for his 'solo effort' in the past to bring movie filming to Oklahoma." Spradlin also credited his contacts with Nigh as "what started me thinking about coming home."

The Only Way Home, which began production in late August 1971 was often touted in the state's press—and, at one point, by Lieutenant Governor George Nigh himself—as the first feature to be shot entirely in Oklahoma. Of course, it wasn't even the first feature to be shot entirely in Oklahoma in the '70s; the below-the-radar *This Stuff'll Kill Ya!* had

Behind the scenes on *The Only Way Home*. Bo Hopkins stands near the car. (Photo courtesy of the Randy Johnston Collection)

wrapped less than a year earlier. Homegrown theatrical movies, as we have seen, went all the way back to the silent westerns produced by Oklahoma lawmen, outlaws, and the 101 Ranch.

"Homegrown," however, is the key term here. Pictures as diverse as 1915's *Passing of the Oklahoma Outlaw* and 1962's *Stark Fear* were created by Oklahomans working within their state (although sometimes with imported talent both in front of the camera and behind the scenes), not by filmmakers coming in from elsewhere. True, Spradlin had been a Hollywood resident for a few years when he decided to make a film in Oklahoma, but he was from the Sooner State, and that made all the difference. As Nigh said in a *Tulsa Tribune* article dated June 13, 1972, eight days before *The Only Way Home*'s world premiere, "Bringing this picture to the screen is an important accomplishment. Not only was it produced in our state, but the company which produced it was local."

Shot under the banner of Spradlin's Washita Films, Inc., *The Only Way Home* began production in Tulsa, moving after only a day of filming to locations in Oklahoma City, Jones, and Norman and adhering to a six-week shooting schedule. In addition to producing and directing, Spradlin took the smallest of the four starring roles, all essayed by Hollywood actors. He played a wealthy man, heading for a lake retreat with his wife (Beth Brickell). A flat tire interferes, and when two young drifters (Steve Sandor and Bo Hopkins) show up, an offer to help soon becomes a violent quarrel. After apparently offing Spradlin's character, the two kidnap his wife and head off, trying to figure out what to do next. There's a wild card with these two jokers, however, and it's the wife, a repressed, neurotic mess who ultimately finds romantic and physical satisfaction with one of the lowlifes. (One wonders how this PG-rated encounter played to audiences of the day, considering that Brickell's highest-profile role up to that time had been as the mother in the family-oriented TV series *Gentle Ben* [1967–69].)

None of those actors had any ties to the state before being tapped by Spradlin for the film. But at least one, the Brooklyn-born Sandor, was talking like an adopted son by the time filming was over. John Acord III told of Sandor's newfound love for the state in a June 23, 1972, *Daily Oklahoman* piece—two days after the film had world-premiered at Oklahoma City's Will Rogers Theatre. Sandor had returned to the state to appear at the premiere, and he apparently enjoyed being in the heartland once again:

> "I worked on the movie here for more than five weeks. By the end of that time I wasn't even looking forward to going back to Los Angeles.
>
> "L.A. is a town I hate and love at the same time. Because of the business I am in, acting, you almost have to live there."
>
> Sandor went on to say that he hates Los Angeles because it is too full of superfluous nonsense.
>
> "Oklahoma is really a great place to work. The people are friendly and the feeling you get while you are staying here makes it hard to leave."

Supporting Sandor, Brickell, Hopkins, and Spradlin were a number of Oklahoma-based actors—including Oklahoma City theater regular George Clow, who'd made a memorable screen villain a decade earlier in the state-lensed *Stark Fear*. A June 13 *Tulsa World* piece announcing the Oklahoma City premiere of *The Only Way Home* noted:

> The picture has a distinct Oklahoma flavor in addition to the location and story line.
>
> Of 37 major speaking parts, 34 roles are filled by Oklahoma actors and actresses. Other Sooners fill in as extras.
>
> The technical crew was dominated by Oklahomans, and the film's musical score was composed, orchestrated and recorded by Okies.
>
> Financing also was obtained in the state.

The story quoted Spradlin: "The Hollywood hierarchy is watching us with skepticism and apprehension. They think this is going to be an amateurish, home movie type film."

It wasn't, but the notices *The Only Way Home* received on Spradlin's home turf were decidedly mixed. Reviewers sometimes damned with faint praise or wrote ambiguously about the film, as though they were striving mightily to say something good about it. Jon Denton of the *Oklahoma City Times*, for instance, wrote the following in his "Cinema Critique" column, published the day after the premiere. (Longtime movie fans will recognize the first line as a play on a famous phrase from the 1967 film *Cool Hand Luke*.)

> What we have here is the ability to communicate.
>
> G. D. Spradlin's new film, *The Only Way Home*, is now out of the gate, the premiere is over in Oklahoma City and this business of word-of-mouth takes over.
>
> In Oklahoma the word should be good. . . .
>
> The director moves us through one day when three lives mix in violence and tragedy. The newspapers are full of things like this and even if Oklahoma were not the setting, you could believe it happened to people you know.

Denton went on to give Hopkins and Sandor high marks, while calling Brickell a "puzzle" in her role, and concluded by calling *The Only Way Home* "a movie very obviously made in Oklahoma."

Down the Turner Turnpike in Tulsa, however, the *Tribune*'s Bill Donaldson disagreed. In his "Showcase" column for August 7, he not only slammed the picture but even spent a significant amount of ink debunking the notion that it was "very obviously made in Oklahoma," as Denton had written:

> While the state is happy to have had the movie industry discover it, even if in the person of a native who functioned as both producer and director, there is nothing in the film that could not have been filmed in half a dozen other states save for the skyline of Tulsa in one brief shot. . . .
>
> And there are much more interesting and picturesque locations in Oklahoma than were shown in *The Only Way Home*. If Lt. Gov. George Nigh is going to attract any substantial movie business to the state, he should point some of these out to potential producers and directors.
>
> In the final title, the caption "Made Entirely in Oklahoma" is shown. It is, in the last analysis, of little more than academic interest. Nothing is really said about, or done with[,] the state that makes it uniquely of this area.

Perhaps Donaldson—who in the same column flatly stated, "It isn't a very good movie" (laying the blame mostly on an "incredible script")—was cranky about having to watch the movie at the 11th Street Drive-In, which ended up as the location of the Tulsa premiere, rather than inside an air-conditioned indoor theater. By August 2, when *The Only Way Home* debuted under nature's own canopy in Tulsa, it had already finished a multiweek run in Oklahoma City, another factor that might have subtly colored the opinions of Tulsa reviewers.

As reported in an August 1 "Viewpoint" column, Spradlin told the *Tulsa World*'s Ron Butler—Donaldson's morning-newspaper counterpart—that plans to open the movie in June in Tulsa fell through because of an "error in booking the Village Theater," and the drive-in in August was the next available option in town. Two days later, at the end of his own review of the picture, Butler noted the aesthetic problems with the drive-in showing: "The sound levels are soft and those speakers just don't do the job. Add an occasional semi on 11th Street or a jet overhead, and you've really got problems.". The beginning of Butler's column seemed to encapsulate the problems Oklahoma reviewers had in writing about the picture:

> Don't expect to see a cinematic milestone in any artistic sense if you try G. D. Spradlin's (and Oklahoma's) first film. You will see some familiar territory and hear some familiar dialect in *The Only Way Home,* but the bursts

of promise and the interesting ideas are sprinkled too thinly to make the picture more than a fairly routine B picture.

After the great statewide interest in the picture and after finding Spradlin an intelligent and likable spearhead for film-making in Oklahoma, it's sad to have to report the dissatisfaction.

Still, this is Spradlin's first attempt at directing and producing his own picture (though he's acted in several earlier films). Perhaps with better writing and a little less self-consciousness Spradlin will evolve into a better director. There are those occasional flashes of ability.

Spradlin's flash as a director, however, would be confined to this movie and one other, the Vietnam War home-front feature *Outside In*. Released in 1972 by novelist Harold Robbins's company Robbins International (and reissued in '75 as *Red, White, and Busted*), it found Spradlin sharing directorial credit with TV veteran Robert Hutchinson. *Outside In* also seems to be the only other movie-writing credit for *The Only Way Home*'s critically maligned Jeeds O'Tilbury, a colorful name that just possibly was a pseudonym—maybe even for Spradlin himself.

Reliable Jon Denton, writing in the *Sunday Oklahoman*'s *Showcase* magazine this time (the *Oklahoman* and *Times* were, respectively, morning and afternoon papers owned by the same family), reported on July 9 that "Spradlin is negotiating with several [distribution] firms and has a 'serious' discussion going with American International Pictures" regarding *The Only Way Home*. The movie ended up without a major distributor, however, and was released to theaters across the country by regional outlets on a piecemeal basis. The movie, shot on 16 mm film and blown up to 35 mm, hadn't cost much by Hollywood standards—Denton reported that it had been brought in for $300,000. Still, without a national distribution company pushing it, it probably didn't make its money back. Abandoning his plans to make a second film in the state titled *Ice Castles* ("It will be another attempt," Spradlin told Denton, "to make a serious exploration of the psyche and the anxieties, the hostilities, the tensions and joys which I see in my fellow Oklahomans"), Spradlin returned to Hollywood and a noteworthy career as a character player that lasted until his retirement in 1999, just before his seventy-ninth birthday.

Although Spradlin didn't achieve his noble dream of an Oklahoma-based film industry, at least one of his cohorts on *The Only Way Home* wasn't quite ready to let that vision go. In fact, the film made in the state by Joseph Taft, right on the heels of Spradlin's movie, paralleled *The Only Way Home* in many ways, from its use of Hollywood actors to its tepid critical reception and ultimate failure to find a home with a major distribution company. Like Spradlin, Taft turned out to be a one-off director. But also like Spradlin, he at least got a professional feature in the can.

In the spring of 1972, movie-biz buff George Nigh was riding high. In addition to the Hollywood productions he'd coaxed into the state over the past couple of years, *The Only Way Home*—with its mostly Oklahoma cast and crew—had wrapped and was headed for a summer premiere. And besides that, as a UPI story dated April 17 reported, a second in-state movie, helmed by another Sooner, was on the way:

> Lt. Gov. George Nigh today announced plans for the filming of another motion picture in Oklahoma. He said it would be [the] first fully financed by Oklahomans.
>
> Oklahoma Cityan Joseph Taft will be producer-director for the film *30 Dangerous Seconds*, which Taft describes as a "thriller caper" with an upbeat ending in which justice triumphs.
>
> No nationally known stars have been signed for the film, he said, although negotiations are under way with an actor "whom you would recognize."
>
> Filming is expected to begin in July and take about six weeks, Taft said.
>
> Henning Schellerup, a West Coast movieman who will be associate director, said the film would have a budget of "less than $300,000."
>
> Nigh said the movie would have five principal characters and a lesser cast of about 20 people. He said the film would "use a great deal of Oklahoma talent."

As already noted, resemblances to *The Only Way Home* abound. While Taft's professional film-biz credits weren't on the level of Spradlin's, Taft had been, according to a September 24, 1973, article in the *Tulsa Tribune*, "a television writer and director in Oklahoma, New Mexico and California for nine years." The piece also identified him as assistant director on *The Only Way Home* and added that he'd had a play produced in Oklahoma City.

Another important holdover from Spradlin's crew was Schellerup, director of photography on *The Only Way Home*. At the time, Schellerup had a variety of credits—from camera operator to producer—on a number of mostly exploitation-style films. (His career to date as a director and/or cinematographer cuts across an impressively vast spectrum, ranging from *Dr. Carstair's 1869 Love-Root Elixir*, released the same year as *The Only Way Home*, to 1992's *Ancient Secrets of the Bible*.)

The estimated under-$300,000 budget and six-week shooting schedule for *Thirty Dangerous Seconds*—which got under way in the summer of '72—also echoed the earlier picture, as did the intention to cast all but the main roles with in-state talent. In fact, one of the principal roles ended up going to a non-Hollywood Oklahoman—Josef Peter Hart (also known as Josef Hardt), remembered by Tulsa TV viewers as the host of the '60s late-night horror movie showcase *Fantastic Theatre*. (He would later show up in a major role in the first-ever made-for-home-video feature, *Blood Cult*, which gets its due in chapter 7.)

The other actors Taft got to play his leads were recognizable mostly from television appearances, with the exception of female lead Kathryn Reynolds, who was just beginning her TV and movie career. Evidence suggests that her starring role in *Thirty Dangerous Seconds* was her first credit.

Her three costars, however, all had significant experience before the cameras. The "recognizable" actor Taft mentioned to the UPI was probably Robert Lansing, who'd starred in his own television series, *12 O'Clock High*, in 1964–65 and guest-starred on dozens of episodes of other shows. Michael Dante and Marj Dusay had also done a lot of episodic television work. (At this writing, Dusay is a longtime presence on TV's daytime-drama landscape.)

Rated PG by the MPAA, *Thirty Dangerous Seconds* tells the story of two groups that, unbeknownst to each other, plan to rob the same armored car. On the one side is a down-on-his-luck oil geologist, played by Lansing; on the other, professional crooks (Dusay, Dante, and Hardt), led by Hardt's character, Edward Bizby. Through a combination of circumstances, the amateur is the one who manages to pull off the heist; his rivals for the illicit booty respond by kidnapping his wife (Reynolds) and forcing the geologist to embark on what the September 24, 1973, *Tulsa Tribune* called a "human scavenger hunt."

"He makes contact with several bizarre characters—a clown, a bishop and a dwarf on roller skates—in the nickelodeon room at the Cowboy Hall of Fame, the Rosehill Cemetery, the modernistic Oklahoma Theatre Center and the State Capitol Building," wrote the unnamed reporter. "The sequence features three wild chases and a spectacular car wreck."

In reports of the time, Taft is often credited as producer, director, and writer of the picture. A casting-call notice in the May 17, 1972, *Tulsa World* also named Marston Austin as a coproducer, while a user comment on the film's site at IMDb.com asserts that "James H. Milligan, an intelligent and outstanding businessman," was actually the film's producer. Whatever the case, there's no doubt that Taft was the creative force behind the movie, which, except for one sequence shot in Shawnee, was lensed entirely in Oklahoma City.

When it came time for the premiere, however, *Thirty Dangerous Seconds* made its debut not in the state's capital but in its second city—specifically, at the Fontana 4 Cinema in Tulsa on October 12, 1973. Why Tulsa was chosen is something of a mystery; perhaps it had something to do with Josef Hardt's employment at the NBC-TV affiliate there, where he likely would've been able to generate a lot of publicity.

But as things turned out, Tulsa and the Fontana 4 weren't the best choices for the film's launching pad. Perhaps it was because only four months earlier the city had hosted, with much ballyhoo, the world premiere of director Stanley Kramer's *Oklahoma Crude* (shot in Stockton, California, after Oklahoma had been toured by Kramer and rejected as a filming site), and Taft's little state-shot opus seemed quite modest in the shadow of that big-budget, star-studded picture. Whatever the reason, the grand opening of *Thirty Dangerous Seconds* didn't make a huge impression on the locals.

"Poor management, sloppy weather or a laissez faire attitude toward the event," summed up the *Tulsa World*'s David C. MacKenzie in an October 13 review, "made the much-vaunted world-premiere of *Thirty Dangerous Seconds* a non-happening." MacKenzie, a frequently brilliant and notoriously hard-to-please critic, seemed to like the film well enough, however, calling it "a pleasant robbers-and-robbers escapade with all the quick, disconcerted action and two-dimensional characterizations of a comic book." He even compared it to some of the classic work in American cinema:

> At times, *Thirty Dangerous Seconds* resembles a comic and very lightweight version of *Treasure of the Sierra Madre,* a more definitive study of greed. At others, as principals constantly change sides and conspire with former rivals, the film evidently aspires to—without reaching—the almost ballet-like comic machinations of Ernst Lubitsch's movies of the 1930s.

MacKenzie's counterpart at the rival *Tribune,* Bill Donaldson, wasn't quite as generous, although his thoughts on the picture were less harsh than his assessment of *The Only Way Home* a little more than a year before. About *Thirty Dangerous Seconds,* he wrote:

> The film is a modest little crime melodrama in every respect. Its limited budget is obvious. Its scripting is at times labored and at times downright illogical. . . .
>
> *Thirty Dangerous Seconds* is a pleasant enough diversion for entertainment customers who are undemanding. But it is operating in an area in which television is concentrating this season, and they're doing it better on the tube.
>
> Outside Oklahoma where the film has particular local interest because of the familiar locations, *Thirty Dangerous Seconds* will probably be relegated to booking as the lower half of a double bill.

In fact, *Thirty Dangerous Seconds* probably didn't even get many of those double-bill spots. Like its immediate Oklahoma-shot predecessor, *The Only Way Home,* it failed to land a major distributor, and the buzz about it, even in its home state, gradually faded away.

There was, however, plenty of good movie buzz to replace it. In a column two days before his review of the film appeared, Donaldson told his readers, "With *Where the Red Fern Grows* shooting in Tahlequah, and the recent world premiere here of *Oklahoma Crude,* we're getting into the thick of movie business." Filming on *Where the Red Fern Grows,* based on a best-selling young-readers' novel by Tahlequah native Wilson Rawls, had begun in late September of 1973, the same week that Lieutenant Governor Nigh announced the Tulsa premiere of *The Only Way Home.*

Oklahoma favorite son Ben Johnson (center) played top G-man Melvin Purvis in *Dillinger* (1973). (John Wooley Archives)

The former film would end up having a major impact on filmmaking in Oklahoma. But at the same time all of this activity was going on, there was a little matter of a former public enemy and an Academy Award–winning Oklahoma character actor known to the home folks as "Son."

The production of *Dillinger* had actually started in Oklahoma several months before *Thirty Dangerous Seconds*, and its joint state premieres in Tulsa and Oklahoma City ended up preceding the latter picture's theatrical debut by some four months. The upcoming production of the gangster picture had not been announced from the lieutenant governor's office, as had become customary, but from the office of Governor David Hall. Here's how the UPI story put it on October 2, 1972:

> Gov. Hall today announced plans for Oklahoma to be the location for filming of a movie about the life of gangster John Dillinger.

Warren Oates, seen here with costar Michelle Phillips, played the title role in *Dillinger*. (John Wooley Archives)

Hall said the film would star Warren Oates as Dillinger and Oklahoma native Ben Johnson as the chief FBI investigator.

The schedule calls for seven weeks of filming on locations in or near Enid, Pond Creek, Nash, Goltry, Orienta, Jefferson, Ardmore, Gene Autry, Dougherty, Mannsville and Oklahoma City.

Entire script of the movie will be filmed in Oklahoma by American International Pictures.

"We believe that will add authenticity and historic credibility to the film," Hall said.

The headline in the *Tulsa Tribune* over that wire-service report summed up the major point of interest in the film, at least to Oklahomans: "Ben Johnson to Have Role in State Movie."

The son of a rancher and rodeo star with the same name, Ben Johnson—known as "Son" to the people around Pawhuska—had followed his dad into ranching and steer roping. He got into the movies after delivering several horses to Hollywood, where they were used in the infamous Howard Hughes–produced film *The Outlaw* (1943). Finding horse wrangling and stunt work unexpectedly profitable, Johnson worked in those capacities in Hollywood for a few years before being discovered by director John Ford and cast in a small part in *3 Godfathers* (1948). That appearance began an acting career that saw him quickly ascend to starring and costarring roles.

Like his fellow northeastern Oklahoman Will Rogers, Johnson was a man of strong principles and classic "cowboy" values. Also like Rogers, he would sometimes refer to his home state on-screen. Many Sooner State kids, first encountering the unofficial *King Kong* sequel *Mighty Joe Young* (1949) on TV or the big screen, felt a swell of pride when someone asked Johnson's character, rodeo cowboy Gregg Johnson, if he was from Texas. His reply: "We can ride and rope in Oklahoma, too, y'know."

When Governor Hall announced the impending filming of *Dillinger*, Johnson had been a working actor for just about a quarter of a century—and his stock had never been higher. His new visibility was due to the Oscar for Best Supporting Actor that he'd just won for his role as Sam the Lion, the philosophical movie-house, diner, and pool-hall owner in the dying Texas town depicted in director Peter Bogdanovich's *The Last Picture Show* (1971).

While Johnson was the only Oklahoma native to play a major role in *Dillinger*, he wasn't the only Hollywood resident brought back to the state for its filming. Production manager Elliot Schick had been on the crew of *Welcome Home, Soldier Boys* a year or so earlier, and Warren Oates, playing the title role in *Dillinger*, had costarred in *Two-Lane Blacktop*.

Johnson was cast as G-man Melvin Purvis, archenemy of America's gang element, in this fact-based (and blood-soaked) retelling of the Depression-era bank robber and killer's violent reign at the top of the criminal heap. Some other cast members of note were Richard Dreyfuss as Baby Face Nelson, Cloris Leachman in a small but important role as the famed Lady in Red, and Michelle Phillips, fresh from the hit '60s act the Mamas and the Papas, playing Dillinger's girlfriend Billie Frechette (she received a Golden Globe nomination in the Most Promising Newcomer category for her role). Many Oklahomans were also cast in bit parts or as extras during the production. Their number included *Tulsa World* reporter Wayne Mason, whose humorous dispatch in the December 10, 1972, edition of the paper gave an Everyman's view of the moviemaking process. Wrote Mason, who cameoed as a waiter in a sequence shot in the Tower Ballroom of Oklahoma City's Skirvin Hotel:

You talk about work. We extras "worked" from 3 o'clock in the afternoon until 3 in the morning. And if I blink my eyes I ain't even gonna see me when the movie comes out. And I'll know where and when to look.

Along about the 11 1/2th hour, I had decided I would rather work as a bus boy as play the part of one.

As one wag said, "To hell with this. I'm going back to pickin' cotton."

That really seemed to sum up the feelings of most of the 100 or so local folks who were working as extras. They all decided it didn't take long to take the glamour out of making a movie.

But there's one thing about it, the stars were right there with us. However, they get paid a bit better. We got $10 for the night's work. I heard we did, anyway. . . .

Maybe I better explain about this movie *Dillinger!* They are filming all of it in Oklahoma—at Enid, Ardmore and Oklahoma City. I think they are finished now and it didn't take very long. I don't see how they ever get one finished. After all of us spent all those 12 hours in the ballroom scene, I bet they had maybe five minutes of stuff that will be shown in the theater. That's the way they do, though. They just take those things over and over until they get it right.

Mason also wrote about the specific part of the movie that involved him, obviously enjoying the chance to tell his readers all about it:

The first scene involved Melvin Purvis and his fiancée at an engagement party in this ballroom. Purvis and his girl were seated at a table with about 10 guests (extras, and one of the extras was Ben Johnson's wife, Carol).

Ben was—or Purvis, that is—to make a little four-line speech, announcing his engagement, and propose a toast. He stood to drink the toast and when he lifted his glass to drink you could tell he had spotted somebody across the room. I looked over that way and there wasn't anybody there. But it didn't take me long to figure out he had spotted John Dillinger!

When Ben first arrived that evening, I was sitting with his wife visiting. She told me they had given him a new speech to learn after he had arrived. Then she led him off in a corner to go over it with him. But it wasn't too long and didn't present any big problem.

However, a part of the speech concerned the invention of champagne. Ben said[,] "[C]hampagne was invented by a monk in the 15th century. It was a dangerous job. Sometimes it exploded when it was opened." Or words to that effect. When they started filming the scene, the waiter was to open a bottle of champagne when Ben delivered the words, "sometimes it exploded." Well, about the first four times they tried it, the bottle did "explode" so loudly they had to reshoot.

The assistant director, Don Klune, told the extras they could remain in the ballroom and watch the filming of the "closeup" scenes if they would remain quiet. "When I blow my whistle once it means no noise at all," he said. "When I blow it twice (at the end of a scene) it means you can make a little noise. When I blow it four times, you can make a lot of noise. I never blow it four times."

Don would blow his whistle, somebody yelled "roll it," the sound man yelled "speed" and the director said "action." Once, during a take, a phone started ringing somewhere and Don was fit to be tied! But, "see there, folks, I didn't curse, did I?" he said.

I told Carol that I had felt a sneeze coming on during one take. "Oh my gosh, don't sneeze," she said. "That's worse than a phone ringing."

Another time after a take, Don said, "Now folks, that was a bad one because somebody coughed or something. When little kids do it we drop them down a well."

Dillinger's production had commenced in October, only a few days after Governor Hall's announcement. The director was John Milius, a graduate of the University of Southern California's film program and one of the first film school grads to find significant work in the business. At the time, he'd done scripts for a couple of major productions, cowriting director Sydney Pollack's *Jeremiah Johnson* (1972) and getting sole script credit on John Huston's *The Life and Times of Judge Roy Bean* (also

1972). Sources indicate that American International Pictures had agreed to let Milius break into directing with *Dillinger* if he would also write the screenplay.

The result, as Roger Ebert wrote in his review for the *Chicago Sun-Times,* "is the film, we may speculate, that John Milius was born to make: violent, tough, filled with guns and blood." That assessment echoed earlier lines by the *Tulsa World's* David C. MacKenzie, who'd been able to see the picture before Ebert. (Its official release date was July 20, 1973, which was also the date of Ebert's review.) "It's possible Dillinger and his mob shed blood (theirs and law officers') as profusely as they do on film," wrote MacKenzie in the June 22 *World,* "but the sight of repeated machinegunnings and butchery makes the eyes glaze after a while. Writer-director John Milius . . . digs violence and stipulates that a gun be part of his payment for each script. He probably got an entire Army Surplus store for *Dillinger.*"

The film had premiered in the state's two major cities the day before MacKenzie's notice came out, although—with Michelle Phillips and producer Buzz Feitshans, along with Lieutenant Governor Nigh, in attendance—the Oklahoma City premiere was the official one. A *Tulsa Tribune* story on June 21 related the "squeals of delight [that] drowned out dialogue as people in the audience saw themselves or their friends on screen." It also told of a news conference in which Feitshans said he was "predisposed to return to Oklahoma" for more gangster films "because of cooperation and goodwill shown at the location sites for *Dillinger.*"

Feitshans went on to produce many more features, notably the wildly successful *Rambo* series with Sylvester Stallone. But the late '60s–early '70s miniboom in Depression-era gangster pictures—ignited by the 1967 blockbuster *Bonnie and Clyde*—soon faded, and the possible Oklahoma-lensed biopics on Baby Face Nelson and Pretty Boy Floyd that Feitshans announced at the Oklahoma City news conference ultimately settled into the might've-been bin, the final resting place of innumerable feature film proposals.

But Oklahoma filmmaking, like hope, always seemed to spring eternal. *Dillinger* had hardly left the state for its national run when another feature film outfit made its way into the state. And this time, instead of a blood-drenched tale of profane gangsters, the newly minted company traveled to the state to chronicle the G-rated story of a boy and his dogs.

Although the newspapers and other media of the time didn't record any official queasiness about *Dillinger*'s R-rated violence and profanity, it's certainly possible that some of the state's officials and media members couldn't get wholeheartedly behind the film because of its abundance of coarser elements. In his *Sun-Times* review, Roger Ebert made an example of one scene, a bloody and protracted gun battle following a Purvis raid on the lodge where Dillinger is holed up. "If the massacre at the end of [director Sam] Peckinpah's *The Wild Bunch* was special-effects technology in the service of art," he wrote, "here we have mere overachievement."

So perhaps some secret sighs of relief were breathed when representatives from Doty-Dayton Productions—including director Norman Tokar, best known for helming Walt Disney family fare like *The Happiest Millionaire* (1967) and *The Boatniks* (1970)—headed to Tahlequah to shoot *Where the Red Fern Grows*. Wilson Rawls, the author of the novel on which it was based, was a native of Scraper, about fifteen miles northeast of the main filming location.

Although reports at the time treated Doty-Dayton Productions as though it were an established Hollywood film company, *Where the Red Fern Grows* was actually the group's first production. On top of that, Doty-Dayton had far deeper roots in Utah than it did in Tinseltown. Identifying producer Lyman Dayton as "a devout Mormon, " a January 3, 1977, *Time* magazine piece noted that he had "studied radio and television at Brigham Young University in Provo, Utah, [and] later wound up as a cab driver and part-time film technician in Los Angeles before deciding that the only way he could break into the business in a big way would be to become a film maker himself."

The "Doty" part of Doty-Dayton Productions, according to *Time*, referred to "Dayton's surgeon father-in-law, Dr. George Doty," who had helped with financing on the picture. He's listed in the *Fern* credits as George Ellis Doty, executive producer.

In addition to being made by a brand-new production company, the

A boy (Stewart Petersen) and his dog, from *Where the Red Fern Grows* (1974). (John Wooley Archives)

picture also had a first-timer in the lead juvenile role. Thirteen-year-old Stewart Petersen was cast as a rural Oklahoma kid (just as novelist Rawls had been), whose relationship with his two coonhounds fuels much of the narrative thrust of the movie. The *Oklahoma Journal Fun Guide* for September 16, 1973, told about the Cokeville, Wyoming, boy who had emerged out of the "hundreds" of hopefuls trying out for the role:

> Lyman Dayton, producer of the film—soon to be shot on location near Tahlequah—said that selection of the boy to play the role of Billy Coleman was not easy.
>
> A major talent search for "just the right boy" was conducted over a wide area of the nation. A large number of youths tried out for the part and many of those appearing "showed great potential," Dayton said.
>
> Only after much review and discussion by Dayton and director Norman Tokar and co-producer Jim McCullough was the final decision made. . . .
>
> Young Petersen came to Tahlequah with his mother for a final tryout before the selection was to be made.

Tulsa-area kids Jill Clark and Jeanna Wilson bested hundreds of other young girls to earn featured roles in *Where the Red Fern Grows*. (John Wooley Archives)

"I really didn't think I had much chance," the farm boy said in an interview. "But I figured it would be a good experience to at least try."

Perhaps all of that's true, but it nonetheless seems a bit disingenuous in light of the *Time* article, which identifies young Petersen as Dayton's nephew. (Petersen amassed several other family-film credits in the years immediately following *Fern*, often working with some version of the Doty-Dayton combine.)

Two other unknowns, both locals, were tabbed to play Billy's sisters: Sand Springs' Jeanna Wilson and Tulsa's Jill Clark. Clark, working in various production capacities, would go on to become a leading light in Tulsa's direct-to-video feature-film explosion in the late '80s.

"Six hundred girls auditioned for it," she recalled in an interview with the author for a March 27, 1987, *Tulsa World* story. "I lived on a farm and had an older brother and younger sister, and I loved animals, and that was exactly the kind of person they wanted. I never thought of making

Red Fern as making a movie. I just looked at it as getting out of school for a couple of months."

Despite all the first-timers, including himself, Dayton was savvy enough to place some identifiable actors at the top of his cast. Each of those players also had a connection with Oklahoma, some more tenuous than others.

The latter category included the avuncular character actor James Whitmore, a familiar face and voice from both movies and television, brought in to play Billy's sage grandpa. His tie to the state was his popular one-man stage show called *Will Rogers' USA*, a presentation of humor, commentary, and philosophy from Oklahoma's favorite son. The touring production had also aired as a television special the year before *Fern* began production.

Then there was Beverly Garland, in the role of Billy's mother, returning to the state where, a decade before, she had filmed *Stark Fear*. (This fact never seems to have been brought up in press coverage of *Where the Red Fern Grows*.)

The other two Hollywood actors in the film were both Oklahoma natives. Alva's Jack Ging, a 1954 graduate of the University of Oklahoma, had played football under legendary OU head coach Bud Wilkinson before heading west for a film and TV career. Lonny Chapman, born in Tulsa, had played the father of Joe Don Baker's character in *Welcome Home, Soldier Boys*, although Chapman apparently wasn't in any Oklahoma-filmed scenes. Ging played Billy's dad; Chapman was the sheriff who oversees a coon hunt that's pivotal to the film's plot.

The September 18, 1973, edition of the *Tulsa Tribune*, published just after filming had begun, featured a lengthy Bill Donaldson piece that included a visit with both Ging and Garland. After praising young Peterson for having "some marvelous instincts despite his lack of experience," Garland went on: "He's going to steal the picture, you know. Between the dogs and the little kids and the puppies we (the adult actors) haven't got a chance. . . . But I thought it was a wild script when they sent it to me. It's so important to have this kind of movie today. It's a picture for everyone. It could turn out to be a classic, I think."

Describing the film's main setting as being "on a spectacularly picturesque bend in the Illinois River," Donaldson noted, "In a move that was rather extraordinary, the producers decided to film the movie on the actual locations described in the book." Two and a half months later, with filming virtually complete, *Fern*'s producer reinforced Donaldson's words in an interview with an unnamed reporter for the *Broken Arrow Ledger* newspaper:

> Lyman Dayton . . . said the location near Tahlequah was chosen as the major site for a number of reasons. "For one thing," he said, "the story takes place here. We've been shooting in the approximate area described by the author."
>
> He said the major reason that Green Country was chosen as the site for the film was because it had just about everything to offer. "It's ironic," he said, "but many movies about a particular spot are often filmed thousands of miles away."
>
> But here the scenery, the setting, the weather, the climate and the people all seemed to be just right.

After noting that the picture's town scenes were filmed in Vian, where "merchants and residents there were most agreeable in having their storefronts and buildings 'touched up a bit' to resemble a 1930 Oklahoma village," the story offered a thorough description of the main location:

> The majority of the production was shot in a clearing next to the Illinois River just off State Highway 10 about five miles north of Tahlequah. Members of the Cherokee Nation Construction company crew spent about three weeks reconstructing a typical and authentic rural home of the 1930's, including a barn and other outbuildings. Prior to filming, a garden was planted and fencing added to give the set a "truly realistic appearance." Within a few weeks, the home will be torn down and re-constructed on Cherokee Tribal property, 4 miles south of Tahlequah, where it will be used as a tourist attraction.

Another story on the production—this one written by Pat Crow for the October 20 edition of the *Tulsa World*—gave the location as "just north of No Head Hollow along Oklahoma 10," adding a slightly sinister note to the G-rated proceedings. Crow also noted that additional shooting was done at Qualls, Dripping Springs, Golda's Mill, and "various parts of the Cherokee Hills," telling of a scene with a "red-bone coon hound" named Blue:

Blue's big part came in a scene where the farm family buries another hound which was raised with Blue.

The red dog had two tough scenes in the sequence: to lie on the fresh grave and refuse to leave, and to look back forlornly as he was carried away.

Filming of the sequence took about four hours, but prompted by trainer Gerry Warshauer, Blue eventually played his part perfectly.

As Stewart Petersen, 13, carried Blue away from the mock grave, Mrs. Warshauer, who was standing beside the camera, repeatedly called "Blue, Blue," to keep him looking over Peterson's shoulder. After several tries, Blue performed beautifully.

The other scene was tougher. Blue had to walk to the grave, lie on it, and lower his head to his paws. After about a dozen tries, Blue went through his motions perfectly.

But the camera ran out of film midway. After a few more attempts, Blue did it even better.

That brought applause from the crew, which had been waiting nearly three hours to eat lunch.

As Crow's description indicates, *Where the Red Fern Grows* has its tear-jerking moments involving youngsters and the dogs they love. Its very title, in fact, came from a Native American legend about a red fern that grew between the bodies of two lost children, frozen to death in a blizzard. Author Rawls, a carpenter by trade, told the *Tulsa World*'s Beth Macklin that he'd written five novels by the time of his 1960 marriage—including *Where the Red Fern Grows*, his first. "I burned 'em all the week before I was married," he said in a story that ran on May 14, 1974. "My spelling was terrible and my punctuation was practically zero. I didn't want my wife to know I was that bad."

Once his wife found out about his ambition to write, however, she encouraged him, helping with grammar and syntax and typing his manuscripts. With her help, he knocked out a new version of *Where the Red Fern Grows* and sold it as a serial to the *Saturday Evening Post* the year after they were married. Doubleday picked it up and released it in hardcover, and while it didn't do much out of the gate, it was ultimately discovered by young readers. Several reports at the time of the *Fern* filming put sales of the largely autobiographical kids' novel at two hundred thousand.

Rawls returned from his home in Idaho Falls, Idaho, to attend the

Oklahoma premiere of the film, held at Tulsa's Southeast Cinema on May 21, a week after Macklin's story ran and almost two months after the movie's world premiere in Salt Lake City, Utah. Also in attendance at the show, which was a benefit for the Planned Parenthood Association of Tulsa and the Tulsa County Association for Mental Health, were producer Dayton and star Garland, along with the youngsters who played her kids: Petersen, Clark, and Wilson. Other local actors who'd had roles in the film also got their turn in the premiere spotlight, as did Lieutenant Governor Nigh.

But according to a story filed the next day by the *World's* Ron Butler, "Perhaps the biggest hit with the crowd of several hundred—especially with the many children on hand—were the two canine stars of the show, Rowdy and Blue. . . . Their handler, George Kerr of California, said they'd 'almost had all the hair petted off them' during visits to Tulsa and Oklahoma City schools the past week, but they seemed in good form for the premiere and got plenty of attention."

Butler was less impressed with the film itself, calling it "rather enjoyable, if routine" with a "conclusion that unfortunately resorts to cloying sentimentality" in an advance review that ran on May 5. Bill Donaldson, in the *Tulsa Tribune*, weighed in with his own evaluation the day after the Tulsa premiere:

> *Where the Red Fern Grows* is not a great film. But it is an enormously effective one. And it offers a terribly scarce commodity: a movie that the whole family can attend and enjoy.
>
> Its values—family unity and basic religion—are not often found in films these days. Producer Dayton says, "We believe there are still a lot of people in America who identify with these values and who find the sophistication of modern life discomforting.
>
> "Those people are coming to see the film wherever it has opened. In some small towns where it has played, more people have seen the film than the total population of the town.
>
> "We're getting the audience that has been left out all these years."
>
> *Where the Red Fern Grows*, then, is doing the job it was designed for and doing it very well indeed.

Donaldson and Dayton were both correct. The *Time* magazine profile of Dayton and his operation, cited earlier, asserted, "*Fern* cost $500,000 but already has grossed $8 million." (Pat Crow's *Tulsa World* story put the budget at "about $200,000.") By the time that 1977 piece appeared, Dayton had turned out four more movies, all making a profit by targeting the audiences he alluded to in Donaldson's piece—those primarily in small-town and rural America, the kind of people who would respond positively to a simple and sometimes lachrymose movie about a farm boy and his rawboned pets.

It should be noted that lightning didn't strike twice for Dayton. In 1999 the filmmaker returned to Tahlequah to begin a multimillion-dollar remake of *Fern*, this time starring Joseph Ashton as Billy, rock star Dave Matthews and Renee Faia as his parents, Dabney Coleman as grandpa, and Ned Beatty in the sheriff's role. Production had almost finished in Tahlequah when the Screen Actors Guild pulled its members from the set, citing nonpayment. A number of Tahlequah merchants were also left holding the bag by Dayton's production company, prompting the involvement of the U.S. Department of Labor.

Rod Walton's *Tulsa World* story of April 24, 2003, reported that Dayton had left the state, promising to bring back the needed capital, but instead stayed away. "California-based Crusader Entertainment bought the movie out of bankruptcy for $975,000, according to The Hook Internet film site," Walton wrote. "Crusader spent another $3 million finishing *Red Fern* under the direction of Sam Pillsbury." The remake, which closely followed the original picture, premiered in May 2003 at New York's Tribeca Film Festival.

"Back in Hollywood, they say Art Leonard is nuts, they say he's senile," seventy-year-old Art Leonard told *Tulsa Tribune* reporter Steve Ward for a December 2, 1977, story. "They are saying he is afraid to come back into Hollywood."

"But," wrote Ward, "Leonard has decided to make movies in Stillwater and 'what Art Leonard wants, Art Leonard gets,' he says."

Like G. D. Spradlin and, to a lesser extent, Joseph Taft, Art Leonard was a man who'd run up a moviemaking resume over the years. But the kinds of features he'd made before moving to Oklahoma in the early '70s put him more in the Herschell Gordon Lewis (*This Stuff'll Kill Ya!*) category. That is, he specialized in producing and directing movies that, for the most part, earned their money outside of mainstream channels. Lewis made exploitation films without any real stars or big budgets, finding his major audiences in Southern drive-ins and inner-city grind houses. Leonard, on the other hand, had made his mark in movies for African American patrons, playing them almost exclusively in all-black theaters during the segregated days of the '30s and '40s (the same venues that welcomed Richard E. Norman's two black-cast Oklahoma productions of the 1920s). Leonard's oeuvre as a producer-director in this genre included a couple of 1939 releases featuring the striking African American singer, dancer, and actress Nina Mae McKinney—*The Devil's Daughter* (also known as *Pocomania*) and *Straight to Heaven*—as well as a run of musical features in the '40s. He may also have produced and/or directed a number of theatrical short subjects. The *Tribune* piece told its readers that he "once directed Eleanor Roosevelt in a movie series called *Hobby Lobby*," the name of a popular radio series of the '30s and '40s in which people told about their unusual hobbies. (A *New Yorker* magazine "Talk of the Town" entry from May 18, 1940, reported that Mrs. Roosevelt was having "her first adventure as a motion picture actress" in the city, filming the debut *Hobby Lobby* short with Dave Elman, host of the radio show.)

Less convincing was another section of the story—obviously based on information from Leonard—which stated, "In the '40s and early '50s he directed a series of films with all black casts and was ostracized from the industry." He probably wasn't so much ostracized as ignored, since several people, both black and white, emerged from the African American movie industry to carve out nice careers for themselves in the mainstream— even if the mainstream didn't know or care much about their previous work. But then again, simply admitting that his work in that field was dismissed by the big studios wouldn't have made much of a story. And Art Leonard was a man who liked a good story. Take a look, for instance, at the one he told *Tribune* writer Ward about becoming an Oklahoman:

> Leonard came to the state seven years ago as a land promoter after he had sold the last of a series of nightclubs he had owned. He was stranded in Oklahoma City during a tornado and ended up wandering around

northwest Oklahoma City with his pet poodle because his rented car was destroyed in the storm. He moved into a hotel, married a woman who was working there and says he just "kind of liked Oklahoma."

Somewhere in there, Leonard had also realized something that other producers—including the itinerant filmmaker Melton Barker, whose multiple productions of *The Kidnappers' Foil* are discussed in chapter 4—knew about the middle of the country: The simple fact that one was really making movies, or had done so at some time in the past, opened a lot of doors. A person who'd been even marginally successful in the film business, someone with a legitimate credit or two, could become king of the hill on the Oklahoma filmmaking landscape. It was the classic big-frog, little-pond scenario.

And Leonard not only knew it. He talked about it to anyone who would listen.

"'I like this state because here I could be No. 1' among movie producers, Leonard said, since no other feature film companies are headquartered in Oklahoma," wrote Associated Press reporter David Egner in a story filed June 6, 1978. "In Oklahoma, [Leonard said,] 'you're not governed by studio bosses, you're doing your own thing.'"

In another story, this one appearing in the November 10, 1978, edition of the Oklahoma State University newspaper the *Daily O'Collegian*, Leonard was also up-front with student reporter Chris Day. "It's an ego thing," he said. "I want to be number one and I'm number one in Oklahoma while I might be number 5,627 in California."

The AP's Egner wrote that Leonard was sixty-three years old—seven years younger than the age he'd given the *Tribune*'s Steve Ward six months earlier—and that he'd "worked for 20 years as a producer for Warner Brothers and Columbia studios, but always on B-grade films." Leonard continued, "We can do anything here we can do in California. I'm trying to start an excitement here. . . . I want to bring the film and TV industry to Oklahoma."

By the time both those stories appeared, Leonard's first Sooner State film had been completed. Despite his ideas and plans for state moviemaking and his role in it, however, it would be his last.

Alien Zone, an anthology film that began life under the title *Five Faces*

Cover of the pressbook for *Alien Zone* (1977). (Courtesy of the L. R. B. Scott Collection)

of Terror, was shot in Stillwater, Yale, and Ponca City during the winter of 1977, under the auspices of Leonard's grandly named Myriad Cinema International, Inc., based in Enid. "Enid, with a population of about 45,000, became the movie capital of Oklahoma because it is the home of Leroy and Marvin Boehs," wrote the AP's Egner, "two oilmen who've agreed to supply $500,000 in financing for each of six Myriad films, Leonard said. There are also smaller investors in the company."

Key technicians were brought in from out of state, as were many of the picture's stars, a group that toplined the busy TV guest star and B-picture lead John Ericson, along with the familiar faces of such character players as Ivor Francis, Charles Aidman, and Bernard Fox. Many of the people involved in the production, however, had Oklahoma ties, including director Sharron Miller, an Enid native and a graduate of Stillwater's Oklahoma State University, and production manager Steve Sherry, who was from Yukon. Tulsa's Ayn Robbins wrote the lyrics for the two songs featured in *Alien Zone*; not long before, she'd been nominated for an Oscar for cowriting the lyrics to "Gonna Fly Now," the theme from the huge 1976 hit *Rocky*.

"A wonderful jazz musician named Stan Worth and I wrote what I consider to be a song that stood up to the test of time, 'The Sound of Goodbye,' and a sweet lullaby called 'Bless All the Children,'" said Robbins recently. "Both songs are attempts at irony. I consider the words to 'Goodbye' to be among the best lyrics I've written." "The Sound of Goodbye" ended up being "an homage to Stan," she added. "He built his own stunt biplane and completed it shortly after we completed the songs. On his first test flight, he took it up, put it in a dead stall, and crashed and burned, literally. It was devastating to the industry and to me personally." Worth was best known as a composer for television, creating music for such well-remembered '60s and '70s efforts as *Hollywood Squares* and the animated series *George of the Jungle*.

On the other side of the camera, OSU grad Burr DeBenning came back from Hollywood, where he'd carved out a nice career for himself, to take one of the major roles. Although he was best known as a television actor, he'd nabbed a starring role in the science fiction film *The Incredible Melting Man*, which went into wide release from American International

Pictures the same year DeBenning returned to emote at his alma mater.

Oklahoma State University wasn't used only as a backdrop for some of the scenes in *Alien Zone*. Because of the significant involvement of an OSU faculty member, who helped Leonard put cast and crew together, students at the university were hired to complete the crew.

"One of the radio-television-film professors there was a man named Bill Jackson, who was my adviser," recalled Rick Scott recently. An OSU student at the time, Scott was hired as a grip on the picture. "Bill had experience in Hollywood; he'd worked in some films. I don't know if he knew Art previously, but I know there was some connection between him and Art."

According to the *Tribune* story, Leonard "decided to go to one of the state schools for help in organizing a company because he says that was the only way he could get back into the business," a statement that doesn't indicate that he had a prior relationship with Jackson. Regardless of how or why the connection happened, however, when it all shook out, Jackson had become the titular producer of the picture, with Leonard the executive producer.

Scott remembers that key crew members came in from Utah, where they had been working on the TV series *The Life and Times of Grizzly Adams* for the Schick Sunn Classics company. (With ties to both Utah and Hollywood and similar kinds of product and marketing strategies, Schick Sunn had a lot in common with Doty-Dayton Productions, the company that made *Where the Red Fern Grows*.) That particular crew was hired because of director Sharron Miller, who'd helmed several *Grizzly Adams* episodes.

"They were a great bunch of guys," recalled Scott. "We heard a lot from 'em about [series star] Dan Haggerty and their *Grizzly Adams* days. We were all college students, so we were excited to meet guys who were actually out there making a living doing this kind of stuff.

"We were the grips, the bottom feeders, and we did all the grunt work—but we were glad to do it," he added. "And we did get paid. We got enough money to buy beer."

In fact, Scott said, that particular libation helped them all get through the four-week shoot, which took up most of their December.

"I remember it being *very* cold," he said. "There was a lot of alcohol being consumed at one, two, three in the morning, just to stay awake and to stay warm, just to try and keep going. The students who were working on the film saw how exciting it could be, but we also found out there was a lot of hard work involved. A lot of long hours and *hard* work."

In the style of the better-known horror pictures made by the British studio Amicus (including 1972's *Asylum* and 1973's *The Vault of Horror*), *Alien Zone* was an anthology film, composed of four short stories connected by an overarching narrative that's resolved at the end. The narrative involves Ericson as an unfaithful husband, in town for a plumber's convention, who gets dropped off at the wrong location by his cabbie during a rainstorm. Seeking shelter in a doorway, he's invited in by a sinister-looking man (Francis) who turns out to be a mortician. Although Ericson's character isn't all that interested, the mortician insists on showing him a roomful of clients in caskets, and as he opens each one up, the film dissolves to a new story. As scripted by David O'Malley—whose credits at the time included an episode of *Grizzly Adams*—each of the unfortunate occupants of the caskets deserves his or her fate, although sometimes the punishment outweighs the crime. A teacher (Judith Novgrod) who shows her disdain for kids gets brutally murdered by a group of them, while a rude businessman (Richard Gates) who mistreats a wino is systematically turned into a pitiful alcoholic.

Ultimately, the film was nationally released by the tiny Jupiter Pictures, of Burbank, California—but not before a Hollywood-style send-off in Oklahoma. "Prior to the premiere in Stillwater, I went to a showing in Oklahoma City—I guess it was a rough cut—that Sharron Miller and [editor] Steve Sherry had put together," remembered Scott. "This thing ran like two hours. It was shown at the Will Rogers Theatre in Oklahoma City, and it was obvious to everybody that it was way too long. So it was cut down to the length [82 minutes] we saw at the premiere.

"The premiere was a big deal, a huge deal, in Stillwater. They had searchlights, and, if I remember right, Sharron Miller and Bill Jackson showed up in a hearse. It was the world premiere of, as they billed it, a major Hollywood picture. So it was pretty packed, and there was a lot of excitement, because most of the people there were crew people, people who had something to do with the film, and their families. There was a lot of anticipation about it. Everybody was anxious to see it."

For him and his OSU cohorts, who had gotten their first taste of the movie industry with *Alien Zone*, it was an eye-opener. "I think we all thought there were some parts that were better than we thought they would be," he said. "And there were some parts that obviously did not work."

The whole film didn't work well enough to keep Myriad, Leonard, or the brothers Boehs in the feature film business, and yet another shot at building a movie industry in Oklahoma had fallen short of its mark.

Still, Lieutenant Governor Nigh and the rest of the state's film boosters pressed on, continuing to talk Oklahoma up to Hollywood. And, in the late '70s, one of those helpful boosters was Jesse Vint, the Tulsan who, with his brother Alan (of *Welcome Home, Soldier Boys*), was doing quite well as a player in youth-market pictures in the drive-in style. In April 1977, Tulsa's United Artists Annex 3 Theater hosted a premiere of *Black Oak Conspiracy*, the story of a Hollywood stuntman who returns to his home in Arkansas to find that a mining company with dishonorable intentions has moved in on his town. Although it was filmed outside of the state, *Black Oak Conspiracy* was touted in an April 6 *Tulsa Tribune* article as "the first movie for which all the money was raised in Tulsa." (In fact, that distinction probably belongs to one of the silent films of the '10s or '20s or, in the talking-features department, to the aforementioned *Just between Us*.)

Added the unnamed writer, "It's largely the work of two Tulsa natives. *Black Oak Conspiracy* was produced by Jesse Vint, son of Jesse Vint Jr., president of Unit Rig & Equipment Co. here; and Tom Clark, president of Tulsair Beechcraft Inc. Vint was also co-writer of the screenplay and is the star of the film. Young Vint and Clark have been friends for many years."

A couple of years later, on April 15, 1979, the *Sunday Oklahoman* ran a story on the then current feature *Fast Charlie . . . The Moonbeam Rider*, a period film from Universal Pictures starring David Carradine and Brenda

Oklahoma boy Whit Clay and David Carradine in *Fast Charlie . . . The Moon-beam Rider* (1979). (John Wooley Archives)

Vaccaro and coproduced by legendary low-budget auteur Roger Corman. Not only had it been filmed almost entirely in Oklahoma in the summer of 1978, but it also starred Jesse Vint. The Tulsa native played a character named Calvin Hawk, the main rival of Fast Charlie Swattle (Carradine) in a transcontinental motorcycle race held following the World War I armistice. Chances seem good that Vint had something to do with the company's filming in Oklahoma.

If he did, it's possible that he felt a tinge of regret about it before the shooting wrapped. As the unbylined *Sunday Oklahoman* piece noted, filming began in Lawton in the dead heat of an Oklahoma summer, and "the cast and crew often sweltered in 100–110 degree temperatures coupled with stifling humidity." That group would've included Vint himself, of course.

On the plus side, the story showed that Oklahoma sites could be used for just about any location that was needed, at least for this particular picture:

> The beginning of the motorcycle race, supposedly at the St. Louis Fairgrounds, was shot at a deserted fairground in Lawton that was dressed up with bands and marching units, passenger-carrying balloons, vintage airplanes, a World War I–uniformed and horse-drawn artillery drill team provided by nearby Fort Sill, and hundreds of local extras, recruited with help of the Lawton Community Theatre. . . .
>
> Even the "San Francisco" that is seen at the end of the race was filmed in Oklahoma, at Guthrie, where the houses and brick streets look like their Bay Area counterparts of 1920.

Cache, a movie location since the days of marshal Bill Tilghman, was also used, thanks to "period buildings . . . on display in an amusement park." The crew even filmed a jailbreak in Marietta, "using the real local jail with bonafide prisoners." Sheriff Wesley Liddell, around to keep an eye on things, ended up being cast as an extra in the picture. He was one of many Oklahomans who ended up in the PG-rated film, some with substantial roles. Six-year-old Whit Clay, for instance, whose father was an army officer stationed at Fort Sill, was cast as Wesley Wolf III, the son of waitress Grace Wolf (Brenda Vaccaro), *Fast Charlie*'s female protagonist. Her boyfriend was played by Jack Brennan, a sergeant from Fort Sill. Even the Oklahoma Tourist Commission's Peggy Weems, assigned by the state to assist the film company with locations and other arrangements, took a part as a landlady.

According to the *Sunday Oklahoman* story, only one scene in the entire picture was shot outside of the state. It involved "a train of 1880 vintage, which was located in Sonora, 350 miles north of Los Angeles."

While costarring in *Fast Charlie*, Tulsa native Jesse Vint wrote his first script "during lulls in the filming," according to Bruce Westbrook's *Daily Oklahoman* story of May 22, 1979. "I had a lot of free time, so I sat down and wrote a screenplay of my adventures as a teen-ager in high school in Tulsa," Vint told the reporter. "Max had been looking for a good screenplay for three years, and decided he wanted to do it."

"Max" was Max Baer, Jr., the former star of TV's *The Beverly Hillbillies* and the producer and cowriter of 1974's *Macon County Line*, a huge hit for Vint and his actor brother Alan. With Baer as both producer and director, Vint's script was the basis of *Hometown USA*, a picture released in 1979 by Film Ventures International, which specialized in exploitation and horror movies for the drive-in trade.

Shot in California, *Hometown USA* came along in the wake of the '50s-set coming-of-age pictures that had begun with the 1973 blockbuster *American Graffiti*. In an interview with the *Tulsa Tribune*'s Bill Donaldson for a May 18, 1979, piece, Vint acknowledged as much when he described the picture as "my *American Graffiti*, about a string of experiences I had when I was attending Edison High School in 1958."

In the same interview, he aired a difference of opinion he'd had with Baer over the movie's content. "Max and I differed widely on the nature of the film," Vint told Donaldson. "I thought it should be shot as a PG-rated film. He thought it should be a 'hard' R because that was more commercial. The man with the money usually wins. He calls my morality 'dated.' The print that will open in Tulsa will be R-rated. But the picture is being re-edited right now to get a re-classification to PG."

Perhaps it was reedited. But the only version of *Hometown USA* widely available for home viewing at this writing remains a racy R version.

Two summers before Vint came to Oklahoma to act in *Fast Charlie*—and write his *Hometown USA* script—another feature started up in many of the same locations Fast Charlie would use. *The Charge of the Model T's*, which began filming in the Wichita Mountains around Lawton and Cache on July 5, 1976, was a G-rated comedy involving a World War I German spy (Louis Nye) who, with the aid of Mexican guerrillas and a specially equipped automobile, hopes to disrupt the war effort by making trouble on the U.S.-Mexico border. His efforts are countered by those of an army lieutenant (John David Carson) and his men, who roll into battle in Model T Fords.

Released regionally in early 1979, the film had actually been completed in 1977. According to a November 5, 1977, Associated Press release—

published in conjunction with the film's official premiere in Lawton—producer-director Jim McCullough had lensed the picture in locations that also included Eagle Park and Fort Sill, using somewhere around one hundred locals as extras. A *Daily Oklahoman* story from two days earlier noted, "*Charge of the Model T's* is the second movie to premiere here [in Lawton] since the 1948 grand opening of *Prince of Peace*, a film on the Easter pageant at the Holy City of the Wichitas." There were to be "two days of community activities" in conjunction with the premiere, with star Carson and supporting players John Doucette, Louisa Moritz, and Bill Thurman expected to attend.

In addition to its shooting-location similarities with *Fast Charlie*, *Charge of the Model T's* also had a connection to *Where the Red Fern Grows*. McCullough's first significant credit had been as an associate producer on *Fern*, while his son, Jim McCullough, Jr. (who had a supporting role in *Charge of the Model T's*), had been a production assistant on it. The two films also shared the same cinematographer, Dean Cundey. Released in 1974 and 1979, respectively, *Fern* and *Charge* sandwiched the feature that would bring Cundey much of his early fame—the 1978 horror blockbuster *Halloween*.

The elder McCullough planned to return to the state to film "the story of Oklahoma Indian outlaw Ned Christy" the next year. Although that never happened, he managed to amass several other production credits, often working with his son. They include the down-home comedy *Soggy Bottom U.S.A.* (1980), *Mountaintop Motel Massacre* (1986), and *Where the Red Fern Grows: Part 2* (1992), which moved the location of the story to Louisiana and featured Doug McKeon as a returning World War II vet who is given a pair of dogs by his grandfather (Wilford Brimley) to help ease him back into civilian life. McCullough Sr. also directed this straight-to-home-video release, which is not to be confused with the troubled 1999/2003 remake of *Fern*.

A huge country-music festival, called 48 Hours in Atoka and held the last weekend of August 1975, brought—by some accounts—nearly one hundred thousand souls to an amphitheater in the hills about ten miles

SHOT IN OKLAHOMA

outside that southeastern Oklahoma community. Featuring such top-flight country acts as Willie Nelson, Larry Gatlin, Don Williams, Freddy Fender, Red Steagall, and Oklahoma natives Hoyt Axton and Don White, it was dubbed by some—including the *Daily Oklahoman*'s Edwin Maloy—"the Woodstock of country music."

Maloy reported on the event in a front-page *Oklahoman* story from August 31, which was accompanied by a Woodstock-like scene of a young woman in a headband, grooving by herself in front of a crowd of longhairs, shirtless and otherwise. Buried inside that edition, another story (unbylined, but likely Maloy's) told of the filming of the event:

> Chuck Bowman of Bowman-Davis productions, a Los Angeles motion picture company, said Saturday his company plans a full-length motion picture or television specials of the state's musical extravaganza.
>
> Bowman said he is directing the filming and Bob Davis is producer.
>
> "We brought 15 people from California and hired another five from the area for the project," Bowman said. Ten cameras and 16-track sound equipment were brought to the southeast Oklahoma festival to gather raw material for the film, he said.
>
> "With this equipment the sound should be mixed perfectly with everything isolated," Bowman said.
>
> Bowman said his company and Media Five of Tulsa will view the film and decide whether to use it for theater release or television programs.

Just about four years later—on September 7, 1979—the answer came with a theatrical film titled simply *Atoka*. Opening simultaneously on that date in forty theaters across the state, ranging from venues in Oklahoma City and Tulsa to movie houses in Clinton and Hobart, the advertising material asked: "Were you there in <u>Atoka</u>, Okla. when the last of the great outdoor <u>concerts</u> happened? '48 Hours in <u>Atoka</u>.' The <u>concert</u> is now '<u>ATOKA</u> THE MOVIE.'"

Rated R because of the language used by the highly unpredictable singer-songwriter David Allan Coe and some brief nudity, the picture was soundly thrashed by the *Tulsa Tribune*'s country-music writer, Ellis Widner, when it played his town. The headline—"*Atoka*: The Movie That Should Never Have Happened"—said it all.

"The filming is horrible and the editing is even worse," wrote Widener in a review that ran the day after the premiere. "Camera angles and framing lacked imagination or were totally off the mark." And he was just getting started.

> The film is an amateurish effort—and a poor one at that. It goes beyond what was obviously a low budget. This is just poor filmmaking.
>
> A beginning high school film class could've done a better job.
>
> *Atoka* is a total embarrassment for the filmmakers, the festival and the talent involved.
>
> The movie wastes some of the greatest musical talent ever included on a concert film. . . .
>
> *Atoka*, now showing at the Fontana and Forum Theaters, is a rip-off. Don't waste your money. Even if you get in free, you'll come out on the short end of the deal.

An *Oklahoman* article from the day before, written by David Devane, was kinder to the picture, quoting mostly lukewarm endorsements from people who'd been at the actual event, and noting that it, like the event itself, had "upset some residents of Atoka."

The story gave the distributor as "Innovative Marketing and Movies Distribution," which may have been an ad hoc group put together only for this film. Whether it was or not, it employed an old movie-selling technique known as saturation booking, in which the idea is to get a film into as many theaters as you can, get your money, and get out and go somewhere else before word of mouth can kill it. This strategy was traditionally used to promote films of dubious quality.

The saturation booking of *Atoka*, however, doesn't seem to extend beyond the forty theaters in Oklahoma. After those play dates, the feature-length concert documentary seems to have disappeared without a trace. Even in an age when the most obscure theatrical features are being dug out of vaults and reissued on the home-video market, *Atoka*—despite its big-name stars and relatively recent release—remains unavailable.

Before leaving the '70s, let's take a quick look at two other films that were allegedly shot in Oklahoma during the decade. Both animator Ralph Bakshi's incendiary and still-controversial *Coonskin* (1975) and director Alan Rudolph's comedy-with-music cult favorite, *Roadie* (1980), are often included on lists of made-in-Oklahoma films.

One might well wonder how an animated film like *Coonskin* could've been shot on location. Those who have seen the picture, however, know that the feature-length cartoon—a tough and angry urban spin on the classic Uncle Remus stories of Joel Chandler Harris—is framed by live-action footage of actors Barry White, Philip Michael Thomas, Scatman Crothers, and Charles Gordone, before and after a prison break.

In an interview by Richard von Busak that appeared on the website Metroactive.com (in a "web extra" complementing the February 27–March 5, 2003, issue of *Metro, Silicon Valley's Weekly Newspaper*), Bakshi affirmed that the live-action material—except for some background footage shot in New York—was lensed in Oklahoma. "I used film as sort of an adventure, to get out of Brooklyn," he said. "I went to El Reno to the state prison and filmed there; a week later, they [prisoners]burned it in a riot."

No such evidence of Oklahoma scenes in *Roadie* exists, however. According to the official United Artists press kit, most of the filming was done well across the Red River in Austin, Texas, with additional scenes shot in New York and Los Angeles. The film is one of the best-known works of the great Tulsa character actor and comedian Gailard Sartain, so perhaps that has something to do with the perception of state involvement. (The press kit also referred to the "natural twang" in the voice of one of Sartain's costars, Rhonda Bates, attributing it to her "Oklahoma origin." Later, however, the same press material gave her birthplace as Fayetteville, Arkansas, and her hometown as Evansville, Indiana.)

On January 3, 1979, film-industry booster George Nigh was no longer second in command in Oklahoma. The longtime lieutenant governor now occupied the Governor's Mansion—and he brought his love of movies and movie people with him. By September of that year, he'd formed the Oklahoma Film Industry Task Force. Although the task force still worked through the state's Department of Tourism and Recreation, which had handled all the previous official attempts to bring moviemaking to the state, it was now. as a special Oklahoma supplement to the May 14, 1983, edition of the *Hollywood Reporter* put it, "a legislatively recognized body with one job—selling the film and video industry on Oklahoma."

Wrote Kate Jones, the author of the piece:

> The task force is the fulfillment of a longtime commitment on the part of Oklahoma's governor. . . . Back in the '60s, when Nigh was lieutenant governor, the story goes, he ran into an old friend who'd been in Texas, where *Bonnie and Clyde* was being filmed. Since Oklahoma was one of the bandit couple's favorite haunts, he asked a logical question, "Why wasn't it being filmed in Oklahoma?" The answer seemed to be that no one had asked them to.
>
> That started Nigh on what has become a pet project—luring film and TV companies, and dollars, to Oklahoma.

"Look at the evidence," said Vern Stefanic, whose tenure as the *Tulsa World*'s film critic began in 1979 and lasted into the early '80s. "When George Nigh really started pushing it, he could do it with the all of state of Oklahoma officially behind him. It wasn't just local groups trying to promote their own specific areas.

"There were two things going on: First, Oklahoma needed more diversity of income. Oil and cattle were still big then, but things were starting to change. Second, George Nigh seemed to enjoy celebrity—both his and that of the people he was around. Films attached to the state of Oklahoma a certain coolness. People in this state have always worked to change the Dust Bowl image of Oklahoma. Having filmmakers come in was a way to redefine who we are."

For all that, however, the most famous batch of shot-in-Oklahoma theatrical features—which came along during Stefanic's film-critic tenure—had more to do with one of the best-known writers of young-adult books in the nation than with any official or state entity. Her name was Susan Eloise Hinton, and she just happened to live in Tulsa.

SEVEN

Tulsa—Outsiders and Innovators

There was one point in my life when *Tex* was coming out, we were doing pickup shots for *The Outsiders*, and I was still working on the screenplay of *Rumble Fish*. Matt [Dillon] and I went on a publicity tour for *Tex*, one of those eight-cities-in-five-days kinds of things, and ended up in L.A., where I worked with Francis [Ford Coppola] on the screenplay some more. But at that point in my life, I was shooting a movie, advertising a movie, and writing a movie, all at the same time.

> —S. E. Hinton

Filming of *Tex* in Tulsa Makes Task Force's Job Easier

> —headline in *Tulsa Tribune* (October 26, 1981)

We're not at the point where we'd do a video feature-length movie. We still believe a film should be seen in a theater and then come to home video. We see film production and the videotape market as two separate entities at this point. But things are changing so much in this business that it may be a viable thing for us to do somewhere down the line.

> —Vestron Video's Cathy Mantegna, in an interview with the author for a *Tulsa World* story (May 19, 1985)

To those who were around the scene, it still seems as though everything suddenly lit up and blew through with the velocity and flash of a massive high-plains thunderstorm. In a little more than a year, three Hollywood-studio films had begun and ended shooting in and around Oklahoma's second-largest city—one feature from Walt Disney Studios and two from the Oscar-winning Hollywood heavyweight Francis Ford Coppola.

Indeed, the flurry of Tulsa filmmaking—jam-packed into the months between spring of 1981 and late summer of 1982—remains unprecedented in the annals of Sooner State cinema. To find out what happened, it's necessary to go all the way back to Tulsa in the late 1960s, when a young teenager named Susie Hinton witnessed something so disturbing to her that she just had to get it down on paper.

"I grew up in kind of a borderline greaser neighborhood, and when I was first at Will Rogers [High School], a sophomore, one of my friends got beaten up by some Socs when we were walking home from school," said Hinton recently. "It made me mad, and I began a short story about a kid who got beaten up on his way home from the movies."

That short story, and the incident that inspired it, led to Hinton's renowned novel *The Outsiders*, written while she was still in high school and published in 1967. Its story of uncrossable social-class boundaries between the upscale "Socs" and the wrong-side-of-the-tracks "greasers," along with its meditations on innocence and loss, resonated with young readers everywhere, and it soon became one of the most popular young-adult books of all time. After a long writer's block that followed the unexpected success of *The Outsiders*, Hinton wrote several more well-received novels for that same audience, including the other two picked up for filming in Hinton's hometown, *Rumble Fish* and *Tex*, published in 1975 and 1979, respectively.

The same year *Tex* was published, as Hinton remembered it, she heard from someone at Zoetrope, the studio established by Francis Ford Coppola. "They were the first to call me, but they were not the first to get into production [in Tulsa]," she explained. "They called and said they wanted to buy *The Outsiders* for the studio, and they were going to hire a screenwriter, and then I didn't hear from them for a while."

The Outsiders had been brought to Coppola's attention by a group of junior high students and their librarian in Fresno, California, who had all drafted and signed a letter to the filmmaker telling him what a wonderful movie the book would make. That 1979 call from a Zoetrope representative to Hinton started the process that secured the film rights to the novel.

A couple of months later, Hinton remembered, "Disney called me, wanting to do *Tex*. And then, the next thing I knew, I had the *Tex* screenwriter-director out. When I met Tim Hunter, I knew we had a good connection. And to this day, he's one of my best friends."

Hinton took Hunter around Tulsa, showing him some of the real-life locations she'd used in the book. What he saw on those trips, coupled with Hinton's and *Tex*'s connection to the area, impressed him enough to lobby for Tulsa as a filming location.

In a March 14, 1981, *Tulsa World* story announcing that the Tulsa area had been chosen by *Tex*'s filmmakers, Vern Stefanic wrote that just a few days earlier Stockton, California, was still being considered as a possible location. But executive producer Jerry Baerwitz told Stefanic, "We wanted to shoot it here, because this is where the story takes place. "The book is based here . . . so we'll shoot the total picture here."

Cameras began rolling on May 11, with outdoor scenes filmed around Tulsa and the nearby community of Bixby. Matt Dillon starred as Tex McCormick, a happy-go-lucky rural teen who loves his horse (played in the film by S. E. Hinton's horse) and his best friend's sister (Meg Tilly). He lives with his older brother, Mason (Jim Metzler), who's assumed most of the parenting duties because their rodeo-drifter father (Bill McKinney of *Deliverance* fame) isn't around much. After an encounter with a hitchhiker causes certain revelations about the family to come to light, Tex is faced with some tough choices—and he doesn't always make the right ones. Emilio Estevez, in his motion picture debut, plays Tex's best pal, Johnny.

The film was Tim Hunter's debut as a director as well, although he had written the disaffected-youth picture *Over the Edge*. That 1979 film also marked the cinematic debut of Dillon, who would star in all three of the Tulsa-shot movies. "Tim told me later that the kids in *Over the Edge* who had never read *anything* had read *The Outsiders*, and the ones who had read *everything* had read *The Outsiders*," Hinton said. "Matt kept bugging Tim [during the *Over the Edge* filming], saying, 'Why don't you guys do S. E. Hinton books? They're my favorite books.' That got Tim into *Tex*. Matt got Tim into *Tex*, and Tim didn't really have anybody else in mind for the role."

The movie also brought Oklahoma favorite son Ben Johnson back home to play the patriarch of the Collins clan, which includes the young characters played by Estevez and Tilly. He'd last filmed in the state four years earlier, as one of the stars of *Dillinger*. That film had been rated R; *Tex* was going for a PG. Still, because of the production company behind *Tex*, Johnson expressed some reservations about the proposed rating to the *Tulsa Tribune*'s David Jones. "This is the first Disney film made that's a little off color," Johnson said in a story from May 20, 1981. "I'm not sure how it's going to be accepted. It's a decent script, but it's different from what you'd usually expect from Disney. Yeah, it bothers me a bit that Disney is doing this." (Although *Tex*, at the time, was thought by many to be the first PG movie from Disney, known as a purveyor of squeaky-clean G-rated fare, that distinction actually goes to the science fiction feature *The Black Hole*, released by the studio in 1979.)

Not many locals appeared to share the veteran actor's concern. A crowd estimated by *Tribune* writer Ray Formanek at more than 1,500 began lining up at 6 o'clock on a late June morning outside the Broken Arrow High School gym, hoping to get passes for a special basketball game between the Broken Arrow and Bixby squads that was being staged for the *Tex* cameras. Although they received no pay—except for complimentary concessions—and had to wear clothes suitable for the autumn basketball season, many, if not most, of the volunteer extras hung in there until filming was complete. Wrote Formanek in his June 24 story, "The crowd—most of whom were wearing the long pants that the Disney studios had requested them to wear—began filing into the gymnasium at about 1:30 P.M. hoping to escape the 93-degree-heat. "Once the gym had filled, however, it became apparent that the film's extras were in for one long, hot afternoon," which would include lots of time between scene setups when there wasn't much to take the crowd's mind off the stifling indoor temperature.

By 4 P.M., according to Formanek, "heat had taken its toll on the extras" and the remaining spectators—which the writer figured to be about half of the original group—had to be moved to the north side of the stands, so it would look as though the gym was full. And the gratis concessions were going fast.

"So far, we've poured over 200 gallons of Pepsi, used 120 pounds of popcorn and given away 800 bags of Fritos," property master Jack

Eberhart told the reporter. "All that in just four hours and 15 minutes." Eberhart estimated the 4 P.M. temperature at the top of the stands at 130 degrees—which would go a long way in accounting for the Pepsi consumption that afternoon.

Given the heat of that long-ago Oklahoma summer, it's not surprising to read publicist Howard Green's assessment of the local shooting, published in a companion *Tribune* report the same day. "I think a lot of us thought Tulsa was a hick town," he told writer Kevin Harrison. "I was surprised to see people like Liza Minnelli and Pavarotti coming through town. And there is a lot of culture around here. Some of the crew has gone to museums.

"I have never encountered nicer people anywhere I have been," he added. "We have all been favorably impressed with everything except the weather."

"It was summer when the last of the *Tex* people left," recalled S. E. Hinton. "That fall was when Francis first contacted me." Francis was, of course, Francis Ford Coppola, who was holding casting calls for *The Outsiders* in a number of American cities, including the place where the book was born.

"Francis wasn't going to shoot it himself, not originally," revealed Hinton. "It was bought for Zoetrope Studios. But he was in an airplane and read the book, and he decided he wanted to do it. There was already a screenplay written by a woman named Kathleen Rowell [who gets screenwriter credit for *The Outsiders*], but he tossed it. Didn't even look at it. I read it. It was modernized and basically, other than the names, it didn't have much to do with the book.

"So he came to Tulsa for a casting session [on October 21] and asked if I'd come down to meet him. I did, and we hit it off real well. He said, 'Show me the places you were thinking of when you were writing this.' I'd already done this with Tim Hunter, and after I'd driven Tim around, he'd decided to shoot in Tulsa. So I drove *Francis* around, and *he* decided to shoot in Tulsa, and he and I wrote the screenplay."

It probably didn't hurt Tulsa's chances to have Coppola's longtime collaborator Gray Frederickson, an Oklahoma City native and University of Oklahoma graduate, on board as coproducer (with Fred Roos). And the presence of George Nigh's Oklahoma Film Industry Task Force, eager to do whatever it could to get someone of Coppola's stature to film in the state, made for another plus.

By mid-November, Vern Stefanic could write in the *World* that Tulsa was "the leading candidate" for the shooting, with the final decision to be made within a month.

"This week Roos, in a telephone interview from his Hollywood office, said Zoetrope "is pretty sure it's going to be in Tulsa," wrote Stefanic in a November 13 piece. "'The obvious reason why is because that's where the story is set,' Roos said. . . . But another reason surfaced as the movie makers took several tours of Tulsa, scouting for possible filming locations: 'We liked Tulsa very much,' Roos said."

S. E. Hinton especially remembers one of those trips. She was showing Coppola a locally famous drive-in theater, where, years before, she had personally witnessed an encounter between a greaser boy and Soc girls that had inspired a scene in her book. "When Francis said, 'Show me what you were thinking about [with that scene],'" I took him to the Admiral Twin Drive-In," she recalled. "I'll never forget it, because it was February and it was really cold, the wind was really sharp, and he had this big video camera—in those days they were huge—on his shoulder, shooting. Something got jammed up, so we all ended up in the ladies' room, where it was warm, and he fixed his camera with his Swiss Army knife. I still remember standing there thinking, 'Am I standing in the ladies' room at the Admiral Twin Drive-In while Francis Ford Coppola fixes his camera with a Swiss Army knife?' It was surreal."

That same month, all of America heard of his plans—even if the announcement wasn't exactly official. "Francis Ford Coppola let the cat out of the bag on national TV late Monday night when he told talk show host David Letterman that yes, he was coming to Tulsa to film his next movie, *The Outsiders*," wrote Stefanic in a February 10 *World* piece. "Unfortunately, his revelation led to a few red faces in both Tulsa and Hollywood. No one else knew Coppola was going to make that statement."

Among those Coppola's revelation caught by surprise was coproducer

Frederickson, who told Stefanic he'd like the official announcement to come from Governor Nigh's office, since the Oklahoma Film Industry Task Force had "played a big part" in getting the filmmakers to town and helping scout locations. On the other hand, Mary Nell Clark—the task force coordinator who would be a major figure in '80s and '90s Oklahoma filmmaking—demurred, saying she hadn't yet gotten official confirmation from Zoetrope. A couple of weeks later, however, everyone ended up on the same page, and the next month, Coppola and the crew flew in and began setting up shop. Shooting ran from March 29 to May 15, at locations in Tulsa and the neighboring communities of Skiatook, Sperry, Owasso, and Sapulpa. (Coppola and his crew filmed incidental, or pickup, shots in the area for several months after that, however.)

"Originally, he was going to try to go with unknowns, with no experience or anything," said Hinton, referring to Coppola's initial casting plans. "But I think the only real unknown he got was Darren Dalton [from Albuquerque, New Mexico], who played Randy. All the rest of the boys had had some kind of experience, and Matt [Dillon] was the only one who had any kind of a name."

A case could also be made for the name recognition of cast member Leif Garrett, playing one of the main Socs. Not long before, Garrett had been a teen-magazine cover boy and recording artist, known for such pop hits as 1978's "I Was Made for Dancin'" and the 1977 remake of "Runaround Sue." But for the rest of the principals, *The Outsiders* was the vehicle that helped propel them to stardom. By now, the roster of young up-and-comers in the movie has become legendary. In addition to Dillon, Garrett, and Dalton, the stars included C. Thomas Howell (as the viewpoint character, Ponyboy), Tom Cruise, Emilio Estevez, Ralph Macchio, Rob Lowe, and Patrick Swayze, along with Diane Lane as the Soc girl who crosses the greasers' path. Michelle Meyrink, as another Soc, also made her debut in the film. Dillon and Estevez had starred in *Tex*, but neither had hung around Tulsa after the filming was complete.

"I'd given Matt riding lessons [for *Tex*], and we'd become really good friends," said Hinton. "When Francis was casting *The Outsiders*, nobody was looking at Matt, and I thought, 'Well, it's because he just did a movie with me.' But I got Fred Roos—the producer who also cast—one day, and I said, 'When you're in New York, look at Matt, because he'd be really good for [the part of] Dallas.' And as soon as Francis saw him, he cast him."

In order to hammer a psychological wedge between the Socs and the greasers, Coppola gave the actors playing the Socs leather-bound scripts, while the greaser actors got regular ones. The living quarters of the two groups were also segregated, with Soc actors put up on a higher floor of the Excelsior Hotel, where the cast stayed. And, Hinton noted, "they had them play football against each other, but the Socs got really nice track suits, and the boys got regular old gray sweats. But they all ended up getting the same per diem, because the boys' agents thought that [different pay rates] would be carrying things a little bit too far."

In one of the movie's major scenes, a group of Socs corner Ponyboy and attempt to drown him in a fountain. (The scene took place in Tulsa's Crutchfield Park, where Coppola would later host a wrap party, inviting the whole neighborhood.) In the interview section of her book *Some of Tim's Stories* (2007), Hinton told interviewer Teresa Miller that Howell "had the flu—bad—the night we were drowning him in the fountain. It was in the upper thirties. We did have heaters around, but by the time you were dragged out of that fountain and put in front of a heater, you could get pretty cold. Tommy toughed it out, though. Nobody whined."

Meanwhile, Hinton continued, back at the hotel, "the other cast members, in a show of camaraderie, were pretending to drown each other in the hotel fountain." She added, "A few years later, I went back to the hotel and the fountain was gone. I think I know why."

The Outsiders premiered on March 22—just about ten months after the Oklahoma shooting officially wrapped—at Tulsa's Williams Forum Cinema. Attended by Howell, Swayze, and Hinton, the benefit screening netted nearly $25,000 for the Rainbow House, a local family crisis center.

Not long after that official unveiling, *The Outsiders* debuted on some nine hundred movie screens nationwide. Seventeen days later, an April 13 *Tribune* announcement stated that the picture was grossing an average of a million dollars a day. It was a hit, despite lukewarm reviews—including one tinged with disappointment from the *Tulsa World*'s Vern Stefanic, who had been very close to the filming. In a March 25 notice he wrote

Francis Ford Coppola (in beret) directs *Outsiders* stars C. Thomas Howell, Ralph Macchio, and Matt Dillon in a scene outside a drive-in restaurant. (John Wooley Archives)

that the film "doesn't live up to expectations of greatness. It doesn't come close, although the ingredients for greatness are obvious in every frame of the movie." He felt that "too much post-production work may have robbed the film of a logical exposition, flow and several elements crucial to plot and character development." Describing the score by Carmine Coppola (Francis's father) as "beautiful—but totally out of place," he added, "This is a movie about street-tough thugs; the music, except for snatches of [the rock 'n' roll classic] 'Gloria,' sounds like 101 Strings. It's annoying and alarming."

Much later, both of Stefanic's concerns—shared with several other reviewers across the country—were addressed in a director's-cut version called *The Outsiders: The Complete Novel*, released on DVD in 2005. It added twenty-two minutes of new footage and jettisoned much of the elder Coppola's sound track in favor of rock 'n' roll songs from the '60s.

"My problems were simply with the feel of the original release, which relied heavily on his father's music," explained Stefanic, more than twenty-five years after writing his initial review. "The music was too grand and sentimental and didn't fit with the story. When it was recut and given a new soundtrack, that put the emphasis back where it needed to be, on Susie's story about a personal, intimate struggle.

"My comments in the review were not about the quality of the film—everything was beautifully done—but about the artistic choices," he added. "I believe the recut served the story better."

Like its 1983 predecessor, *The Outsiders: The Complete Novel* also had a benefit premiere in Tulsa. Held on September 8, the invitation-only event was a fund-raiser for Tulsa's Street School. On hand for the 2005 screening were Hinton and Howell—who'd attended the first premiere—as well as costar Ralph Macchio. Among the attendees was Kim Connor, who'd been a senior at Nathan Hale High School when Howell et al. had come to town to shoot the picture. "The big thing to do then was you had to see the movie twice," Connor told the *World*'s Jason Collington in a September 9 story. "You saw it the first time to see where everything in town was, and then saw it a second time to actually watch the movie."

By October of that same year, 1983, Connor and the other young Tulsans entranced by *The Outsiders* would have a chance to see a second Coppola-Hinton collaboration, once again starring Dillon. This one, however, would be something a little . . . different.

"Halfway through the shoot of *The Outsiders*," Hinton remembered, "Francis turns to me and says, 'Well, Susie, you and I work together real well. Have you got anything else I can do while I'm here? I've got a crew. I've got some actors.'

"I said, 'Well, I've got this weird book called *Rumble Fish*, and nobody gets it.'

"One day, he comes running in, waving a copy. He says, 'I love this book. It's so weird. We'll make it weirder. You and I will write the screenplay on Sundays'—because we were shooting six days a week on *The Outsiders*. So that's what happened."

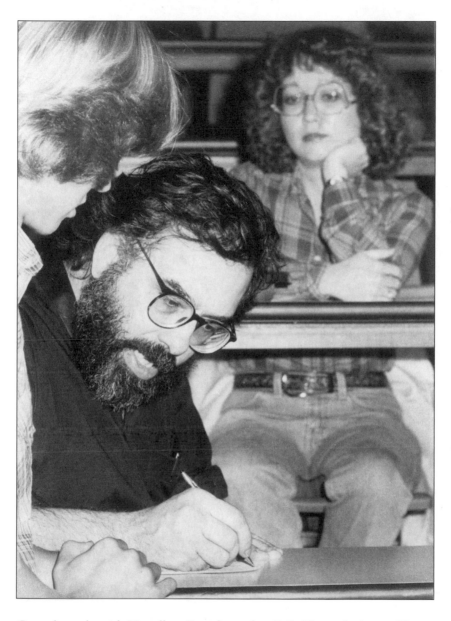

Coppola works with Howell as *Outsiders* author S. E. Hinton looks on. (Courtesy of the *Tulsa World*)

Mickey Rourke studies Siamese fighting fish in *Rumble Fish* (1983), the third
S. E. Hinton novel adaptation filmed in Tulsa. (John Wooley Archives)

The story of a young tough named Rusty-James and his older brother,
a former gang leader and near-mythological figure known as the Motorcycle Boy, *Rumble Fish* was also a favorite novel of *Tex* and *Outsiders* star
Dillon. "When we were on *Tex*, Matt had told me that if we ever got a
movie of *Rumble Fish* going, he wanted to play Rusty-James," revealed
Hinton. "We were in his trailer at one of the high schools, and there were
all these screaming fans outside, and we were just trying to hold a nor-
mal conversation. He said, 'You know, Suze, I really want to play Rusty-
James. But if I'm too old to play Rusty-James, I'll play the Motorcycle
Boy. And if I'm *really* old, like twenty-seven, I'll direct.'"

On July 12, 1982, when filming commenced on *Rumble Fish*, Dillon
was nineteen—a little old to play the junior high protagonist of the
novel, but still young enough to convincingly play a high schooler. So,
for the movie, Rusty-James was closer to that age. Rising tough-guy
star Mickey Rourke was the Motorcycle Boy, Dennis Hopper was their
dysfunctional dad, and *The Outsiders'* Diane Lane played Rusty-James's

girlfriend. As was the case with the first Coppola-Hinton collaboration, the cast was studded with young up-and-comers—including Vincent Spano, Laurence Fishburne, and Coppola's nephew Nicolas Cage.

Much of the filming was done in and around Tulsa's Greenwood Avenue, the "Black Wall Street" that had been a focal point of one of the biggest race riots in history back in 1921. When Coppola and his team moved in, however, it was hardly even a skeleton of its former self. Wrote Vern Stefanic in the August 20, 1982, edition of the *Tulsa World:*

> It once looked like the land that time forgot—to say nothing about the land that people trashed. Buildings there had been deserted for years, life was gone, and Greenwood Avenue looked like a ghost town. That is, until this week.
>
> Now the magic of Hollywood has changed the historic area into a carnival setting of neon lights and throbbing, pulsating humanity, a place where hundreds of people meet nightly to create a world that many Tulsans may have never seen. . . .
>
> The change is temporary—as soon as production there is completed, the fabrications will be gone.

That was undoubtedly fine with city leaders—including the Greenwood Chamber of Commerce, one of the entities that allowed Coppola to dress and use the area. The garish storefronts effectively represented the neon-lit underbelly of urban America, with signs advertising X-rated films, a massage parlor, tattooing, and faux businesses like Lindy's Lingerie and The Pleasure Place. Those weren't exactly the kinds of enterprises likely to be touted in a chamber of commerce brochure.

In fact, that place wasn't even supposed to be Tulsa. In his own August 20 report on the filming, the *Tulsa Tribune*'s Bruce Westbrook explained: "Overall, the crowded, garish avenue looks nothing like Tulsa, and it won't be Tulsa on film. The street scene, which was designed by Dean Tavoularis, depicts an unnamed urban area in the near future—a place where the film's rebellious youths go for some action."

In that way, and in many others, the film echoed the setting of Hinton's novel. "I purposely made the book vague," she told Stefanic, adding, "I'll tell you one thing. When this movie comes out, people won't think of me as a kid's writer." Although her success in the young-adult field was hardly obliterated by the film, the R-rated picture—which featured, among other things, a fair amount of graphic language—undoubtedly surprised some of Hinton's fans.

With Fred Roos and former Tulsan Doug Claybourne as producers, *Rumble Fish* continued its principal photography in Tulsa through most of September. On September 26, Coppola flew back to Southern California. There, according to an October 3 *World* report by Stefanic, the director completed the picture "with several studio shots—including some action shots involving star Matt Dillon and a cemetery scene, footage which Coppola tried to film here but was unsatisfied with the results." Before he left, Coppola brought in Stewart Copeland, founder and drummer of the influential rock band the Police, to record a sound track for the movie at Tulsa's Long Branch Studios.

"We worked 70 hours in four days," chief engineer Bill Belknap told the *Tribune*'s Ellis Widner in a story published October 11. "Copeland is very creative, energetic and competitive. I'm not surprised he is at the top in rock 'n' roll."

Starting with "clock sounds," Belknap noted, "we added all kinds of things—car horns, piledrivers—everything we could think of that is percussive and implies rhythm. We used other effects, like breaking glass, pool balls and a car engine running. It wasn't easy getting the sound effects on the same beat—in synch."

That unorthodox approach to a movie sound track was surely in sync with the film Coppola was crafting, which would end up fulfilling his promise to S. E. Hinton to make the movie version of *Rumble Fish* even weirder than her novel. (On Hinton's website, at www.sehinton.com, she calls *Rumble Fish* "the easiest [of her books] to read, the hardest to understand.") In *On The Edge: The Life and Times of Francis Coppola* (1989), authors Michael Goodwin and Naomi Wise wrote that Coppola prepared cast and crew—including cinematographer Steve Burum—for the filming by showing them a group of movies that included the 1920 German expressionist horror classic *The Cabinet of Dr. Caligari*, which Goodwin and Wise call "Coppola's stylistic prototype" for *Rumble Fish*. *Caligari*'s expressionism—one of the few filmed manifestations of an artistic movement that grew out of Germany following World War I—included tilted and otherworldly-looking sets, creating a dreamlike, disorienting viewing experience.

Expressionism, a kind of reaction to realism in art, was meant to reflect reality as seen through the eyes of an individual artist—or, in the case of movies, a character. *Rumble Fish*'s black-and-white cinematography (with only a few splotches of color, when the titular Siamese fighting fish are shown) and distorted reality (some of the shadows are painted onto the scenery, à la *Caligari*) can be seen as a representation of the world that's filtered through the eyes of the Motorcycle Boy (and perhaps the other members of his family as well), whose perception has been altered by years of physical and mental damage.

Rated R for language, violence, and brief nudity, *Rumble Fish* officially opened at the New York Film Festival on October 7, 1983, the same evening that a sneak preview of the film unreeled in Tulsa. Reported David Wilson in the next day's *Tulsa World*, "Tickets . . . went fast, but 'the response wasn't very good,' said Roger Block, manager of Tulsa's Annex Theater. 'All the people who appeared in the movie liked it real well, but most seemed to feel it was confusing, with not much plot.'"

The wide variance in opinions about the film extended to the New York screening. As Wilson observed, "Boos mixed with a few cheers as the film ended. Comments. . . ranged from 'stupid' to 'funny.'"

Similar opinions continued to be expressed as *Rumble Fish* rolled out from Universal Pictures two weeks later. Unlike *The Outsiders* (which had been released by Warner Bros.), it was not a hit, although in the subsequent years it has been hailed by some as one of Coppola's masterpieces.

S. E. Hinton succinctly sums up the attitude toward the picture *Rumble Fish* on her website. "Rumble Fish is a very strange movie (R-Rated!) and people love it or hate it," she wrote. "I love it."

Because the 1979 novel *Tex* was the first of S. E. Hinton's books to be filmed, there's a widespread perception that it had something to do with getting Coppola to consider Tulsa's possibilities as a film site. Not so, said Hinton in her interview for this book. While Tim Hunter's movie and Coppola's two films were all based on her novels, that was where the connection ended. For Coppola and his crew, *Tex* might as well have been filming on a different continent.

"They weren't paying any attention to *Tex*," she explained. "As a matter of fact, when *Tex* came out, and we were still shooting *The Outsiders*, I remember telling Gio [Gian-Carlo] Coppola, 'Look. This is a great review for *Tex*.'

"Man, if reviews had been box office, *Tex* would've been a gold mine. We got great reviews, and this one said something like, 'Even Francis Coppola will have a hard time equaling this.'

"And Gio—he was eighteen, Francis's oldest kid, and our associate producer—says, 'Well, I'm sure it's a nice little movie, but let's not be *ridiculous.*'"

Of course, not all of the feature filmmaking in Oklahoma in the early '80s boasted the star power of the S. E. Hinton trilogy. Well before director Tim Hunter headed east from Hollywood to film *Tex*, a thirty-three-year-old auteur named Pat Poole had begun filming a western comedy for the family trade called *Oklahoma Bound*. Working out of an unair-conditioned office in Collinsville that he co-leased for $37.50 a month—according to a May 30, 1980, piece by the *Tulsa Tribune*'s David Jones—the Oral Roberts University graduate had nothing if not a clear motive for becoming a filmmaker, which he expressed to Jones:

> "I was born in Dallas and grew up with the cowboy heritage. The heroes of my youth were John Wayne and Roy Rogers and Gene Autry. That was when you could tell the good guys from the bad guys.
>
> "But as I grew older I became alarmed at the power of the media. After all, TV and movies and newspapers do plant seeds in young minds, and they all seemed to be making looser morals more acceptable.
>
> "I've always been interested in entertainment. I've promoted and produced and performed in many Tulsa concerts, usually as a humorist. So I decided to make a clean movie."

"Poole knew what kind of movie he wanted to make . . . one with lots of action and fights and laughs, and strictly aimed for a G rating," wrote Jones. So the fledgling filmmaker borrowed $10,000 and got to work producing, directing, and starring (as Clint Poole) in a film made from his own script. None of the principal actors, including Poole, had ever been in a movie before. They included Strother Martin lookalike F. E. Bowling, an antique-car dealer from Okmulgee; Dan Jones, a service station manager from the same city; and Jones's wife, Shirley, who acted under the name of "Sheryl Rose" (because, as the *Tribune*'s Jones—no relation to the actors—noted dryly, "There already is a Shirley Jones").

The story involved an older guy (Bowling) and his nephew (Poole), living on a ranch near Buffalo Flats, Oklahoma, and the trouble old uncle gets into when he goes in debt to gamblers, including Dirty Dan (Jones) and his accomplice (Rose). This setup is played out amidst a lot of car chases and crashes, with largely comedic intent.

"The cars have proved to be the big expense," Jones wrote. "[Poole] had to pay up to $150 for some of them."

Filming on *Oklahoma Bound* began in August 1979, with principal photography wrapping in early June 1980. Locations included Collinsville, Tulsa, Haskell, and Skiatook. According to Jones's May 30 *Tribune* piece, the crew had begun shooting with a pair of 16 mm Bolex cameras, reshooting in 35 mm when a backer stepped up with a sizable chunk of money for the production.

Reportedly, the budget for the picture was $500,000, with virtually everyone involved working on deferred salaries. Jones wrote that Poole was "negotiating with Paramount, Warner Bros., and Avco Embassy, as well as two distributors for foreign markets."

"You can't blame the cast and crew for being a bit anxious—none of them will receive a cent until the money starts flowing in," Jones added. "Such doubts are not shared by Pat. He is even thinking about his next film, *So You Want to Be a Cowboy?* which he says will have a genuine star in it—Academy Award winner Ben Johnson." Oklahoma native Johnson, as noted earlier in this chapter, would indeed return to his home state the next year to make a movie. But it would be *Tex*, not *So You Want to Be a Cowboy?*—which, despite Poole's ambitions, never made it to the screen.

Oklahoma Bound, however, did. And, showing that he and his Oklahoma Film Industry Task Force weren't just there for the Hollywoodites, Governor George Nigh held a press conference with Poole on Monday,

December 8, 1980, four days before the movie's official premiere. The Collinsville filmmaker used his time in the spotlight to, among other things, take a few potshots at the movie industry in general. *Tulsa Tribune* Capitol Bureau reporter Will Sentell told about it in a December 9 story:

> "It is my opinion that the public has been bombarded with unwholesome and often perverted entertainment," Poole tells reporters. . . .
> "It is great to entertain but with that also goes an obligation, and that is to instill the greatness of our country," Poole declared on a "Poole Productions" press release.
> "One can laugh without eroding and undermining the principles of God and country.
> "I would like you to know that I believe in prayer.
> "How else could you explain a good ol' boy making a feature film?"

Oklahoma Bound debuted at Collinsville's Crown Theater on December 12. Despite the reported negotiations with major studios, the feature ended up being released by Buffalo Pictures, a company formed by a group of Tulsa-area businessmen. In many ways, Buffalo fit the profile of an ad hoc entity, put together merely to release a film that failed to get picked up by a major distributor. However, the company was also something more, at least for a while. The *Tribune's* David Jones, who seemed to be especially intrigued by *Oklahoma Bound*, wrote in a May 1, 1981, story that Buffalo was distributing not just Pat Poole's locally produced effort but others as well, including "movies that failed in previous marketing efforts." These included a St. Louis–lensed picture about shenanigans at a summer camp called *Stuckey's Last Stand* (1980); *The Great Brain* (1978), with Jimmy Osmond of the singing Osmond Family; and a period western, *She Came to the Valley* (1979; shot in south Texas's Rio Grande Valley), featuring Hollywood actors Dean Stockwell, Scott Glenn, and Ronee Blakley (who had composed the original music for the partially shot-in-Oklahoma *Welcome Home, Soldier Boys*), along with country-music star Freddie Fender.

Buffalo general manager Steve Durbin told Jones that the company would work only with G or "mild" PG-rated pictures. "This is a family film company," he said. "The only other ones are Buena Vista (Disney) and Pacific International."

At the time of the story, Jones wrote, Buffalo had been in existence for six months, which would tie its origin in neatly with the big-screen debut of *Oklahoma Bound*. The company seemed to specialize in creating new ad campaigns and using the old concept of saturation booking—releasing a picture to as many theaters as it could at the same time—in hopes of giving films new life. Jones's story pointed out the new newspaper advertising for *Oklahoma Bound*, which emphasized its comedic aspects and featured a cartoon of the Uncle Earl character front and center. The group had even put together a new campaign for the then-seven-year-old *Where the Red Fern Grows*, taking it out for another spin. (Buffalo's tactics recall the wisdom of exploitation-movie kingpin Dan Sonney, who famously said that a movie was like a sack of flour: no matter how empty it seems, if you shake it hard enough, a little more flour will always come out.)

"As time goes on we know more and more theater managers, and this helps us get bookings," Durbin told Jones. "Independent filmmakers already know about us. I imagine we could see 150 films a year if we wanted to."

At the time, Jones wrote, *Oklahoma Bound* was riding its new ad campaign to success in Okmulgee, where, he noted, its box office take had "dwarfed" its major-studio competitor there, the Charles Bronson–Lee Marvin picture *Death Hunt* (1981).

Jones quoted filmmaker Poole: "When I made the movie," Poole said, "I was as green as I could be. I thought all you had to do was shoot the film and then sell it to a distributor. It doesn't work that way. Getting the film in the can is only half the battle."

Poole and Buffalo Pictures battled on, at least for a little while longer, getting up on the screens of mostly small-town theaters with their family-oriented entertainment. It was a laudable effort, but Buffalo never gained a long-term foothold, and it gradually faded away. The independent, family-owned movie houses that might take a chance on a little picture like *Oklahoma Bound* were even then becoming fewer and fewer, as the massive theater chains tightened their stranglehold on America's big-screen entertainment.

Oklahoma Bound's creator, however, seems to have lasted a bit longer in the business. Several film reference sites (including the *New York Times*, at www.nytimes.com) credit a Patrick C. Poole with the direction of two subsequent pictures, both 1986 releases: *French Quarter Undercover*, a story about terrorists at the World's Fair, starring Michael Parks (and featuring Bill Vint, the third acting brother from the Tulsa clan that included siblings Jesse and Alan); and *Shadows on the Wall*, a mystery involving a fifty-year-old murder, with Wilford Brimley. Poole is listed as codirector (with Joseph Catalanotto) on the first, and as writer, producer, and director on the second, which most sources indicate was made for television. The executive producer of the latter was Oklahoma City's E. K. Gaylord II, the filmmaking member of the Gaylord clan—which owns the *Daily Oklahoman* newspaper, among many other holdings. His participation would indicate that this Patrick C. Poole is the same auteur who got *Oklahoma Bound* in the can and on the screen, even if most of those screens lay within the borders of his home state.

Although *Tex* was not responsible for attracting the two Francis Ford Coppola–S. E. Hinton collaborations to northeastern Oklahoma, that film did help bring another youth-oriented picture to Tulsa for a few days of shooting. In early June 1983, first-time director Kevin Reynolds came in with part of the cast of *Fandango* to film several scenes, including a tricky one involving stunt flying. According to reporter David Wilson, who covered the shooting for the *Tulsa World*, the group came to Oklahoma to finish up the movie after doing most of the principal photography south of the Red River.

"Work on the $7 million Warner Bros. adventure-comedy had moved here because of trouble finding locations in Texas," Wilson wrote in a June 8 story. "Producer Tim Zinnemann had filmed *Tex* here and knew what he'd find."

One of the things he found was an overpass on U.S. Highway 244. And with Federal Aviation Administration safety inspector Cleo McGoveran on hand and watching closely, a stunt pilot flew under it several times, making different turns until director Reynolds was satisfied.

The film, released in January 1985, was—like *The Outsiders*—set in an earlier time. It told of an early '70s road trip taken by five students from the University of Texas, all facing the draft and possibly Vietnam. The film's stars included Kevin Costner, Judd Nelson, and Sam Robards, none of whom appears to have made the trek to Tulsa. Model Suzy Amis, an Oklahoma City native, made her big-screen debut as the female lead, and she and actor Marvin J. McIntyre, playing the pilot of the single-engine airplane used in the picture, were on hand for the Sooner State–shot footage.

Wilson's story echoed two things already voiced by other filmmakers who'd come to Oklahoma for summer shooting: They were delighted at the cooperation they found, and they weren't that crazy about the heat. According to Wilson, when asked what they'd do after this, the final day of shooting, "nearly everyone" on the set quickly replied, "Go skating. Ice skating."

Although made-for-television efforts are generally outside the scope of this book, a study of the flurry of filmmaking activity in early '80s Oklahoma wouldn't be complete without looking at a couple of TV movies: the massive 1982 miniseries *The Blue and the Gray* and a 1985 drama about teen suicide called *Surviving*.

Although the four-part, eight-hour Civil War opus *The Blue and the Gray* was shot mostly in Arkansas, the company traveled to Fort Gibson for a couple of days to capture some scenes in and around its historic stockade. Fort Gibson, the military post that gave the northeastern Oklahoma town its name, had existed through most of the 1800s. In the 1930s, it had been reconstructed as a historical site, and since it had been in use during the War Between the States—occupied by both Confederate and Union soldiers at different junctures—it provided a nice degree of authenticity for director Andrew V. McLaglen and his troupe.

The unit traveled to Fort Gibson from Arkansas after Oklahoma Film Industry Task Force coordinator Mary Nell Clark took members of the company on tour to various Oklahoma locales. They were, according to Vern Stefanic's article in the November 13, 1983, edition of *Tulsa World*, "looking for a certain setting for some specific scenes" and found what they needed "when they toured the Ft. Gibson stockade and mess hall area." For the purposes of the film, the preserved stockade was used to simulate the prison at Elmira, New York, where many captured Confederate soldiers wound up at the end of the real war.

Stefanic wrote that the crew would be shooting for at least two days and bringing more than 150 people to Fort Gibson. There, noted the *Daily Oklahoman*'s Sue Smith in a November 26 piece, 136 extras were hired at minimum wage to appear before the cameras. Part of her story followed one man, a colorful local who showed up because he was looking for work. He found it, too, landing a gig as a Confederate prisoner.

> "Nothing's changed. They've taken the unemployed and put 'em in uniform," Fort Gibson's J. W. Sawyer said, grinning a toothless grin, half of his smudged face made up to look like a severe case of whisker burn. . . .
>
> "It don't matter," Sawyer replied when asked how much he thought he'd make as a newcomer to the screen. "I'm hungry. I'm unemployed." Sawyer joined a buffet line with the other starved-looking Reb extras, including three firemen from Springdale, Ark., who said they were hired because they were "skin and bones."
>
> They all sat down to a lunch that included broiled trout, Swiss steak, and marinated vegetables with mushrooms. A California caterer brought in the gourmet victuals, a task-force spokesman said.

"They do it with verve and with fire and seem to enjoy it," producer Hugh Benson said of the locals. "Hollywood extras are blasé. They've done it so often it doesn't mean anything to them anymore. It means something to these people."

The Blue and the Gray, starring Stacy Keach and featuring notable actors playing historical figures (including Gregory Peck as Abe Lincoln, Rip Torn as Ulysses S. Grant, and Sterling Hayden as the abolitionist John Brown) debuted on CBS in the fall of 1982. A year later, it won the People's Choice Award for Favorite TV Mini-Series.

While *The Blue and the Gray* was a sweeping drama with a huge cast, 1985's *Surviving* was a personal tale about two interconnected families dealing with the tragedy of teen suicide. And while the time the former production spent in the state could be measured in hours, the entire five weeks of *Surviving* was lensed in Oklahoma City.

This time, the location was chosen by producer Hunt Lowry, a native of the city. "The story is set in an upper-middle class community in an unnamed city, and Lowry chose his hometown as the location for filming because of its typical, middle-American look," wrote Gene Triplett in the October 7, 1984, *Sunday Oklahoman*. Triplett noted that the outfit had filmed at Classen High School, West Nichols Hills Elementary School, and a couple of local hospitals and in the upscale Nichols Hills area.

The cast was a solid one, including Len Cariou, Ellen Burstyn, Zach Galligan, and River Phoenix as the members of one family, and Paul Sorvino, Marsha Mason, and Molly Ringwald as the other. With the exception of producer Lowry, none of the cast had major state connections, although Sorvino told reporter Triplett, "I've lived here before, when I was a boy, for six months. Tulsa. Oklahoma."

Even though he was playing a deeply troubled young man in *Surviving*, twenty-year-old Galligan—best known at the time for his role in the 1984 theatrical hit *Gremlins*—seemed to be having a swell time in Oklahoma. "It's a total change of pace for me, what with growing up in New York City," he told Triplett. "I like the open spaces and the changeable weather. I've been going out with some friends that I've met here, going to clubs, seeing some movies, shooting a little skeet on Mr. Lowry's ranch. It's kind of a relaxing, kick-back time for me."

Sorvino felt the same way. "I sang about 30 songs at the country club the other night," he said. "I just got up and started singing. There was a very good pianist there. A little Weller's and water and I'll sing all damn night."

Surviving debuted on the ABC television network in February of the next year. And even as it was airing, something was stirring within the state. Although it wouldn't be recognized by many at the time, a group of people in Tulsa were getting ready to create something that would have a profound and lasting effect on movies—changing the very definition of the term for all time.

Bill Blair was a visionary. A longtime film collector and fan, he spent his early adult years primarily as an appliance salesman for a Tulsa concern, installing some of the first color TVs that city had seen. In the early '60s, he began parlaying his obsession with celluloid into a 16 mm film-rental business called United Films. In those prevideo days, the only way to watch a commercial film outside of a movie theater—or sliced up by commercials on one of the three network affiliate stations available in most of America at the time—was to rent it and thread it onto a film projector. Movie clubs and other organizations relied on 16 mm rental outfits like United to provide those reels of film, and Blair's company became one of the best-known in the country.

The thing that made Bill Blair different from many of the other film rental people, however, was that he would always try to sew up all the nontheatrical rights to the movies he acquired. This was, of course, long before there was anything like a home video market, but his sons Bob and Don—who joined Bill in the family film business—believe their father saw it coming.

When the whole idea of videotaped movies for home viewing began to take hold in the late 1970s, the rights that Blair had presciently purchased became the foundation of a whole new business, and his United Video, later VCI Entertainment, became a pioneer in selling movies on videocassette—at first to video rental houses and later, directly to consumers. His pioneering days, however, were just beginning.

By the time the early '80s rolled around, Blair had also gotten in on the burgeoning cable television market, using his movies to provide all the programming for a local cable channel. Working with him on the production end was Linda Lewis, promotions director for Tulsa radio station KRAV. Because her position involved getting publicity for new features coming to Tulsa theaters, she was doing a lot of face-to-face interviews with movie stars, and videotaped versions of those sit-downs were the perfect thing to play between Blair's pictures on the cable station.

"When I started being invited on the interview junkets, I went to Bill Blair and said, 'I have this footage. Would it be something we could work with?'" remembered Lewis recently. "He said, 'If you can learn to edit, you can do whatever you want with it.' So I was working in his back room on his old three-fourth-inch editing machine, putting together these fifteen-minute *Intermission with Linda Lewis* shows."

Lewis's husband, Christopher Lewis, was hosting an afternoon news-magazine show for Tulsa's KOTV at the time—but he was itching to direct a feature film. And he had the pedigree. Not only was he the son of screen legend Loretta Young, but he had also gone to film school at the University of Southern California, where his pals included George Lucas.

Blair knew this, of course. And when his pipeline for new video releases began to shut down, thanks to more and more companies—including major studios—getting into the homevid act, it was probably only natural for him to start thinking about making his own picture.

Truth to tell, he'd thought about it before. He'd even cowritten a script with a then-Tulsa-based neurologist, Dr. Stuart Rosenthal (also the author of 1976's *The Cinema of Federico Fellini*). They came up with a horror-style picture titled *The Sorority House Murders*, which Blair initially wanted to do as a theatrical film with his friend Buster Crabbe—a former screen Tarzan, Flash Gordon, Buck Rogers, and Billy the Kid—in the lead. But Crabbe died in 1983, before Blair could get it going, and the script went into a drawer.

Then one day Blair brought it back out—and showed it to the Lewises. "He said, 'I've got this script. What would it cost us to do a movie on it?'" recalled Christopher. "So we looked at it and we said, 'Well, maybe $25,000.' I made a couple of additions to the script—they had a snake in it that got in and scared somebody, but I wrote it out because it was too hard to get a rattlesnake. A couple of things like that. I said, 'If you want to make it, here's what we'll do. We'll see if we can talk Sony into giving us Betacams.' The Betacams were very portable cameras, [using] half-inch tape, and all the TV stations were just getting them. They were just coming in. So we called Sony, and they said, 'Yeah, we'll give you a couple of the cameras and an editing system if you'll say it was recorded on Betacams.' Actually, I think they charged us a thousand bucks or something, but it was a very good deal."

Lewis's idea was to shoot a feature film like a TV soap opera. He'd gotten the idea from his sister, actress Judy Lewis, who had produced some episodes of the daytime drama *Texas* in the early '80s. "I knew they taped an hour show every day, and I thought if we used videotape instead of film, and edited it ourselves, we could do it," remembered Lewis. "Then, if we used the crew from [the KOTV show] *PM Magazine*, and we all took our week-off vacation at the same time, with the weekend we'd have nine days to shoot."

Although the film ended up costing a couple thousand dollars more than Lewis estimated, and a few pickup shots had to be done after the nine days were over, director Christopher and producer Linda were right in the ballpark with both their estimates. "We had to be right about the shooting schedule," said Christopher. "We all had to be back at our jobs on Monday."

Although *Blood Cult*—as the movie was ultimately titled—was a local production in every sense of the word, its cast featured one actor who had a handful of theatrical-feature credits; Julie Andelman was her name. A former Tulsan, her resume included the 1980 horror picture *The Silent Scream*. In *Blood Cult*, Andelman was top-billed as Tina, daughter of the local sheriff, who gets involved in a series of killings on campus that point to a dog-worshipping cult.

"I think Bill Blair brought her up," recalled Linda. "I think he knew she was a Tulsa girl, and we didn't have to pay for a hotel if she was from Tulsa—she could stay at her mom's place. That's how cheap we were."

The cast was rounded out by Tulsa-based actors Charles Ellis (in the sheriff role originally written for Crabbe), Josef Hardt (the TV announcer who'd previously costarred in the Oklahoma-produced *Thirty Dangerous Seconds*), Bennie Lee McGowan, and James Vance. McGowan was a local theater veteran, while Vance was a writer, an award-winning playwright, and a well-known Tulsa actor. (Most recently, he's made his mark as the highly acclaimed scripter of the graphic novels *Kings in Disguise* and *On the Ropes*.)

"One thing about everybody we used: they all hit their lines and did their thing," noted Christopher Lewis. "They were theater people who knew their stuff, and they were *good* at it. Everybody took it really seriously and did a good job."

Despite its ultralow budget, the production was also aided by the reliable Oklahoma Film Industry Task Force and its coordinator, Mary Nell Clark. "Mary Nell really helped us in getting locations," Christopher said.

"We didn't have enough money to pay anybody, so we pulled in favors."

Even with Clark's help, though, things could get a little rocky. Among the locations she found for the shooting was Cascia Hall, a private Tulsa high school where much of the dormitory footage was shot. Because this was a horror-exploitation film, there were lots of scantily clad young women present, along with a considerable amount of fake blood and gruesome makeup effects. A combination calculated to draw young male viewers to the movie, it also drew them to the filming.

"We had to take the boys who actually lived there and move them over so we could shoot in that part of the dormitory," explained Christopher. "The girls were all in their little skimpy stuff, you know, and it was like heaven for the boys. They were drooling, looking through windows, all of that stuff, and word got around Cascia Hall that night that we weren't on the up-and-up and maybe we were doing a porno film. So we wrap it up there about one in the morning, and we're due the next morning at the big library at the University of Tulsa. Mary Nell and I had called the president and personally cleared it through him. He'd okayed it a week or two before. But we show up the next morning and the security people tell us we can't set up. We can't film."

As it turned out, the president, Dr. J. Paschal Twyman, was traveling and couldn't be reached, and the group was told that no one else on campus had the authority to let them shoot. Christopher, however, believes that they were kept away from the campus because "word came over from Cascia Hall that we were doing a porno film." He also recalled that a young woman had been violently assaulted on the campus not long before, and perhaps school officials thought that the *Blood Cult* crew was intending to exploit that incident.

"I didn't even know about it," Christopher said. "That was the farthest thing from our minds. All we wanted to do was do our story, and Paschal Twyman knew what the story was about. But someone who was in charge while he was out of town took on the responsibility of not letting us in there."

Clark jumped to the rescue, securing a new location on the fly—Tulsa's Central Library—and the production lost only a few hours. But it

Promotional flyer for *Blood Cult* (1985), the world's first made-for-home-video feature. (John Wooley Archives)

gained a tagline, one that ran across much of the promotional material that heralded *Blood Cult*'s release to video stores: "A movie so gruesomely realistic, it was banned from two mid-western campuses!"

Shot during March of 1985, *Blood Cult* was ready for distribution (at a cost of $59.95 per cassette) by August. It received a lukewarm notice in the August 21 issue of *Variety*, which found reviewer "Lor" taking positive note of director Christopher Lewis's development of "some effective atmosphere, especially in night scenes"; the convincing work of special-effects makeup artists Dave Powell and Robert Brewer; and director of photography Paul MacFarlane's "wide angle shots and moody lighting [that] prove horror via video can compete with the filmed variety."

The people behind *Blood Cult* found out their film could compete in the video marketplace as well. According to Christopher Lewis, "It cost $27,000 to make. VCI spent $100,000 promoting it. But on the opening day of its release, because cassettes were selling at that time for sixty bucks a shot, it made $400,000." The direct-to-video feature ended up grossing well over a million dollars and is still available from VCI.

Before *Blood Cult*, VCI had released a movie now and again that had never seen a legitimate theatrical release and had subsequently been acquired from filmmakers looking to cut their losses. Certainly, that was true for an early '80s movie called *Copperhead*, made in Sedalia, Missouri, by a filmmaker named Leland Payton. He had shot it on one-inch videotape, hoping to bump it up to 35 mm for theaters. But that never happened, and Blair acquired it for VCI and took it directly to home video.

Copperhead, in fact, is sometimes cited as the first real made-for-home-video movie, and Blair in fact mentioned it in interviews as an inspiration for his own efforts. But the distinction is not so much about the medium as it is about intent. Payton and those auteurs before him went into their projects with the idea of being seen on the big screen, whether they were shooting on 35 mm or 16 mm film or—in Payton's case—one-inch videotape. Blair and the Lewises and *Blood Cult* did not have that intention—and that makes all the difference. As Bill Blair told the author in an interview for a May 19, 1985, *Tulsa World* story: "There are three markets in the movie industry that command big, big dollars. Those are the home video market, the theatrical market, and the television market.

The way we feel is that when you can hit two out of three, you're doing pretty well."

They did more than pretty well with *Blood Cult*. They changed the face of the industry forever. The release of *Blood Cult* in August 1985 represents nothing less than the line of demarcation between the old definition of a movie and the new one, which continues to evolve even as these words are being written.

Epilogue

And *Then* What Happened?

> Nobody was producing movies strictly for the home video market. We were the first. That was even written in *Variety* and *Hollywood Reporter* at the time. So, yeah, we stuck our necks out a little bit. It was all new. We were kind of making it up as we went along. And it did start a huge part of our industry. I don't know how many hundreds of made-for-video movies have been made since *Blood Cult.*
>
> —VCI Entertainment president Bob Blair

> I don't think we knew the industry was going to take notice of it. I know we did not know that. We didn't understand that it could revolutionize anything.
>
> —*Blood Cult* producer Linda Lewis

> Before the Lewises, everybody thought you needed millions of dollars and a big studio machine behind you to make a movie. What they did was the first inkling of the democratization of filmmaking.
>
> —former *Tulsa World* film critic Dennis King

It wouldn't be completely accurate to place the entire responsibility for a massive industry change solely on the shoulders of a few moviemakers from Oklahoma. But Bill Blair and the Lewises deserve a great deal of credit for taking an entertainment innovation that was just hitting its stride—movies as on-demand home entertainment—and moving it beyond its dependence on theatrical features.

When *Blood Cult* hit the scene, cable television's Home Box Office and other movie channels had been around for several years, offering subscribers Hollywood fare at home. Then home video had come along, freeing consumers from the scheduling imposed on them by the cable channels and free TV channels. "Home video" meant just what the term implied: a movie recorded on videotape that could be enjoyed at home whenever a person chose.

But even though the technologies of cable and home video revolutionized the way people could view films, the essential product delivered to the consumer remained the same, at least for a time. The term "movie" meant exactly what it had meant for many decades: a feature that had played at theaters. (This definition discounts the "made-for-TV movie" that arose in the mid-1960s, offered by networks as a changeup from their half-hour- and hour-long programming. Sometimes stand-alone stories, other times special hour-and-a-half or two-hour versions of existing shows—including situation comedies like *Gilligan's Island* and *Green Acres*—made-for-TV movies usually featured familiar television stars and, except for their length, fit almost indistinguishably alongside the network series that surrounded them. Later would come the lengthy miniseries, shown over several nights, including the aforementioned *The Blue and the Gray* and 1989's *Oklahoma Passage*, a five-part, five-hour historical drama bankrolled by the Oklahoma Educational Television Authority and featuring many nationally known and regional actors with Oklahoma ties.)

In bypassing the theaters for home screens, and intending to do so, *Blood Cult* was the harbinger of a massive change in the way people looked at movies. In fact, it even caught the industry by surprise. Contacted by the author for a May 19, 1985, *Tulsa World* story, West Coast film and video executive Joe Wolf seemed to echo the opinion of those in the home video business when he said he felt the market might be big enough to support a "major film" in two or three years.

The term "major" can be debated, but it wasn't long before made-for-video films were cranking up all over the countryside—including in Oklahoma, where Blair and the Lewises combined again for *The Ripper* (1985), bringing noted makeup-effects artist Tom Savini in to star as a modern-day Jack the Ripper, and *Revenge* (1986), a *Blood Cult* sequel that toplined a pair of name actors, Patrick Wayne and John Carradine.

While *Revenge*, like the other two United Entertainment originals, was aimed squarely for the homevid market, it was shot on 16 mm film to give it a higher-quality look. By that time, however, the country was crawling with nascent moviemakers who realized that the exploding array of

Tulsa kid-show host Carl Bartholomew played a western-style vigilante in 1988's *Cole Justice.* (John Wooley Archives)

videotape cameras and accessories, along with their relatively low cost—especially when compared with film and filmmaking equipment—just might enable them to jump onto the made-for-home-video gravy train with their own pictures.

"When Chris Lewis shot *Blood Cult,* the technology was just starting to tilt toward being affordable for nonstudio filmmaking," noted Dennis King recently. As the *Tulsa World's* movie critic from 1986 through 2006, King was in a good position to witness the revolution. "Afterwards, the whole landscape changed," he said, "and it changed very quickly."

The filmmaking picture exploded as quickly in Oklahoma as anywhere else. In the blink of an eye, such video-lensed features as director Larry Thomas's alien-invasion picture *Mutilations* (1986) and Lewis cinematographer Paul MacFarlane's ballroom-dancing feature *Best Foot Forward*

(1987) got under way. Christopher and Linda Lewis and the Blairs split up their trailblazing partnership, but United Entertainment continued to pick up and/or finance straight-to-video efforts like *Terror at Tenkiller* (1986), a stalk 'n' slash picture set at a famous Oklahoma lake (and directed by Ken Meyer, who'd go on to do the TV miniseries *Oklahoma Passage*) and *Blood Lake* (1988), another lakeside chiller, this one shot near El Reno by an Oklahoma City–based production group.

Chris and Linda Lewis, meanwhile, announced in the spring of '87 that their production company, the Entertainment Group—still extant at this writing—would shortly begin a direct-to-video feature called *Death Drive-In* as part of a homevid deal with the Los Angeles–based Prism Entertainment. That picture never saw fruition, but the Entertainment Group found a solid niche as a creator of documentaries, stepping back into the fictional film field in 1990 with the Tulsa-lensed *Dan Turner, Hollywood Detective* (known as *The Raven Red Kiss-Off* in its video release). Debuting in prime time on more than two hundred television stations prior to its video release, it was directed by Chris Lewis and written by the author of this book, from a 1940s pulp-magazine story by Robert Leslie Bellem.

But the "nonstudio filmmaking" cited by King had its downside. True, technology made it easier than ever to get a feature-length movie made. But so many people got into it that it quickly shifted from a seller's to a buyer's market. As James Vance—the playwright and writer who also happened to be one of *Blood Cult*'s stars—put it in his previously cited 1999 article "Rewind to Fast Forward": "Competition for the direct-to-video market had become fierce in a very short time, and simply getting a film in the can was no longer a guarantee that it would be seen."

Certainly, there were exceptions, including a contemporary western picture called *Cole Justice* (1988), the brainchild of Tulsa's Carl Bartholomew, best known locally as the longtime kid-show host Uncle Zeb. His feature was picked up by the Blockbuster video-rental chain as well as the Cinemax movie channel, and, because of the popularity of the film, Bartholomew found himself invited be the grand marshal of a Florala, Alabama, holiday parade—where, he said in a 2006 conversation with the author, he shared the spotlight "with a guy who could pick up twenty chickens."

But for every success story, there were infinitely more Oklahoma-produced features that never found a distributor, ending up as entertainment only for friends and family, or perhaps getting some sort of local, small-scale release. As more and more people with wildly varying degrees of talent got into the act, technology continued to shorten the distance between the home movie and the professional feature film, and by the early '90s the mere making of a film was simply no longer a good enough reason for the press to pay much attention.

"Back when the Lewises were doing it, it *was* newsworthy," said Dennis King, who often found himself confronting angry video-camera-armed auteurs who couldn't understand why he wouldn't visit their sets and do big newspaper stories on their projects. "But once that ground was broken, what followed wasn't necessarily newsworthy, The whole nature of 'film' changed. The technology was in everybody's hands, but not everybody had the talent, drive, or resources to close the deal. I'd tell people, 'If some guy throws up a canvas and starts painting a picture, or if someone starts writing a novel, that's not newsworthy. Make your movie and put it up on a screen for people to see, and we'll talk. But just the fact you're making a movie isn't enough anymore.'"

As this is being written, digital technology, the latest in a long line of advances, has made it more affordable and easier to shoot a movie than it's ever been. Film festivals continue to pop up like mushrooms after a summer rain, and Internet outlets offer all sorts of movie-viewing experiences, most of which can be had at no cost to the viewer. Made-for-homevid features wildly outnumber theatrical releases, and rare is the dwelling space that doesn't have some sort of movie library. Films on disc are for sale everywhere, including supermarkets and deep-discount houses. Sometimes you can get two former theatrical features for a dollar. At times, all of this calls into mind the poet Judson Jerome's famous statement about how poetry, next to zucchini, is the most overproduced commodity in America. These days, it would be easy to make the case that it's not poetry but films. And like poets, many moviemakers appear to be doing what they do mostly for those who are doing the same thing.

Even though the classic Hollywood dream still wields considerable power in the national imagination, the terms "movie" and "filmmaker" today have a far different resonance than they did a quarter of a century ago, when a group of Oklahomans turned out a low-budget horror picture in nine days and nudged it into the video marketplace to see what would happen. (Of course, the years of post–*Blood Cult* filmmaking in Oklahoma have their own wonderful stories—including several concerning state-shot theatrical features, a selected listing of which appears in the appendix.) And so we're stopping here, during the mid-'80s, at a time when cracks had begun to spiderweb across the old assumptions about feature films, when the dreamers had started to rouse and realize that maybe they, too, could get in the movie game without having to leave home for the uncertainties of a new life elsewhere.

Many of them, in fact, did stay in Oklahoma, turned on their cameras, and watched what happened—not unlike those pioneers from a hundred years earlier, when moviemaking was dawning in the state. These new auteurs, brandishing equipment that would've seemed positively otherworldly to someone like Bennie Kent or Bill Tilghman, continue to shoot and watch and record, their numbers increasing exponentially, as Sooner cinema rolls on into its second hundred years.

Appendix

Shot-in-Oklahoma Theatrical Features, Post-1985

As outlined in the epilogue, the whole definition of the term "movie" changed forever in 1985, thanks in large part to Oklahoma movie-makers Christopher and Linda Lewis and the Tulsa-based video distributor United Entertainment. That is precisely the reason for ending the main text of this book after that year; it marked, quite simply, the end of one way of thinking about feature films and the beginning of a paradigm shift. As a result, multimillion-dollar features from major studios and no-budget video-camera efforts, along with a multitude of pictures that lay between those two extremes, would all come to be considered "movies" in the public mind.

Nevertheless, the theatrical pictures, pumped onto America's screens by major distributors and hyped by advertising campaigns, have continued to draw the largest audiences by a long shot, especially when one considers their eventual distribution to the home entertainment market. Some made-for-TV movies come close to matching this kind of audience penetration, but television, too, has changed greatly since the mid-'80s. TV broadcasting—long exemplified by the three over-the-air networks that dominated in the precable era—has now been sliced, and sliced again and again, into ever narrower outlets, with hundreds of specialty channels now vying with those of general interest on cable and satellite systems.

So, with no disrespect meant to the Oklahoma-shot television movies (including the aforementioned *Oklahoma Passage* series and a personal favorite, 1999's dandy little high school football film *Possums*, filmed in Nowata, which went to a cable movie network after a very limited theatrical release), nor to the many worthwhile direct-to-video features, here's a chronological and admittedly subjective list of the most important theater-exhibited features filmed in the state since *Blood Cult* came along. This group includes only pictures with a substantial amount of Oklahoma-lensed material, which means that the likes of *Phenomenon* and *The Frighteners*—both released in 1996 and both allegedly containing a very small amount of footage shot in Tulsa—won't be found here (although they are included in the filmography presented in the next section of the book).

Rain Man (1988)

Half a decade after his role as just one of the boys in the Tulsa-shot *The Outsiders*, Tom Cruise returned to the state as a major star, pairing with Dustin Hoffman in what is probably the most-awarded picture involving Oklahoma locations. This story of an autistic savant (Hoffman) taken on a cross-country trip by his glib.and egocentric hustler brother (Cruise) earned Academy Awards for screenwriters Ronald Bass and Barry Morrow, director Barry Levinson, and actor Hoffman, in addition to taking Best Picture honors.

Oklahoma locations included El Reno, which represented Amarillo, Texas, in the picture, along with Hinton, Cogar, and Oklahoma City, where the production stayed for two weeks. The scenes at the Guthrie clinic, where Cruise's Charlie takes Hoffman's Raymond to the doctor, were actually filmed in Guthrie.

"Five scenes, about 25 minutes of the movie, were shot at authentic Oklahoma locations, with authentic Oklahoma faces in the background," noted Ann DeFrange in a *Daily Oklahoman* story datelined January 3, 1989.

The '80s Movie Rewind website (www.fastrewind.com) identifies the El Reno motel room where Raymond and Charlie stay as room 117 at the Budget Inn. Other sources indicate the location was, instead, the town's Big 8 Motel.

UHF (1989)

"When I told people I was going to Tulsa to make a movie, their reaction was, 'Oh. You're doing a Western?'" song parodist "Weird Al" Yankovic told the *Tulsa Tribune*'s Ron Wolfe for a story that ran July 21, 1989.

The first feature film to star Yankovic (who was also its cowriter), *UHF* is certainly no western. The story of young dreamer George Newman, whose uncle (Stanley Brock) turns a run-down low-power television station over to his nephew after winning it in a card game, the picture is essentially a spate of movie, television, and music spoofs stitched together by a slight but amusing story. Michael Richards, only a year or so away from beginning his run as Kramer on TV's *Seinfeld*, plays the station's janitor and George's right-hand man. Several local actors are featured in humorous bits, with an especially memorable job done by Tulsa theater veteran Lisa Robertson Stefanic (wife of former *Tulsa World* entertainment editor Vern Stefanic), who plays an exuberant contestant on a game show called *Wheel of Fish*.

UHF's executive producer and production manager was Gray Frederickson, the Oklahoma City native who'd produced *The Outsiders* in Tulsa a few years earlier. He undoubtedly had something to do with the production's coming to Oklahoma.

My Heroes Have Always Been Cowboys (1991)

E. K. Gaylord II, the filmmaking member of the Oklahoma newspaper publishing dynasty, was a producer of this rodeo-rider drama, with much of the action taking place in and around Guthrie, site of Gaylord's Lazy E Arena. In addition to lead Scott Glenn, the cast included noted Oklahoma stars Gary Busey, Ben Johnson, and Clu Gulager in featured roles, with Sooner actor Rex Linn and well-known rodeo announcer and state political figure Clem McSpadden in cameos.

"I was amazed at how beautiful, how really, really pretty this country is," Glenn said at a luncheon held before the film's Oklahoma City premiere, according to a story written for release on February 27, 1991, by the Associated Press's Owen Canfield. "It's a great place to shoot a film."

My Heroes Have Always Been Cowboys was the final feature film credit for Stuart Rosenberg, the director of such well-known pictures as 1967's *Cool Hand Luke* and 1979's *The Amityville Horror*.

Twister (1996)

Oklahoma's reputation as the tornado magnet of America was reinforced by this big-budget disaster film, in which a group of University of Oklahoma weather researchers encounter the mother of all storms. The scientists include Bill Harding (Bill Paxton) and his wife, Jo (Helen Hunt), whom he wants to divorce in order to marry another storm chaser (Jami Gertz). Jake Busey, son of Tulsa's Gary, had a secondary role as a lab technician.

Although a July 9, 1995, *Tulsa World* article put the budget at "$30 million-plus," which is certainly impressive enough, the website IMDbPro estimated it at $92 million (with a worldwide return, as of early 2010, of nearly $495 million). What did the production company get for that kind of outlay? Among other things, permission to annihilate much of a northwestern Oklahoma town.

In the *World* piece, writer Dennis King noted that "the city fathers of Wakita, a community of 500 located at the end of Oklahoma 11-A, volunteered about 37 homes (which were already slated to be torn down) plus several other town business structures for demolition by the filmmakers. Warner Bros. ended up destroying five downtown business locations and about 15 houses. After crews finished filming in Wakita, the studio contracted with Midwest Wrecking Co., an Oklahoma City demolition firm, to clean up the mess."

Some two hundred Oklahomans were hired as crew members, and many more as extras. In addition to Wakita, other state filming locations included Guthrie, Maysville, Norman, Pauls Valley, Ponca City, and Waurika.

A Simple Wish (1997)

In October of 1996, Bob Davis, then director of the Oklahoma Film Commission, announced that a Hollywood crew was coming in to film several scenes at Oklahoma's Tallgrass Prairie near Pawhuska. "The Tallgrass Prairie matched perfectly with the producer's ideas for this film," Davis told the *Tulsa World*'s Barbara Hoberock for an October 27 story. "We are thrilled that such a noted director and cast have decided to come to Oklahoma."

The director was Michael Ritchie, known for such blockbusters as *The Candidate* (1972), *The Bad News Bears* (1976), and *Semi-Tough* (1977). And the cast was a good one, featuring comic actor Martin Short as a fairy godfather and Kathleen Turner as his nemesis, with Teri Garr, Amanda Plummer, and Ruby Dee also on board. In his July 17, 1997, review, the *Tulsa World's* Dennis King wrote that "one extended scene" shot at the Tallgrass Prairie had made it into the final film.

A PG-rated kids' picture, *A Simple Wish* was not a box office success, although it seems to have found a following in subsequent years. As was the case with Stuart Rosenberg and *My Heroes Have Always Been Cowboys*, *A Simple Wish* was the theatrical-feature swan song of a major director. Ritchie died in April 2001, some four years after completing his only Oklahoma movie.

Elizabethtown (2005)

Director-writer Cameron Crowe's quirky air/road-trip tale included footage taken in some of the same Sooner State towns that provided locations for *Rain Man* nearly two decades earlier. Crews filmed for two days in Oklahoma City, spending some of that time at the Oklahoma City National Memorial, and shot in Guthrie, Anadarko, and El Reno as well. (The Cherokee Trading Post outside El Reno can be seen in the finished film.)

The meandering tale of a big-time shoe designer (Orlando Bloom) and the flight attendant (Kirsten Dunst) he meets on his way back to Kentucky to pick up his father's remains is also noteworthy to fans of Oklahoma films because of the presence of Tulsa's Gailard Sartain, playing Elizabethtown's mortician. Sartain, the reader may recall, went (along with Gary Busey) from the fondly remembered early '70s late-night local *Uncanny Film Festival and Camp Meeting* show to a lengthy and successful movie career.

The Killer Inside Me (2010)

In a story released June 16, 2009, the Associated Press reported that this picture was "considered the biggest movie to be shot in Oklahoma since *Twister* in 1996." Although its budget, estimated by IMDbPro at

$13 million, was a fraction of *Twister's*, *The Killer Inside Me* boasts substantial star power, including Kate Hudson, Jessica Alba, Bill Pullman, Ned Beatty (who'd been in the state for the troubled *Where the Red Fern Grows* remake a few years earlier), and Casey Affleck. Affleck plays Lou Ford, the deputy sheriff of a small Texas town, whose bland demeanor masks a vicious homicidal nature.

In the AP story, producer Brad Schlei spoke of Oklahoma's "fabulous film subsidy" (the rebate given by the state to filmmakers who shoot there), adding, "Really, we went to Texas, we went to New Mexico, we went location scouting all over the place and (director Michael Winterbottom) really loved it here. It has everything we need."

Apparently, what they needed included two cities, Tulsa and Oklahoma City, with the architecture and general look that enabled them to play 1950s Texas locations. The Oklahoma shoot, estimated at five weeks, also entailed work in Cordell and Guthrie, among other towns.

The Killer Inside Me, first published in 1952 as a paperback original, has come to be regarded as a classic noir novel. First filmed in 1976 with Stacy Keach in the role of Ford, it's the best-known work of author Jim Thompson, an Anadarko native.

A couple of other theatrical features with Oklahoma ties from the post–*Blood Cult* period include the cult horror picture *Near Dark* (1987) and the Pauly Shore comedy vehicle *In the Army Now* (1994). The latter includes scenes taken at Fort Sill; for the former, "the majority of the filming was done on Oklahoma roads and rural locations." That's according to Adam Knapp's "Top 10 Movies Filmed in the State of Oklahoma," in the About.com Guide (okc.about.com). *Near Dark* represented still another kind of movie—the "limited theatrical release" feature.

There was nothing new about modest-budgeted films being released to a limited number of theaters by small, often regional, distributors and road-showmen, the latter sometimes physically hauling a print of their picture from town to town. With the advent of home video, however, the practice increased, and bookings on a few (or, in the case of *Near Dark*, a couple of hundred) big screens allowed a homevid distributor to tout the picture as a theatrical release, giving it extra cachet with rental stores and their customers.

This section closes with two of those. One helped take a pair of Tulsa filmmaker brothers to the next level. The other one, despite a cast full of reliable actors, simply misfired. The blame has been laid at the feet of its two main players, a Hollywood pair with a checkered background, collaborating on their first—and so far only—feature film to see completion.

Dark before Dawn (1988)

Based on an idea by a Kansas wheat farmer named Jeff Cox, *Dark before Dawn* told a dark story of corporate greed, murder, and—oddly—a group of violent farmers who worship a strange deity. Produced by E. K. Gaylord II's Lazy E Productions and shooting in both Kansas and Oklahoma—including some scenes filmed inside the Oklahoma Supreme Court's courtroom in Oklahoma City—it boasted a fine supporting cast full of familiar faces (including Ben Johnson, Morgan Woodward, Doug McClure, Rance Howard, Buck Taylor, Billy Drago, and singer-songwriter Red Steagall), as well as good smaller performances from Oklahoma-based film players like Bill Buckner, Eldon G. Hallum, Lee Gideon, and Randy Whalen. Rex Linn, who'd go on to a solid Hollywood career, can also be seen here, in one of his earliest film appearances, while rodeo announcer and well-known Oklahoma political figure Clem McSpadden starts off the film with a cameo appearance. Director Robert Totten was known for his westerns and family films, as well as for helming a number of episodes of the classic TV show *Gunsmoke*.

Scriptwriting credit went to Reparata Mazzola, a Hollywood-based writer-actress brought in by Cox. She also took the female lead, playing TV reporter Jessica Stanton. Her moviemaking partner, Sonny Gibson, was top-billed as Jeff Parker, an area farmer who teams with Stanton to expose a deep-rooted conspiracy.

Gibson and Mazzola had earlier collaborated on his alleged biography, *Mafia Kingpin*, published in 1981 and later debunked by Los Angeles Times writer William K. Knoedelseder, Jr. In an extensive two-part special report for the December '94 and January '95 issues

Reparata Mazzola, scripter and female lead of *Dark before Dawn* (1988). (John Wooley Archives)

of *Premiere* magazine titled "The Grifters," John H. Richardson told the frequently outrageous story of Gibson's film-biz machinations, including the involvement he and Mazzola had with *Dark before Dawn*:

> The problem was, Gibson and Mazzola were terrible actors. The evidence is still there on the videotape, released in 1989 by Vestron. Gibson is so stiff and flat that he's like a bad boy trying to act innocent in the principal's office, and Mazzola . . . well, there's no good way to put this: She comes off looking like a cross between Patti Smith and Margaret Hamilton. . . . The editor cut around them as much as possible.

In his review of the picture, Chuck Davis of the *Daily Oklahoman*—the newspaper owned by the family of *Dark before Dawn* executive producer Gaylord—was more succinct: "Gibson can't act," he wrote. "Mazzola can't act."

In a recent conversation, Steagall, who played an honest government employee targeted by the corrupt corporation, said, "I have no idea where that couple came from, or what they were doing in the movie. I'd known Sonny a little bit in Hollywood, so I recognized him—even though he was about two hundred and fifty pounds lighter than when I'd seen him last. He used to show up out there at the golf course in a big white limousine."

Steagall recalled that he and many of the cast members—along with director Totten and producer Ben Miller, star Ben Johnson's nephew— were old friends who shared cowboy backgrounds. They spent a lot of their time between scenes taking turns roping a dummy steer.

"They were definitely outsiders," Steagall said of Gibson and Mazzola. "I think ol' Sonny would've liked to have joined us and been one of the guys, but she kind of kept him off to the side, away from us."

"I was proud to be a part of the film," he added, "because of all my buddies that were a part of it."

Eye of God (1997)

Put together by Tulsa brothers Tim Blake Nelson (director, writer) and Mike Nelson (producer), *Eye of God* fared much better with its city's movie critic than *Dark before Dawn* had. Wrote the *Tulsa World*'s Dennis King in his October 31 review, "Independent filmmaking—that is, storytelling on a shoestring that gives voice to fresh, original cinematic visions—seldom gets better than *Eye of God*."

A meditation on sin and retribution, Old Testament–style, in a small Oklahoma town (shooting locations included Collinsville, Skiatook, and Avant), the picture starred Martha Plimpton and Kevin Anderson as a waitress and the paroled con she marries, with downbeat results. Noted actress Mary Kay Place, a Tulsan, appeared in a cameo role. In a companion piece published the same day as his review, King wrote that "several supporting cast members and about 80 percent of the behind-the-scenes talent were locally recruited," giving Mike Nelson as his source for the information.

Both of the Nelsons had legitimate Hollywood credits before returning home to shoot *Eye of God*. Mike, in fact, now best known as a producer and production manager on pictures like *The League of Extraordinary Gentlemen* (2003) and the underrated satire *Idiocracy* (2006), was an executive at (Duncan native) Ron Howard's Imagine Entertainment at the time. A few years later, 2000's *O Brother, Where Art Thou?* would establish Tim Blake Nelson as a movie star; at this writing, he continues to act in, write, direct, and produce movies, performing all four functions on 2009's *Leaves of Grass,* shot in Louisiana but set in Oklahoma.

Filmography

The following filmography includes the shot-in-Oklahoma movies mentioned within these pages. In most cases, each entry lists distribution company, year of release, and, if known, stars, director, writer, and cinematographer. The author acknowledges with gratitude information gleaned from the IMDbPro website (http://pro.imdb.com), along with numerous reference books (listed in works consulted), studio promotional material, and the *Tulsa World* archives.

Note: A reel is approximately ten minutes of film.

Alien Zone
(Jupiter Pictures, 1978) 82 minutes
John Ericson, Charles Aidman, Bernard Fox, Ivor Francis, Burr DeBenning, Judith Novgrod, Richard Gates, Elizabeth MacRae, Kathie Gibboney, Leslie Paxton, John King
Director: Sharron Miller
Writer: David O'Malley
Cinematographer: Ken Gibb
Synopsis: A horror anthology framed by an adulterous plumber (Ericson) who seeks shelter in a mortuary. Shot in and around Stillwater with Oklahoma State University students as a part of its crew.

All on Account of an Egg
(Universal Film Manufacturing Company, 1913) one reel
Director: William F. Haddock
Synopsis: Adaptation of an O. Henry short story filmed at Pawnee Bill's Buffalo Ranch.

Around the World in Eighty Days
(United Artists, 1956) 175 minutes
Cantinflas, Finlay Currie, Robert Morley, Ronald Squire, Basil Sydney, Noel Coward, Sir John Gielgud, Trevor Howard, Harcourt Williams, David Niven, Martine Carol, Charles Boyer, Evelyn Keyes, Jose Greco

Director: Michael Anderson

Writers: James Poe, John Farrow, S. J. Perelman, Jules Verne (source novel)

Cinematographer: Lionel Lindon

Note: Producer Michael Todd's three-hour-long blockbuster, shot on 70 mm film and featuring dozens of stars in cameo appearances, included footage filmed in Oklahoma's Wichita Mountains.

Atoka

(Innovative Marketing and Movies Distribution, 1979) approximately 90 minutes

Willie Nelson, Larry Gatlin, Freddy Fender, Don Williams, Marty Robbins, Red Steagall, Hoyt Axton, David Allan Coe, Freddy Weller, Don White

Director: Chuck Bowman

Writer: unknown

Cinematographer: unknown

Note: A musical documentary chronicling the 1975 country-music festival called 48 Hours in Atoka, this feature seems to have disappeared after getting saturation booking in dozens of Oklahoma theaters.

The Bank Robbery

(Oklahoma Natural Mutoscene Company, 1908) two reels

Al Jennings, William M. Tilghman, Quanah Parker, John R. Abernathy, Heck Thomas, Chris Madsen

Director: William M. Tilghman

Cinematographer: J. B. Kent

Synopsis: A gang robs a bank in Cache, Okla., only to be captured by the forces of the law.

Best Foot Forward

(Show Productions [direct-to-video], 1987) 86 minutes

Bill Cole, Wade Tower, Jamie Breashears, John Bliss, Bill Buckner, George Hummingbird

Director: Paul MacFarlane

Writers: Diedre Simone Hill, David Gonzales

Cinematographer: Paul MacFarlane

Synopsis: A young man faces many obstacles in the way of his becoming a professional ballroom dancer. Shot in the Tulsa area, it features performances from real-world ballroom-dance pros. It's unclear what, if any, distribution the film received.

Black Gold

(Norman Studios, 1928) six reels

Lawrence Criner, Kathryn Boyd, Steve "Peg" Reynolds, Alfred Norcom, L. B. Tatums

Cinematographer: Richard E. Norman

Synopsis: Filmed in the all-black town of Tatums—and featuring its founder—the film tells an allegedly true tale of chicanery in the oil fields.

Blood Cult

(United Entertainment Pictures [direct-to-video], 1985) 89 minutes

Julie Andelman, Charles Ellis, Josef Hardt, Bennie Lee McGowan, James Vance, David Brent Stice

Director: Christopher Lewis

Writers: Stuart Rosenthal, James Vance (additional dialogue)

Cinematographer: Paul MacFarlane

Notes: This story of gruesome killings on a college campus was the first-ever made-for-home-video feature, shot in and around Tulsa and released by the Tulsa-based home-vid distributor, United Entertainment, also known as United Home Video.

Blood Lake

(United Entertainment Pictures [direct-to-video], 1988) 82 minutes

Doug Barry, Angela Darter, Mike Kaufman, Travis Krasser, Christie Willoughby, Tiny Frazier

Director: Tim Boggs

Writer: Doug Barry

Synopsis: Young people at a lake cabin are stalked by a maniacal killer. Produced by star and writer Barry, an Oklahoma City resident, and shot on a private lake near El Reno.

The Blue and the Gray

(CBS-TV miniseries, 1982) eight hours, including commercials

Stacy Keach, John Hammond, Lloyd Bridges, Rory Calhoun, Colleen Dewhurst, Warren Oates, Geraldine Page, Rip Torn, Robert Vaughn, Sterling Hayden, Paul Winfield, Gregory Peck, Bruce Abbott, Diane Baker

Director: Andrew V. McLaglen

Writers: Ian McLellan Hunter, Bruce Catton (story), John Leekley (story)

Cinematographer: Al Francis

Note: A small portion of this award-winning Civil War epic was lensed in Fort Gibson.

The Blue Ribbon Hijack

(unreleased, shot in 1956) unfinished

Jim Davis, Jan Young, Bill Hale, Bob Tafur, Billy Coppedge, Bob Green, Lee Couch, Mrs. Josh Evans, John Lindsey, Russ Stamper, Vincent Elliott, Walter "Buckshot" Pope

Director: Harry Donahue

Writer: Ed Erwin

Note: The first in a projected series of half-hour TV shows revolving around Brangus cattle, this pilot episode was never completed. Footage was shot at Raymond Pope's Clear View Ranch outside of Vinita.

A Brush between Cowboys and Indians

(Edison Manufacturing Company, 1904) short

Gilbert M. [later "Broncho Billy"] Anderson

Cinematographer: A. C. Abadie

Synopsis: Indians on horseback chase a group of mounted cowboys.

Bucking Bronco

(Edison Manufacturing Company, 1904) short

Cinematographer: A. C. Abadie

Synopsis: A 101 Ranch cowboy rides a fierce bronc.

The Buffalo Hunters

(Pawnee Bill's Buffalo Ranch Film Company, 1910) short

Gordon "Pawnee Bill" Lillie

Note: Shot on Pawnee Bill's ranch.

The Bull-Dogger

(Norman Film Manufacturing Company, 1921) 32 minutes

Bill Pickett, Bennie Turpin, Steve "Peg" Reynolds, Anita Bush

Cinematographer: Richard E. Norman

Synopsis: Shot in the all-black town of Boley, with Pickett re-creating some of his best-known rodeo tricks in a tale of outlawry on the U.S.-Mexico border. Although sources indicate it was a five-reeler, the Library of Congress print runs only a little over half an hour.

Charge of the Model T's

(Ry-Mac, 1979) 90 minutes

John David Carson, Carol Bagdasarian, Louis Nye, Herb Edelman, John P. Fertitta, Arte Johnson, Jim McCullough, Jr., Bill Thurman, John Doucette, Louisa Moritz

Director: Jim McCullough

Writer: Jim McCullough

Cinematographer: Dean Cundey

Synopsis: A World War I German spy (Nye) tries to make trouble on the U.S.-Mexico border, only to be thwarted by an army lieutenant (Carson) and his Model T brigade. Filmed in the Wichita Mountains around Lawton and Eagle Park near Cache.

The Cherokee Strip

(Oil Field Amusu Company, 1925) unknown length

Herbert Bethew, Lucille Mulhall

Note: A film shot by the 101 Ranch crew featuring the outfit's top female performer.

A Close Shave

(Slipshod Productions, 1958) unknown length

Eldon Seymour, Luther "Luke" Graham, Barbara Powell, Bob Berry, Cliff King, Jim Shadid, John Gumm

Cinematographer: Ernie Crisp

Synopsis: Filmed at the Frontier City amusement park in Oklahoma City, this noncommercial parody of TV's *Gunsmoke* featured local television professionals in front of and behind the cameras.

Cole Justice

(Raedon Entertainment Group [direct-to-video], 1989) 91 minutes

Carl Bartholomew, Keith Andrews, Matt Bailey, Willard Clark, Tyler Sweatman, Michael Shamus Wiles, Nick Zickefoose, Noel Fairbrothers, Ayn Robbins, Mickey Blackwell, Michelle Merchant, Lisa Robertson Stefanic, Amy Grueber

Director: Carl Bartholomew

Writers: Carl Bartholomew, Doug Crain

Cinematographer: Jeff Steinborn

Synopsis: A college professor (Bartholomew) becomes an Old West–style vigilante in this made-in-Tulsa picture, the brainchild of longtime local kid-show host Bartholomew.

Coonskin

(Bryanston Distributing Company, 1975) 100 minutes

Barry White, Charles Gordone, Scatman Crothers, Philip Thomas, Danny Rees, Buddy Douglas, Jim Moore

Director: Ralph Bakshi

Writer: Ralph Bakshi

Cinematographer: William A. Fraker

Synopsis: An animated urban spin on the classic Uncle Remus tales, framed by live-action footage of a prison break filmed almost entirely at the Federal Correctional Institution in El Reno.

Cotton and Cattle
(Westart Pictures, 1921) unknown length
Al Hart, Jack Mower, Robert Conville, Edna Davies
Director: Leonard Franchon
Writer: William M. Smith
Cinematographer: A. H. Vallet
Note: Produced in Tulsa.

The Cowboy Ace
(Westart Pictures, 1921) unknown length
Al Hart, Jack Mower, Robert Conville, Ethel Dwyer, Red Bush
Director: Leonard Franchon
Writer: William M. Smith
Cinematographer: A. H. Vallet
Note: Produced in Tulsa.

Cowboys and Indians Fording a River in a Wagon
(Edison Manufacturing Company, 1904) short
Cinematographer: A. C. Abadie
Synopsis: Mules pull a wagon full of cowboys and Indians across a river.

The Crimson Skull
(Norman Film Manufacturing Company, 1922) six reels
Anita Bush, Lawrence Chenault, Bill Pickett, Steve "Peg" Reynolds
Cinematographer: Richard E. Norman
Synopsis: A masked outlaw called the Skull terrorizes the all-black town of Boley.
    Probably produced back-to-back with *The Bull-Dogger.*

Crossroads of Tulsa
(William M. Smith, 1924) unknown length
Director: Arthur S. Phillips
Writer: Arthur S. Phillips
Note: May have been shown only in Tulsa's Rialto Theater.

Dan Turner, Hollywood Detective (also known as The Raven Red Kiss-Off)
(LBS Communications [television], Fries Entertainment [home video], 1990) 93
    minutes
Marc Singer, Tracy Scoggins, Nicholas Worth, Arte Johnson, Clu Gulager, Miriam
    Byrd-Nethery, Paul Bartel, Eddie Deezen, Daniel Kamin, Brandon Smith, Susan
    Brooks, Bethany Wright, Barry Friedman, James Frank Clark, Eldon G. Hallum,
    Bill Belknap

Director: Christopher Lewis

Writers: John Wooley, Robert Leslie Bellem (story)

Cinematographer: Steve McWilliams

Synopsis: A private detective (Singer) goes on location to shadow the movie-star wife (Scoggins) of a Hollywood producer (Kamin), and murder and mayhem ensue. Set in the 1940s, it features a well-known character from the pulp magazines of that era.

Dark before Dawn

(PSM Entertainment, 1988) 95 minutes

Sonny Gibson, Reparata Mazzola, Morgan Woodward, Doug McClure, Ben Johnson, Rance Howard, Buck Taylor, Jeff Osterhage, Red Steagall, Rex Linn, Francis Zickefoose, John L. Martin, Clem McSpadden, Charles Dickerson, E. K. Gaylord II, Paul Newsom, William Buckner, Eldon G. Hallum, Billy Drago, Lee Gideon, Randy Whalen

Director: Robert Totten

Writer: Reparata Mazzola

Cinematographer: Steve McWilliams

Synopsis: Farmers who live around a small Kansas town are being cheated by a giant Texas grain company, which is trying to corner the market by storing grain illegally—and getting rid of those who find out about the scheme.

The Daughter of Dawn

(produced by the Texas Film Company, 1920; no general release?) six reels

Esther LeBarre, White Parker, Hunting Horse, Jack Sankadoty, Wanada Parker

Director: Norbert A. Myles

Writers: Norbert A. Myles and Richard E. Banks

Synopsis: A conflict between members of the Comanche and Kiowa tribes plays out as a love triangle in this all-Native American cast picture, filmed in the Wichita Mountains.

Death Rides the Range

(amateur production, 1942) unknown length

O. W. Rogers, Betty Crosson, Eugene Heflin, Velma Wolf, Al Nicholson, E. J. Holzbehlein, Buster Garrett, Bob McCoy

Producers: Fritz Holzberlein and Eugene Heflin

Note: An amateur western feature produced in Oklahoma City.

A Debtor to the Law

(Peacock Pictures/Norman Distributing Company, 1919) unknown length

Henry Starr, Paul Curry, William Karl Hackett, Patrick S. McGreeney
Director: George Reehm
Writer: Patrick S. McGreeney
Synopsis: Based on the life of outlaw Starr and produced by Tulsa's Pan-American Motion Picture Company.

Dillinger

(American International Pictures, 1973) 107 minutes
Warren Oates, Ben Johnson, Michelle Phillips, Cloris Leachman, Harry Dean Stanton, Geoffrey Lewis, John Ryan, Richard Dreyfuss, Steve Kanaly, John Martino, Roy Jenson
Director: John Milius
Writer: John Milius
Cinematographer: Jules Brenner
Synopsis: The story of the battle between G-man Melvin Purvis (Johnson) and America's Depression-era gangsters, especially John Dillinger (Oates). Shot at various Oklahoma locations, it marked Milius's directorial debut.

Driving Cattle to Pasture

(Edison Manufacturing Company, 1904) short
Cinematographer: A. C. Abadie
Synopsis: Cowboys move their stock on the 101 Ranch.

11:59 A.M.

(Slipshod Productions, 1954?) unknown length
Cinematographer: Ernie Crisp
Synopsis: A noncommercial parody of *High Noon*, with settings that include an Oklahoma City gravel pit.

Elizabethtown

(Paramount, 2005) 123 minutes
Orlando Bloom, Kirsten Dunst, Susan Sarandon, Alec Baldwin, Bruce McGill, Judy Greer, Jessica Biel, Paul Schneider, Loudon Wainwright, Gailard Sartain, Paula Deen,
Dan Biggers, Alice Marie Crowe, Tim Devitt, Ted Manson, Maxwell Moss Steen
Director: Cameron Crowe
Writer: Cameron Crowe
Cinematographer: John Toll
Synopsis: A hotshot shoe designer (Bloom), whose latest creation has failed miserably, travels to the titular Kentucky town where his father has died and ends up taking a road trip with dad's ashes and a flight attendant (Dunst) he met on the trip

South. Among their stops is the Oklahoma City National Memorial, on the site of the bombed Murrah Building.

Evening Star
(Pan-American Motion Picture Company, 1919?) unknown length
Henry Starr
Note: The second picture made by Oklahoma outlaw Starr and Tulsa-based Pan-American, following *A Debtor to the Law.* It's unclear whether it was ever finished or released.

Eye of God
(Castle Hill Productions, 1997) 84 minutes
Martha Plimpton, Kevin Anderson, Hal Holbrook, Nick Stahl, Mary Kay Place, Chris Freihofer, Woody Watson, Margo Martindale, Wally Welch, Larry Flynn, Richard Jenkins, Maggie Moore, Vernon Grote, Gary Ragland
Director: Tim Blake Nelson
Writer: Tim Blake Nelson
Cinematographer: Russell Lee Fine
Synopsis: A young drive-in restaurant worker (Plimpton) marries a paroled ex-con (Anderson) with whom she's been corresponding, only to find his fundamentalist vision of their life together closing in on her. Shot in and around Collinsville, Skiatook, and Avant by Tulsa brothers Tim Blake Nelson and Michael Nelson, who produced.

Fandango
(Universal Pictures, 1985) 91 minutes
Kevin Costner, Judd Nelson, Sam Robards, Chuck Bush, Brian Cesak, Marvin J. McIntyre, Suzy Amis, Glenne Headly, Pepe Serna, Elizabeth Daily, Robyn Rose
Director: Kevin Reynolds
Writer: Kevin Reynolds
Cinematographer: Thomas Del Ruth
Note: Filmed mostly in Texas, this tale of five college pals on a road trip includes footage shot in and around Tulsa.

Fast Charlie . . . The Moonbeam Rider
(Universal, 1979) 98 minutes
David Carradine, Brenda Vaccaro, L. Q. Jones, R. G. Armstrong, Terry Kiser, Jesse Vint, Noble Willingham, Ralph James, Bill Bartman, David Hayward, Stephen Ferry, Tracy Harris, Whit Clay, Jack Brennan
Director: Steve Carver
Writers: Michael Gleason (script), Ed Spielman and Howard Friedlander (story)

Cinematographer: William Birch

Synopsis: The story of a transcontinental motorcycle race held just after the end of World War I, with shooting done in Lawton, Cache, Guthrie, and Fort Sill.

The Frighteners

(Universal, 1996) 110 minutes

Michael J. Fox, Trini Alvarado, Peter Dobson, John Astin, Jeffrey Combs, Dee Wallace-Stone, Jake Busey, Chi McBride, Jim Fyfe, Troy Evans, Julianna McCarthy, R. Lee Ermey

Director: Peter Jackson

Writers: Fran Walsh, Peter Jackson

Cinematographers: John Blick, Alun Bollinger

Synopsis: After a serious car accident, a young man (Fox) finds out he can talk to ghosts. Although its filming location was New Zealand, some footage was reportedly shot in Tulsa.

The Frontier Detective

(Pawnee Bill's Buffalo Ranch Feature films, 1910) short

Gordon "Pawnee Bill" Lillie

Note: Shot on Pawnee Bill's ranch.

Gold Grabbers

(Merit Film Corporation, 1922) five reels

Franklyn Farnum, Shorty Hamilton, Al Hart, Genevieve Berte

Director: Francis Ford

Writer: William Wallace Cook

Cinematographer: Reginald Lyons

Note: Made in Tulsa by William M. Smith Productions.

The Grapes of Wrath

(Twentieth Century-Fox, 1940) 129 minutes

Henry Fonda, Jane Darwell, John Carradine, Charley Grapewin, Dorris Bowdon, Russell Simpson, O. Z. Whitehead, John Qualen, Eddie Quillan, Zeffie Tilbury, Frank Sully, Frank Darien, Darryl Hickman, Shirley Mills

Director: John Ford

Cinematographer: Gregg Toland

Note: Nominated for seven Academy Awards and winner of two (Best Supporting Actress, for Jane Darwell, and Best Director), this classic film about Oklahomans contained some, but not very much, footage shot in the state.

Greasepaint Indians

(Universal Film Manufacturing Company, 1913) one reel

Lamar Johnstone, Hal Wilson

Director: William F. Haddock

Synopsis: A western-themed comedy filmed at Pawnee Bill's Buffalo Ranch.

He Could Not Lose Her

(Universal Film Manufacturing Company, 1913) one reel

Director: William F. Haddock

Synopsis: A western-themed comedy filmed at Pawnee Bill's Buffalo Ranch.

Hearts and Crosses

(Universal Film Manufacturing Company, 1913) one reel

Lamar Johnstone, Lucille Young

Director: William F. Haddock

Synopsis: Adaptation of an O. Henry short story filmed at Pawnee Bill's Buffalo Ranch.

Home in Oklahoma

(Republic Pictures, 1946) 72 minutes

Roy Rogers, George Hayes, Dale Evans, Carol Hughes, George Meeker, Lanny Rees, Ruby Dandridge, the Flying L Ranch Quartette, Bob Nolan and the Sons of the Pioneers

Director: William Witney

Writer: Gerald Geraghty

Cinematographer: William Bradford

Synopsis: A small-town newspaper editor, played by Rogers, tracks down a rancher's killers.

In the Army Now

(Buena Vista, 1994) 91 minutes

Pauly Shore, Andy Dick, Lori Petty, David Alan Grier, Esai Morales, Lynn Whitfield, Art LaFleur, Fabiana Udenio, Glenn Morshower, Peter Spellos, Barry Nolan

Director: Daniel Petrie, Jr.

Writers: Ken Kaufman, Stu Krieger, Daniel Petrie, Jr., Fax Bahr, Adam Small, and Steve Zacharias, Jeff Buhai, Robbie Fox (story)

Cinematographer: William Wages

Synopsis: Former MTV star Shore plays a bumbling Army recruit whom the film follows through basic training and onto the African desert, where he and his fellow soldiers take on a renegade Arab nation. Some of the training scenes were shot at Fort Sill.

In the Days of the Thundering Herd

(General Film Company, 1914) five reels

Tom Mix, Bessie Eyton, Red Wing, Wheeler Oakman, John Bowers, Major Gordon [Pawnee Bill] Lillie

Director: Colin Campbell

Writer: Gilson Willets

Synopsis: The only two survivors of a wagon train attack run into Indian trouble again.

It Happened Out West

(Merit Film Corporation, 1923) five reels

Franklyn Farnum, Shorty Hamilton, Virginia Lee, Al Hart

Director: Francis Ford

Synopsis: Farnum plays a Texas Ranger investigating the smuggling of Chinese immigrants across the Mexico-Texas border.

Note: Made in Tulsa by William M. Smith Productions.

Jim Thorpe, All-American

(Warner Bros., 1951) 107 minutes

Burt Lancaster, Charles Bickford, Steve Cochran, Phyllis Thaxter, Dick Wesson, Jack Bighead, Suni Warcloud, Al Mejia, Hubie Kerns

Director: Michael Curtiz

Writers: Everett Freeman, Douglas Morrow, Russell J. Birdwell, James Thorpe

Cinematographer: Ernest Haller

Synopsis: A major-studio biopic about Oklahoma's famous American Indian athlete, filmed partially in and around Muskogee.

Just between Us

(Pax Films, 1960) feature-length

London, Marcia Becton, Rue McClanahan, Billy Pitcock, David Sipes, Ed Niebling, Tom Cunliff, Billy Pappert

Director: John Patrick Hayes

Writer: Chuck Eisenmann

Note: This film, about a little girl (Becton) and her German shepherd (London) debuted in two Tulsa theaters, but it may never have seen national distribution. McClanahan was also a makeup artist on the picture.

J.W. Coop

(Columbia Pictures, 1972) 112 minutes

Cliff Robertson, Geraldine Page, Cristina Ferrare, R.G. Armstrong, R. L. Armstrong, John Crawford, John Crawford, Wade Crosby, Marjorie Durant Dye, Paul Harper, Son Hooker

Director: Cliff Robertson

Writers: Gary Cartwright, Cliff Robertson, Edwin Shrake

Cinematographer: Frank Stanley

Synopsis: An imprisoned cowboy (Robertson) returns to the rodeo world upon his release, only to find that lots of things have changed since his incarceration. Partially shot at the Oklahoma State Penitentiary in McAlester, the film features many personalities from the real-life world of rodeo, including well-known Oklahoma political figure and rodeo announcer Clem McSpadden.

The Kidnappers Foil

(Melton Barker Productions, 1946) two reels

Harold Nix, Ruella Yates, Melton Barker

Director: Melton Barker

Writer: Melton Barker

Note: Itinerant filmmaker Barker made this picture dozens of times in dozens of American towns, always using local kids. A slight tale about the kidnapping and subsequent release of a young girl, the story allowed for musical interludes and large numbers of young people to participate (for a fee). The version listed here was shot in Shawnee and has been archived by the Oklahoma Historical Society.

The Killer Inside Me

(Revolution Films, 2010) 148 minutes

Kate Hudson, Jessica Alba, Casey Affleck, Simon Baker, Bill Pullman, Liam Aiken, Elias Koteas, Ned Beatty, Rosa Pasquarella, Brent Briscoe, Tom Bower, Jay R. Ferguson

Director: Michael Winterbottom

Writers: John Curran, Michael Winterbottom, Jim Thompson (source novel)

Cinematographer: Marcel Zyskind

Synopsis: The most recent adaptation of Oklahoma writer Jim Thompson's paperback noir classic, featuring Affleck as a small-town Texas deputy whose bland exterior masks a psychopathic killer.

The Last Stand of the Dalton Boys

(The Atlas Company, 1912) three reels

Note: Supervised by Emmett Dalton, the only survivor of a botched Coffeyville, Kansas, bank robbery he attempted with his two brothers. Evidence suggests that at least some of the filming was done in Red Fork and Sand Springs.

Mad Dogs and Englishmen

(MGM, 1971) 117 minutes

Leon Russell, Joe Cocker, Chris Stainton, Bobby Keys, Jim Gordon, Jim Keltner, Carl Radle, Don Preston, Chuck Blackwell, Bobby Torres, Jim Horn, Rita

Coolidge, Sandy Konikoff, Claudia Lennear, Emily Smith, Denny Cordell, Jim Price

Director: Pierre Adidge

Cinematographer: Dave Myers

Synopsis: A musical documentary chronicling the massive early '70s rock 'n' roll tour with headliner Joe Cocker, this film featured several scenes shot in Leon Russell's hometown of Tulsa.

Mutilations

(Baron Video [direct-to-video], 1986) 67 minutes

Al Baker, Katherine Hutson, Bill Buckner, Harvey Shell, John Bliss, Shelly Creel, Richard Taylor, Matthew Hixenbaugh, Jackie Shook, William Jerrick, Pamela Michaels

Director: Lawrence Thomas

Writer: Lawrence Thomas

Cinematographer: Steve Wacks

Synopsis: An alien invader traps an astronomy professor (Baker) and his field-tripping students in an old house.

My Heroes Have Always Been Cowboys

(Samuel Goldwyn Company, 1991) 106 minutes

Scott Glenn, Kate Capshaw, Tess Harper, Gary Busey, Ben Johnson, Balthazar Getty, Clarence Williams III, Mickey Rooney, Dub Taylor, Clu Gulager, Dennis Fimple

Director: Stuart Rosenberg

Writer: Joel Don Humphreys

Cinematographer: Bernd Heinl

Synopsis: A rodeo rider (Glenn) comes home to face his past and the people who care about him in this made-in-Guthrie feature.

Near Dark

(De Laurentiis Entertainment Group, 1987) 94 minutes

Adrian Pasdar, Jenny Wright, Lance Henriksen, Bill Paxton, Jenette Goldstein, Tim Thomerson, Joshua Miller, Marcie Leeds, Kenny Call, Ed Corbett, Troy Evans, Bill Cross

Director: Kathryn Bigelow

Writers: Kathryn Bigelow, Eric Red

Cinematographer: Adam Greenberg

Synopsis: When an Oklahoma farm boy (Pasdar) is bitten by an attractive vampire (Wright), he becomes involved with a group of bloodsuckers traveling the back roads of America's heartland.

North of 36

(Paramount Pictures, 1924) feature-length

Jack Holt, Ernest Torrence, Lois Wilson, Noah Beery, David Dunbar, Stephen Carr, Guy Oliver, William A. Carroll, Clarence Geldart, George Irving, Ella Miller

Director: Irvin Willat

Writer: Emerson Hough (source novel)

Synopsis: A sequel to Paramount's 1923 epic *The Covered Wagon,* also based on a Hough novel, detailing the adventure of a cattle drive.

Oklahoma As Is

(Warner Bros., 1937) one reel

Cal Tinney, David Tinney

Writer: Cal Tinney

Synopsis: Little is known about this one-reel comedy, ostensibly an entry in the Vitaphone series of movie shorts, in which the town of Oologah is lampooned as "Oolala" by Tinney, a Tulsa-based humorist.

Oklahoma Bound

(Buffalo Pictures, 1980) feature-length

F. E. Bowling, Dan Jones, Sheryl Rose, Patrick C. Poole [as Clint Poole]

Director: Patrick C. Poole

Writer: Patrick C. Poole

Cinematographer: Robert P. Perry

Synopsis: A G-rated rural comedy about the trouble an old man (Bowling) gets into when he goes in debt to gamblers. The film debuted in Collinsville in December 1980 and apparently received only regional bookings after that.

Oklahoma Holiday

(?, 1956) 28 minutes

Synopsis: A noncommercial travelogue offered free to interested schools and organizations by Oklahoma's Planning and Resources Board.

Oklahoma Newsreel Cameraman

(Oklahoma Educational Television Authority, 1994) 60 minutes

Producers: Bill Moore and Bill Thrash

Cinematographer: Arthur Ramsey

Synopsis: A made-for-television documentary about pioneering Oklahoma newsreel photographer Arthur Ramsey that first aired on OETA stations.

Oklahoma Passage

(Oklahoma Educational Television Authority, 1989) five hours

Ben Johnson, Daniel Kamin, Robert Knott, Rex Linn, Jeff MacKay, Jeanette Nolan,

Dale Robertson, G. D. Spradlin, Whitman Mayo, Michelle Merchant
Director: Kenneth A. Meyer
Writer: Kevin Meyer
Cinematographers: Steve Schklair, James W. Wrenn
Synopsis: An award-winning TV miniseries covering 150 years in the history of Oklahoma, produced by OETA at a cost of more than $1 million.

The Oklahoma Story

(Continental Nationwide Films, 1952?) short
Producer: Hal Ayers
Writer: Ruth Ayers
Synopsis: A noncommercial travelogue, touting Oklahoma as a vacation destination, made available to both movie theaters and television. See also *The Tulsa Story*.

The Only Way Home

(regional distribution, 1972) 86 minutes
Bo Hopkins, Beth Brickell, Steve Sandor, G. D. Spradlin, Walter Jones, Jack Isaacs, Jean Abney, Maurice Eaves, Stanley Zenor, Jane Hall, Lynn Hickey, George Clow
Director: G. D. Spradlin
Writer: Jeeds O'Tilbury
Cinematographer: Henning Schellerup
Synopsis: Shot entirely in Oklahoma, the film is a psychological thriller about an abducted woman (Brickell) who falls for one of her captors.

Osage

(unreleased, shot in 1949) unfinished
Edward Norris, Noel Neill, Smith Ballew, Johnnie Lee Wills, Lon Chaney, Jr., Pamela Blake, Lee "Lasses" White, Spade Cooley, Robert Gilbert, Elizabeth Marshall, Robert Curtis, Joe Gilbreath, Kay Mullendore, Ewing Brown, Theresa Dean
Director: Oliver Drake
Note: Lensed in Oklahoma locations including the Mullendore Cross Bell Ranch near Pawhuska and the John Zink Ranch near Skiatook, this picture was apparently never completed. Some of the footage may have shown up in 1957's *The Parson and the Outlaw*.

Out of the Clouds

(Westart Pictures, 1921) unknown length
Al Hart, Jack Mower, Robert Conville
Director: Leonard Franchon
Writer: William M. Smith

Cinematographer: A. H. Vallet

Note: Produced in Tulsa.

The Outsiders

(Warner Bros., 1983) 91 minutes

C. Thomas Howell, Matt Dillon, Ralph Macchio, Patrick Swayze, Rob Lowe, Emilio Estevez, Tom Cruise, Glenn Withrow, Diane Lane, Leif Garrett, Darren Dalton, Michelle Meyrink, Tom Waits, Gailard Sartain, William Smith, S. E. Hinton, Darcy O'Brien

Director: Francis Ford Coppola

Writers: Kathleen Knutsen Rowell, S. E. Hinton (uncredited; also source novel), Francis Ford Coppola (uncredited)

Cinematographer: Stephen H. Burum

Synopsis: A story of the conflicts between students of different social classes in the 1960s, as seen through the eyes of Ponyboy Curtis (Howell), a wrong-side-of-the-tracks "greaser." This is the second of three films based on Hinton novels that were shot in and around Tulsa in the early 1980s.

Note: In 2005 a director's-cut version of the film was released on DVD. Titled *The Outsiders: The Complete Novel*, it ran twenty-two minutes longer and featured a musical score altered in favor of period rock 'n' roll.

Passing of the Oklahoma Outlaw

(Eagle Film Company, 1915) four reels

William M. Tilghman, E. D. Nix, Chris Madsen, John Hale, James F. "Bud" Ledbetter, Arkansas Tom Jones

Director: William M. Tilghman

Writer: Lute P. Stover

Cinematographer: J. B. Kent

Synopsis: Lawmen capture and/or kill some of Oklahoma's most famous lawbreakers.

A Pawnee Romance

(Universal Film Manufacturing Company, 1913) one reel

Director: William F. Haddock

Synopsis: A western-themed comedy filmed at Pawnee Bill's Buffalo Ranch.

Phenomenon

(Buena Vista, 1996) 123 minutes

John Travolta, Kyra Sedgwick, Forest Whitaker, Robert Duvall, Jeffrey DeMunn, Richard Kiley, David Gallagher, Ashley Buccille, Tony Genaro, Sean O'Bryan, Michael Milhoan, Troy Evans, Bruce Young, Vyto Ruginis, Brent Spiner

Director: Jon Turteltaub
Writer: Gerald Dipego
Cinematographer: Phedon Papamichael
Synopsis: After seeing a bright light in the sky, an ordinary guy (Travolta) develops extraordinary mental powers.

A Poem Is a Naked Person
(Flower Films, 1974) 72 minutes
Leon Russell, Willie Nelson, George Jones
Director: Les Blank
Writer: Les Blank
Cinematographer: Les Blank
Synopsis: Seldom-seen musical documentary filmed in 1972–74 while Blank was living at Leon Russell's recording-studio complex on Grand Lake O' The Cherokees. Some of the footage was also shot in Tulsa.

Possums
(Monarch Home Video, 1999) 97 minutes
Mac Davis, Cynthia Sikes, Greg Coolidge, Andrew Prine, Dennis Burkley, Monica Creel, Jay Underwood, Jerry Haynes, Clive Revill, Rodney Lay, Barry Switzer, Zac Sherman
Director: J. Max Burnett
Writer: J. Max Burnett
Cinematographer: Christopher Duskin
Synopsis: A hardware store owner and radio announcer (Davis) finds himself having to field a real high school football team after his made-up exploits of an imaginary squad attract attention outside his hometown. Shot in Nowata.

Prince of Peace (I)
(Principle Films, 1948?) 72 minutes
Millard Coody, Darlene Bridges, A. S. Fischer, Hazel Lee Becker, Knox Manning (announcer)
Director: Harold Daniels
Writer: DeVallon Scott
Cinematographer: Henry Sharp
Synopsis: A straightforward filming of the annual Lawton passion play, with a small amount of wraparound material, all shot on location in Oklahoma. Some of this footage was used in the later *Prince of Peace,* also titled *The Lawton Story* (see entry for *Prince of Peace* [II]).

Prince of Peace (II) (also known as The Lawton Story)

(Hallmark Productions, 1949) 100 minutes

Ginger Prince, Forrest Taylor, Millard Coody, Gwyn Shipman, Ferris Taylor, Maude
Eburne, Willa Pearl Curtis, Hazel Lee Becker, A. S. Fisher, Darlene Bridges

Directors: William Beaudine, Harold Daniels

Writers: W. Scott Darling, DeVallon Scott, Mildred Horn (story)

Cinematographer: Henry Sharp

Synopsis: In this version, six-year-old Ginger Prince takes over center stage from
Jesus and the other Easter story characters. She's the focus of a schmaltzy scenario
that finds the whole cast touched by the wonder of the pageant. The 1949 *Prince
of Peace* souvenir program noted that 40 percent of this version was shot in
Hollywood, with 60 percent consisting of the original Lawton-lensed footage. At
this writing, this *Prince of Peace* remains a lost film.

Queen of the Buffalo Ranch

(Pawnee Bill's Buffalo Ranch Feature Films, 1910) short

May Lillie

Note: Shot on Pawnee Bill's ranch with his wife in the lead role.

Rain Man

(MGM/UA, 1988) 133 minutes

Dustin Hoffman, Tom Cruise, Valeria Golino, Jerry Molen, Jack Murdock, Michael
D. Roberts, Ralph Seymour, Lucinda Jenney, Bonnie Hunt, Kim Robillard, Beth
Grant

Director: Barry Levinson

Writers: Barry Morrow, Ronald Bass

Cinematographer: John Seale

Synopsis: Hoffman plays the long-lost, autistic savant brother of Cruise, a West
Coast hustler who begins his relationship with Hoffman's character by trying to
rook him out of an inheritance, only to end up forming a familial bond with him.
Partially shot in several Oklahoma locations. Winner of four Academy Awards.

Ranch Life in the Great Southwest

(General Film Company, 1910) one reel

Pat Long, Charles Fuqua, Johnny Mullens, Tom Mix, Henry Grammar

Director: Francis Boggs

Producer: William Selig

Note: Between stints at the 101 Ranch, Mix makes his film debut here, busting a
bronc.

The Range Pirate
(Westart Pictures, 1921) unknown length
Al Hart, Jack Mower, Robert Conville
Director: Leonard Franchon
Writer: William M. Smith
Cinematographer: A. H. Vallet
Note: Produced in Tulsa.

Revenge
(United Entertainment Pictures [direct-to-video], 1986) 89 minutes
Patrick Wayne, John Carradine, Bennie Lee McGowan, Josef Hardt, Stephanie
    Knopke, Fred Graves, Charles Ellis, David Brent Stice, John Bliss, Andrea Adams
Director: Christopher Lewis
Writer: Christopher Lewis, James Vance (story, uncredited)
Cinematographer: Steve McWilliams
Synopsis: This sequel to *Blood Cult* features many of the same cast members (and
    a story by *Blood Cult* star James Vance), along with Hollywood veterans Wayne
    and Carradine. The former plays a man returning to his hometown to investigate
    the death of his brother; the latter, a leader of the Cult of Caninus, the dog-
    worshipping bunch first seen in *Blood Cult*.

The Ripper
(United Entertainment Pictures [direct-to-video],1985) 103 minutes
Tom Savini, Tom Schreier, Wade Tower, Mona Van Pernis, Andrea Adams
Director: Christopher Lewis
Writer: Bill Groves
Cinematographer: Paul MacFarlane
Synopsis: An ancient ring turns a college professor (Schreier) into a modern-day
    incarnation of Jack the Ripper (Savini).

Rock Island Trail
(Republic Pictures, 1950) 90 minutes
Forrest Tucker, Adele Mara, Adrian Booth, Bruce Cabot, Chill Wills, Jeff Corey,
    Grant Withers, Barbra Fuller, Roy Barcroft
Director: Joseph Kane
Writer: James Edward Grant, from Frank J. Nevins's novel *A Yankee Dared*
Cinematographer: Jack Marta
Synopsis: A young railroad man (Tucker) expands his operation, despite opposition
    by a stagecoach and steamship magnate (Cabot).

Rounding Up and Branding Cattle
(Edison Manufacturing Company, 1904) short
Cinematographer: A. C. Abadie
Synopsis: Cowboys and their stock on the 101 Ranch.

A Round-Up in Oklahoma
(Oklahoma Natural Mutoscene Company, 1908) one reel
Director: William M. Tilghman
Cinematographer: J. B. Kent
Synopsis: Cowboys are harassed by Indians during a cattle drive.

Rumble Fish
(Universal Pictures, 1983) 94 minutes
Matt Dillon, Mickey Rourke, Diane Lane, Dennis Hopper, Diana Scarwid, Vincent
    Spano, Nicolas Cage, Christopher Penn, Larry Fishburne, William Smith,
    Michael Higgins, Glenn Withrow, Tom Waits, Herb Rice, Maybelle Wallace,
    Nona Manning, S. E. Hinton, Bob Maras
Director: Francis Ford Coppola
Writers: Francis Ford Coppola, S. E. Hinton (also source novel)
Cinematographer: Stephen H. Burum
Synopsis: In this final entry in the trilogy of Tulsa-shot films based on Hinton's
    novels, a young tough (Dillon) tries to emulate his older brother (Rourke), a
    near-mythological figure known as Motorcycle Boy.

Rustlers of the Night
(Westart Pictures, 1921) unknown length
Al Hart, Jack Mower, Robert Conville
Director: Leonard Franchon
Writer: William M. Smith
Cinematographer: A. H. Vallet
Note: Produced in Tulsa.

A Season of Visions, a Dwelling of Mine
(not commercially released, 1968) 45 minutes
Norman Hawk, Kelsey Bartholic, Louise Larrabee, Paul England, Jean and John
    Kennedy, David Hon, Kenneth Nero, Daniel Fields, Larry Holmes, Zyggy
    Kilian, Vicki and David Ward, Marilyn Pelton, Irma Carrasco
Director: Dale Pelton
Writer: Dale Pelton
Cinematographers: Dale Pelton and David Ward
Synopsis: A man (Hawk) longs to escape his bleak life in a small Midwestern town.

A Simple Wish

(Universal Pictures, 1997) 89 minutes

Martin Short, Kathleen Turner, Teri Garr, Amanda Plummer, Mara Wilson, Robert
    Pastorelli, Ruby Dee, Francis Capra, Jonathan Hadary, Deborah Odell, Alan
    Campbell,

Lanny Flaherty, Clare Coulter, Neil Foster, Jaime Tirelli, Jack McGee

Director: Michael Ritchie

Writer: Jeff Rothberg

Cinematographer: Ralf Bode

Synopsis: A little girl (Wilson) tries to get her carriage-driver father (Pastorelli) a part
    in a Broadway musical, relying on her bumbling fairy godfather (Short). Includes
    a substantial scene shot near Pawhuska at the Tallgrass Prairie.

So This Is Arizona

(Merit Film Corporation, 1922) five reels

Franklyn Farnum, Francis Ford, Shorty Hamilton, Al Hart, Genevieve Bert, Art
    Phillips

Director: Francis Ford

Writers: Marie Schrader, C. C. Wadde

Cinematographer: Reginald Lyons

Note: Made in Tulsa by William M. Smith Productions.

The Stampede

(Selig Polyscope Company, 1909) short

Hobart Bosworth, Betty Harte, Tom Santschi

Director: Francis Boggs

Producer: William Selig

Note: A western shot, at least in part, at the 101 Ranch.

Stark Fear

(Ellis Films, 1962) 86 minutes

Beverly Garland, Skip Homeier, Kenneth Tobey, Hannah Stone, George Clow, Paul
    Scovil, Edna Neuman, John Arville, Carey Mount, Cortez Ewing, Bob Stone,
    Barbara Freeman, Darlene Dana Reno, Joseph Benton

Director: Ned Hockman

Writer: Dwight V. Swain

Cinematographer: Robert Bethard

Synopsis: A young married woman (Garland) has to deal with the increasingly
    bizarre behavior of her husband (Homeier) and the weirdness of his Oklahoma
    hometown of Quehada (actually Lexington) in this homegrown psychological
    thriller.

State Fair

(Twentieth Century-Fox, 1962) 118 minutes

Pat Boone, Bobby Darin, Pamela Tiffin, Ann-Margret, Tom Ewell, Alice Faye, Wally Cox, David Brandon, Clem Harvey, Robert Foulk, Linda Heinrich, Edward "Tap" Canutt

Director: José Ferrer

Writers: Richard L. Breen, Philip Stong (source novel)

Cinematographer: William C. Mellor

Note: The third film version of this classic tale of romance and adventure in a state fair setting was partially shot on the Oklahoma State Fairgrounds in Oklahoma City.

Surviving

(ABC-TV movie, 1985) 143 minutes

Ellen Burstyn, Len Cariou, Zach Galligan, Marsha Mason, Molly Ringwald, Paul Sorvino, River Phoenix, Heather O'Rourke, William Windom, Marc Gilpin, Paddi Edwards

Director: Waris Hussein

Writer: Joyce Eliason

Cinematographer: Alexander Gruszynski

Synopsis: Two families deal with the problem of teen suicide in this made-for TV movie, filmed in Oklahoma City.

Terror at Tenkiller

(United Entertainment Pictures [direct-to-video], 1986) 87 minutes

Mike Wiles, Stacey Logan, Dean Lewis, Michelle Merchant, Dale Buckmaster

Director: Ken Meyer

Writer: Claudia Meyer

Cinematographer: Steve Wacks

Synopsis: Vacationing in a remote cabin beside Oklahoma's Lake Tenkiller, two young women are harassed by a murderer.

Tex

(Buena Vista, 1982) 103 minutes

Matt Dillon, Jim Metzler, Meg Tilly, Bill McKinney, Frances Lee McCain, Ben Johnson, Phil Brock, Emilio Estevez, Jack Thibeau, Zeljko Ivanek, Tom Virtue, Pamela Ludwig, Jeff Fleury, Jill Clark, S. E. Hinton

Director: Tim Hunter

Writers: Charlie Haas, Tim Hunter, S. E. Hinton (source novel)

Cinematographer: Ric Waite

Synopsis: A rural teen (Dillon) with a dead mother and an absentee father

(McKinney) has to make some tough choices about life. The first of three films based on S. E. Hinton novels to be shot in the Tulsa area nearly back to back, it marked the film debut of Estevez.

Thirty Dangerous Seconds
(regional distribution, 1973) 75 minutes
Robert Lansing, Kathryn Reynolds, Michael Dante, Marj Dusay, Josef Hardt, Campbell Thomas
Director: Joseph Taft
Writer: Joseph Taft
Cinematographer: Henning Schellerup
Synopsis: Two groups of criminals—one amateur, the other professional—set out to rob the same armored car in this caper flick, shot mostly in Oklahoma City.

This Stuff'll Kill Ya!
(Ultima Productions, 1971) 100 minutes
Jeffrey Allen, Tim Holt, Gloria King, Ray Sager, Erich Bradly, Terence McCarthy, Ronna Riddle, Larry Drake, John Garner, Billy Mays, Lee Danser, Carol Merrell
Director: Herschell Gordon Lewis
Writer: Herschell Gordon Lewis
Cinematographer: Eskandar Ameri (Alex Ameripoor)
Synopsis: A gore-accented action-comedy about a moonshine operation run out of a backwoods church, shot in Checotah and Oklahoma City.

Trail Dust
(Rayart Pictures Corp., 1924) six reels
David Dunbar
Director: Gordon Hines
Producer: K. Lee Williams
Synopsis: A story of Oklahoma pioneers in the 1870s.

Trail to Red Dog
(Westart Pictures, 1921) unknown length
Al Hart, Jack Mower, Robert Conville
Director: Leonard Franchon
Writer: William M. Smith
Cinematographer: A. H. Vallet
Note: Produced in Tulsa.

Trail's End
(Merit Film Corporation, 1922) five reels
Franklyn Farnum, Peggy O'Day, George Reehm, Shorty Hamilton, Al Hart, Genevieve Bert

Director: Francis Ford
Writer: Arthur Somers Roche
Cinematographer: Reginald Lyons
Note: Made in Tulsa by William M. Smith Productions.

Tulsa

(Eagle-Lion Films, 1949) 90 minutes
Susan Hayward, Robert Preston, Pedro Armendáriz, Lloyd Gough, Chill Wills,
    Edward Begley, Jimmy Conlin, Roland Jack, Harry Shannon, Lola Albright
Director: Stuart Heisler
Writers: Curtis Kenyon, Frank Nugent, Richard Wormser (story)
Cinematographer: Winton Hoch
Synopsis: A highly fictionalized story of the early Oklahoma oil business, following
    a young woman named Cherokee Lansing (Hayward) who takes over her dead
    father's leases.

The Tulsa Story

(Continental Nationwide Films, 1954) 12 1/2 minutes
Producer: Hal Ayers
Writer: Ruth Ayers
Note: A noncommercial travelogue offered to television stations and theaters. See
    also *The Oklahoma Story.*

Twister

(Warner Bros., 1996) 113 minutes
Helen Hunt, Bill Paxton, Cary Elwes, Jami Gertz, Philip Seymour Hoffman, Lois
    Smith, Alan Ruck, Sean Whalen, Scott Thomson, Todd Field, Zach Grenier,
    Jake Busey
Director: Jan de Bont
Writers: Michael Crichton, Anne-Marie Martin
Cinematographer: Jack N. Green
Synopsis: A romantic triangle among University of Oklahoma storm chasers (Hunt,
    Paxton, Gertz) forms the underpinning for this big-budget, effects-laden thriller
    about killer tornadoes. Shot in several state locations (as well as in Iowa and
    Ontario, Canada), notably the Grant County town of Wakita.

Two-Lane Blacktop

(Universal Pictures, 1971) 102 minutes
James Taylor, Warren Oates, Laurie Bird, Dennis Wilson
Director: Monte Hellman
Writers: Rudolph Wurlitzer, Will Corry

Cinematographer: Jack Deerson

Synopsis: A pair of motorhead drifters (Taylor and Wilson) get involved in a cross-country race with another driver (Oates).

UHF

(Orion Pictures, 1989) 97 minutes

"Weird Al" Yankovic, Victoria Jackson, Kevin McCarthy, Michael Richards, David Bowe, Anthony Geary, Trinidad Silva, Gedde Watanabe, Billy Barty, Fran Drescher, Sue Ane Langdon, Eldon G. Hallum, Lisa Robertson Stefanic, Barry Friedman, Adam Maras

Director: Jay Levey

Writers: Al Yankovic, Jay Levey

Cinematographer: David Lewis

Synopsis: A klutzy young dreamer (Yankovic) gets the opportunity to run a low-power UHF outlet, coming up with off-the-wall programming that turns the station into a surprise hit. Filmed in and around Tulsa.

Union Pacific

(Paramount Pictures, 1939) 135 minutes

Barbara Stanwyck, Joel McCrea, Akim Tamiroff, Robert Preston, Lynne Overman, Brian Donlevy, Robert Barrat, Anthony Quinn, Stanley Ridges, Henry Kolker, Francis McDonald, Willard Robertson, Evelyn Keyes, Regis Toomey, Fuzzy Knight

Director: Cecil B. DeMille

Writers: Walter DeLeon, C. Gardner Sullivan, Jesse Lasky, Jr., Jack Cunningham, Ernest Haycox (source novel)

Cinematographer: Victor Milner

Synopsis: This sprawling epic of the transcontinental railroad included a small amount of footage shot around Cache.

Violin Man

(not commercially released, circa 1970) 20 minutes

Armin Sebran

Director: Paul Stevenson

Cinematographer: Paul Stevenson

Synopsis: A violinist (Sebran) encounters inhabitants of Tulsa's inner city. Shot as a silent film, with a sound track of mostly classical music added later.

Welcome Home, Soldier Boys

(Twentieth Century-Fox, 1972) 91 minutes

Joe Don Baker, Paul Koslo, Alan Vint, Elliott Street, Jennifer Billingsley, Billy Green Bush, Geoffrey Lewis, Francine York, Timothy Scott, Lonny Chapman, Florence

MacMichael, Beach Dickerson
Director: Richard Compton
Writer: Guerdon Trueblood
Cinematographer: Donald H. Birnkrant
Synopsis: Four newly discharged Vietnam vets head out across America, with predictably downbeat results. Partially shot in Cordell.

Western Stage Coach Hold Up
(Edison Manufacturing Company, 1904) short
Cinematographer: A. C. Abadie
Synopsis: Outlaws rob the passengers of a stagecoach and make a clean getaway.

Where the Red Fern Grows (I)
(Doty-Dayton Productions, 1974) 97 minutes
James Whitmore, Beverly Garland, Jack Ging, Lonny Chapman, Stewart Petersen, Jill Clark, Jeanna Wilson, Bill Thurman, Bill Dunbar, Rex Corley, John Lindsey
Director: Norman Tokar
Writers: Eleanor Lamb, Douglas C. Stewart, Wilson Rawls (source novel)
Cinematographer: Dean Cundey
Synopsis: The story of a rural boy (Petersen) and his adventures with his two coonhounds, it was filmed largely around Tahlequah and Vian.

Where the Red Fern Grows (II)
(New City Releasing, 2003) 86 minutes
Joseph Ashton, Dabney Coleman, Ned Beatty, Dave Matthews, Renee Faia, Mac Davis, Andrew Dickison, Stuart Dickison, Lindsey Labadie, Hillary Harwell, Cassidy Spring, Eric Starkey, Rocky Frisco, Kris Kristofferson
Directors: Lyman Dayton, Sam Pillsbury
Writers: Lyman Dayton, Sam Pillsbury, Eleanor Lamb, Douglas C. Stewart, Wilson Rawls (source novel)
Cinematographer: James Jansen
Note: Financial troubles marked the shooting of this remake of the 1974 picture, once again shot in and around Tahlequah.

The White Chief
(Pawnee Bill's Buffalo Ranch Feature Films, 1910) short
Gordon "Pawnee Bill" Lillie
Note: Shot on Pawnee Bill's ranch.

Wild West
(Pathe Exchange, 1925) 10-chapter serial
Jack Mulhall, Helen Ferguson, Ed Burns, Eddie Phillips, Fred Burns, Larry Steers,

George Burton, Milla Davenport, Virginia Warwick, Dan Dix, Gus Saville, Nowata Richardson, Inez Gomez
Director: Robert F. Hill
Writer: J. F. Natteford
Synopsis: A story about a circus and medicine show in the 1890s, shot at the 101 Ranch and featuring many of its performers.

The Wolf Hunt
(Oklahoma Natural Mutoscene Company, 1908) one reel
John J. Abernathy, Al Jennings
Director: William M. Tilghman
Cinematographer: J. B. Kent
Synopsis: John J. Abernathy subdues a wolf with his bare hands in the Wichita Mountains. Filmed at the suggestion of President Theodore Roosevelt.

The Wrecker
(Richard E. Norman, 1919) three reels
R. M. McFarlin, M. A. Breckenridge, Frances Riddle, Albert T. Twist, R. M. Franks, Clarence B. Douglas, Lee Levering, Arlie J. Cripe, Mrs. J. M. Ward, Charles Allen, Rev. J. W. Abel, Charles H. Hubbard, R. C. Adler, Glenn Condon, Frank C. Gow, G. R. McCullough, T. J. Hartman, M. C. Hale, Walter Miller, Lady Bell Baldwin, Mary Delaney
Cinematographer: Richard E. Norman
Synopsis: A railroad drama featuring many of Tulsa's civic and social leaders of the time, including mayor Hubbard and noted oilman McFarlin.

The Younger Brothers (also known as They Never Forgot Mother and Home)
(The Longhorn Company, 1916) three reels
Director: Scout Younger
Synopsis: Tale of the real-life outlaw family, shot in Tulsa.

Works Consulted

In addition to the newspaper and magazine articles, websites, and other sources cited within the text, the following books were consulted during the writing of *Shot in Oklahoma*.

Adams, Les, and Buck Raney. *Shoot-Em-Ups*. New Rochelle, N.Y.: Arlington House, 1978.

Bair, D. Richard, ed. *The Film Buff's Checklist of Motion Pictures (1912–1979)*. Hollywood: Hollywood Film Archive, 1979.

Balshofer, Fred J., and Arthur C. Miller. *One Reel a Week*. Berkeley: University of California Press, 1967.

Bernotas, Bob. *Jim Thorpe: Sac and Fox Athlete*. New York: Chelsea House, 1992.

Cohn, Lawrence. *Movietone Presents the 20th Century*. New York: St. Martin's Press, 1976.

Craddock, Jim, ed. *VideoHound's Golden Movie Retriever*. Detroit: Thomson-Gale, 2004.

Crenshaw, Marshall. *Hollywood Rock*. New York: Agincourt Press, 1994.

DeMarco, Mario. *Yours Truly, Tom Mix*. Worcester, Mass.: privately printed, 1979.

di Franco, J. Philip, ed. *The Movie World of Roger Corman*. New York: Chelsea House, 1979.

Durham, Weldon B. *American Theatre Companies 1888–1930*. Santa Barbara, Calif.: Greenwood Press, 1987.

Everson, William K. *A Pictorial History of the Western Film*. Secaucus, N.J.: Citadel Press, 1969.

Feaster, Felicia, and Bret Wood. *Forbidden Fruit: The Golden Age of the Exploitation Film*. Baltimore: Midnight Marquee Press, 1999.

Fielding, Raymond. *The American Newsreel, 1911–1967*. Norman: University of Oklahoma Press, 1972.

Franklin, Joe. *Classics of the Silent Screen*. New York: Cadillac Publishing, 1959.

Friedman, David F., with Don De Nevi. *A Youth in Babylon: Confessions of a Trash-Film King*. Buffalo, N.Y.: Prometheus Books, 1990.

Gilbert, Douglas. *American Vaudeville: Its Life and Times*. New York: Whittlesey House, 1940.

Goodwin, Michael, and Naomi Wise. *On the Edge: The Life and Times of Francis Coppola*. New York: William Morrow, 1989.

Hinton, S. E. *Some of Tim's Stories*. Norman: University of Oklahoma Press, 2007.

Jennings, Al, and Will Irwin. *Beating Back*. New York and London: D. Appleton and Co., 1914.

Lahue, Kalton C. *Continued Next Week: A History of the Moving Picture Serial*. Norman: University of Oklahoma Press, 1964.

Mazzola, Reparata. *Mafia Kingpin*. New York: Grosset and Dunlap, 1981.

Mix, Paul E. *The Life and Legend of Tom Mix*. New York: A. S. Barnes, 1972.

Oklahoma Almanac 1995–1996. Oklahoma City: Oklahoma Department of Libraries, 1995.

Rainey, Buck. *Heroes of the Range*. Metuchen, N.J.: Scarecrow Press, 1987.

———. *Saddle Aces of the Cinema*. San Diego: A. S. Barnes, 1980.

Rothel, David. *The Roy Rogers Book*. Madison, N.C.: Empire Publishing, 1987.

Slide, Anthony. *Early American Cinema*. New York: A. S. Barnes, 1970.

Wallis, Michael. *The Real Wild West: The 101 Ranch and the Creation of the American West*. New York: St. Martin's Press, 1999.

Wishart, David J., ed. *Encyclopedia of the Great Plains*. Lincoln: University of Nebraska Press, 2004.

Index